NONCONSCIOUS MOVEMENTS
From Mystical Messages
to Facilitated Communication

NONCONSCIOUS MOVEMENTS
From Mystical Messages
to Facilitated Communication

Herman H. Spitz
Princeton, NJ

IEA LAWRENCE ERLBAUM ASSOCIATES, PUBLISHERS
1997   Mahwah, New Jersey

Cover design by Debra Karrel

In Chapter 4, the excerpt from *The Changing Light at Sandover*
by James Merrill, ©1980, 1982 by James Merrill, is reprinted
by permission of Alfred A. Knopf, Inc.
In Chapter 4, the excerpt from Evan C. Vogt and Ray Hyman,
Water Witching U.S.A, ©1959, 1979 by the University of Chicago Press, is reprinted by permission of the University of
Chicago Press.

Lawrence Erlbaum Associates, Inc., Publishers
10 Industrial Avenue
Mahwah, New Jersey 07430

Library of Congress Cataloging-in-Publication Data

Spitz, Herman H.
    Nonconscious movements : from mystical messages to
facilitated communication / Herman H. Spitz.
        p.   cm.
    Includes bibliographical references and index.
    ISBN 0-8058-2563-0. — ISBN 0-8058-2564-9 (pbk.)
    1. Nonverbal communication (Psychology). 2. Facili-
tated communication. 3. Nonverbal communication—Miscellanea. I. Title.
    BF637.N66S65 1997
    152.3′2—dc20   96-33566
                                                                   CIP

Books published by Lawrence Erlbaum Associates are
printed on acid-free paper, and their bindings are chosen for strength and durability.

Printed in the United States of America
10 9 8 7 6 5 4 3 2 1

Contents

Preface

In 1986 I published a book that traced the history of attempts to raise the intelligence of people with mental retardation. I was interested in the subject because for most of my professional life I had been doing research with people of limited intelligence and found them obstinately resistant to change, yet I kept reading about new pedagogical and psychological methods for raising intelligence. If intelligence could be raised, then mental retardation could be cured, so I spent 4 years searching through history for the magic elixir. Alas, I found no magic cures; what I found instead was an astonishing variety of human behavior on the part of those making the claims, ranging from outright fraud to honest self-deception.

How was it possible for so many people to make such assertions, all of which proved to be untrue and many of which were obviously outlandish? My curiosity about the subject of external and internal deception was provoked and it remains a continuing interest. For anyone with such an interest there is no paucity of material; the strangest imaginable claims continue to be made. It was natural, therefore, that my curiosity was aroused by recent claims that a new technique called *facilitated communication* is capable of freeing a heretofore unsuspected inner capacity in people who are severely and profoundly retarded, particularly in those with autism.

Out went the request cards, in went the book orders, and off I trudged to the library. What I found this time surpassed just about anything I had encountered before; a popular delusion was happening not in the past but right before our eyes, presenting an opportunity not to be missed. The unrecognized basis for this latest self-deception is a particular variety of human behavior, involuntary muscle movement, that is natural to all living organisms. The capacity for muscle movement without conscious control is essential for survival, but the failure to understand and appreciate its ubiquity has resulted in a plethora of false beliefs and, of greater concern, in a great deal of unnecessary grief. Being so fundamental to human behavior and yet so little understood, involuntary muscle movements have caused havoc.

Facilitated communication is a fertile medium for the kind of misreading of unconscious muscle movements that underlies many "mysterious" phenomena, and it elicits the same variety of psychological mechanisms by its believers as has been observed in related circumstances throughout history. Consequently facilitated communication serves as a linchpin for the analysis of these related phenomena as well as for an examination of the remarkable fact that they continue to attract believers despite more than a century of contrary scientific evidence. For example, early in the 19th century a small handheld pendulum was used as an instrument for dowsing (finding a hidden supply of water or precious minerals) because the movement of a pendulum had long been thought to have its source in something other than the "unmoving" hand that was holding it. The pendulum continues to be used in this way despite the results of careful experiments performed by Michel-Eugène Chevreul in 1812 and published by him in 1833. In the mid-1800s table turning—in which spirits supposedly moved tables on which the faithful had placed their hands—was all the rage in the United States, England, and elsewhere, despite careful experiments by the great scientist Michael Faraday in 1853 disproving the claims of the spiritualists. The folly continued—and continues—with the divining rod, automatic writing, the Ouija board, mind-reading, and even clever animals who cipher and spell. Yet all these phenomena can be explained by a single principle: involuntary (unconscious) muscle movements, the movement of our muscles without conscious awareness or control.

Although facilitated communication claims to be a legitimate professional movement, the cult-like behavior of those who direct it and those who participate in it is indistinguishable from the behavior of members of many sects and of believers in paranormal phenomena. The people who use facilitated communication deceive themselves, while the leaders continue to proselytize despite the overwhelmingly negative empirical evidence. To explain these and ancillary phenomena it is necessary to mine the wealth of data available in the psychological literature.

In the course of this inquiry I have taken many side trips that I found irresistible, where we meet William James, Gertrude Stein, Houdini, and Arthur Conan Doyle, among others. I hope the reader finds these excursions as fascinating as I did.

In sum, because facilitated communication is currently used throughout the world it provides a living laboratory of one of the most bizarre series of events in the history of psychology and education, as well as a point of departure for the consolidation of numerous related phenomena that have been with us since the dawn of recorded history.

ACKNOWLEDGMENTS

These are among the many people to whom I am grateful. As usual, my family. My wife Ruth, patient and understanding (as well as proofreader *extraordinaire*), who interrupted my long journeys into WordPerfectland only when it was necessary to save my eyes and my back, and whose computer proficiency preserved my sanity. Our son Ken, a phone call away when even Ruth couldn't extricate me, whose computer skills were a source of proud wonder. Our daughter Debra, who provided the latest intelligence on the mental health front to help me navigate the most difficult part of the book.

William Holloway, Research Director of New Jersey's Division of Developmental Disabilities, who opened avenues to much needed information and sent relevant papers that kept me updated, as did David Hoats, my colleague for so many years, who discovered the dowser's tombstone described in Chapter 4. Al Baumeister, at Vanderbilt, for the kind of encouragement that can come only from a friend and colleague in the fight against false prophets and general foolishness that so frequently plague our young science. Gina Green, at the New England Center for Autism (and elsewhere), for discussions I periodically sought and always looked forward to, to keep me from straying too far down some uncertain paths.

The remarkable group at Centurion Ministries—seeking justice for imprisoned innocents—who understood why this particular volunteer was so preoccupied. May their work be blessed.

Ms. Cecilia Johnson, for permitting me to reproduce from the *IARET Newsletter* her moving description of her family's travails following accusations of sexual abuse. Peter Gerhardt of the Eden Institute in Princeton who, as Editor of the Newsletter, not only granted permission to reprint Ms. Johnson's article but also found and borrowed for me a book I had despaired of finding.

Evon Z. Vogt, author with Ray Hyman of *Water Witching U.S.A.*, who took the trouble to find and copy for me William Carpenter's pivotal 1852 article on involuntary muscle movements. Mary Chaikin, psychology librarian, and Linda Chamberlin and Hilda Florentine, Special Collection assistants, at Princeton University's Psychology Library, who were always pleasant and ever helpful. I am not on the faculty of Princeton University but I could not have written this book without access to its superb libraries.

My publisher, Lawrence Erlbaum, who was immediately enthused about the book and both patient and encouraging while waiting for it.

How fortunate I am.

—*Herman H. Spitz*

Chronicle

While I was holding the pendulum with my hand, a muscular movement in my arm, though unfelt by me, made the pendulum leave its resting state, and once the oscillations had begun they were soon augmented by the influence which sight exerted to place me into that peculiar state *of disposition or tendency to movement*.... Hence there is an intimate relationship established between the execution of certain movements and the act of thought relative to them, though that thought may not yet be an act of will commanding the muscular organs. It is in that respect that the phenomena ... seem to me to be of some interest to psychology, and even to the history of science; they prove how easy it is to take illusions for realities whenever we are occupied with a phenomenon where our organs play some role and under circumstances which have not been thoroughly analyzed.
—Michel-Eugène Chevreul (1833, pp. 251–252)

And as we have seen that the *emotions* may act directly upon the muscular system through the motor nerves, there is no *a priori* difficulty in believing that *Ideas* may become the sources of muscular movements, independently either of volitions or of emotions.
—William B. Carpenter (1852, p. 152)

The alternative is, therefore, between the actual transfer of thought from subject to operator, as has been claimed, and the theory of unconscious muscular motion and relaxation on the part of the subject, the truth of which I have demonstrated by numerous experiments.
—George M. Beard (1877, p. 460)

We may then lay it down for certain that *every representation of a movement awakens in some degree the actual movement which is its object; and awakens it in a maximum degree whenever it is not kept from doing so by an antagonistic representation present simultaneously in the mind.*
—William James (1890/1950, Vol. 2, p. 526)

It is important ... to recognize how large a part is played in civilized life by automatic movements—movements which a man does not know he is making, or cannot avoid making, and which give expression to cerebral action of which he is partly or wholly unconscious.

—Frederic W. H. Myers (1886a, p. 214)

The theory formerly accepted was simple enough.... All thought—and particularly if it is concrete, if it is an image—has a tendency to expend itself in movement; it contains within itself a motor germ; more than this, the thought is a movement commencing to outline itself.... It seems to me ... [the theory] should be made a little more complicated by adding to it the simultaneous play of several mental syntheses or consciousnesses. The unconscious movements of normal individuals should be considered ... not as the simple effects of motor tendencies of images, but of the effects of very slight mental duplication.... incomplete fragments or passages from the history of multiple consciousnesses.

—Alfred Binet (1891/1896a, pp. 220–221)

We submit, then, that experimental evidence is overwhelmingly in support of the contention that an idea, or image, of a movement tends to produce the precise movement imagined, or a modified form of it. The strength of this tendency varies from person to person.

—Hans J. Eysenck (1947, p. 196)

1

Facilitated Communication

Prof. Flournoy states that he has endeavored to keep constantly in mind and be guided by two propositions, which he designates respectively the "Principle of Hamlet" and the "Principle of Laplace," the former being, "All things are possible," the latter, "The weight of the evidence ought to be proportional to the strangeness of the facts."
—Translator's preface to Flournoy (1900/1963, p. xxx)

The greater the feat the less indication is there of the use of the scientific method to validate the evidence.
—Boring (1952, p. 537)

Biklen says his experience at the school, and that of others, indicates that facilitation could be used successfully for more than 90 percent of the 350,000 autistic people in America. If that were true, autism itself would have to be redefined.
—Makarushka (1991, p. 36)

HISTORY

Consider this example, a composite of many reports. A 6-year-old girl who has autism and is severely mentally retarded, who has communicated only in single irrelevant words or perhaps not at all, who repeats phrases and echoes what others say, who rocks constantly and performs ritual movements such as hand and arm flapping—is brought to a seat in front of a keyboard and types out readable sentences, sometimes almost at once and sometimes after days or weeks or longer. Sometimes the sentences are grammatically correct although often they have no punctuation. Frequently the words are hidden in strings of letters, but always the communication is startling, coming so unexpectedly from a person who has never been taught to read or write and hardly glances at the keyboard. A miracle, you say. But there is a catch. Someone is holding her hand to steady it, to compensate for her muscular instability and to prevent her from making too many errors. The holder is a *facilitator* and the technique is called *facilitated communication*.

It is conceivable, of course, that the child and not the facilitator actually typed the words. In rare cases children with autism have independently learned to write (Rimland, 1990a). But proponents of facilitated communication claim that hidden aptitudes are not a rarity and that the overt physical disability alone prevents most people with autism and mental retardation from communicating. By means of facilitated communication, they say, normal intelligence hidden beneath a mantle of physical limitations is freed.

The chief spokesperson and driving force for facilitated communication in the United States is Professor Douglas Biklen of the Division of Special Education and Rehabilitation in the School of Education at Syracuse University. In his book *Communication Unbound* (which includes four chapters adapted and expanded from previously published material), Biklen describes how he learned that an Australian educator, Rosemary Crossley, had developed a new technique that enabled people with autism to communicate. He thought little of it, but 18 months later, while in Melbourne, Australia, he visited Crossley's independent, government-supported Dignity through Education and Language (DEAL) Communication Centre.

Crossley had developed her technique while working with people with cerebral palsy who, because of their motor problems, were severely hampered when trying to touch a letter or a picture of a communication device. To help them use this means of communicating, she slowed them down by supporting each client's hand or arm. About this procedure Biklen (1993) commented: "The method was controversial ... because it raised the possibility that the people's choice of letters from a language board, for example, might reflect the facilitator's rather than the learner's choice" (p. 5).

Indeed it might, although it is less likely to happen when motor problems prevent the expression of normal or superior intelligence, as so often is true for people with cerebral palsy. I am reminded of Christy Brown (1970) who despite severe cerebral palsy taught himself to read. He typed out several marvelous books with the little toe of his left foot, and his achievements were beautifully rendered in the film of his book *My Left Foot*. But Christy Brown managed to type by himself; no one supported his foot.

Cerebral palsy is quite a different disability from autism or mental retardation. In many cases of cerebral palsy only the motor areas of the brain are affected, with the intellectual (cognitive) areas remaining intact. Goode (1994) suggested that facilitated communication may be worth trying for some people with cerebral palsy as long as they are bright enough not to "allow words to be placed in their mouths by others" (p. 308). According to Palfreman (1994)—who, based on research for his *Frontline* television program on facilitated communication, has traced its history in Australia—this is in fact what happened in Crossley's most famous case, but the evidence seems inconclusive to me. Palfreman was referring to a a physically disabled institutionalized woman who had been born with the athetoid form of cerebral palsy and who, according to doctors, would never develop beyond a mental age of 2 years. But Crossley announced that she had used facilitated communication to break through this woman's communications barrier and found her patient to be bright and curious. Together (via facilitated communication) they described the woman's passage out of darkness and launched facilitated communication on its fateful journey (Crossley & McDonald, 1980). Reasoning that facilitated communication could also break the barrier she believed surrounded people who were severely mentally retarded without cerebral palsy, including those with autism, Crossley went on to declare success with them as well.[1] In doing so she (and later Biklen) challenged the general consensus of professionals that all persons who are mentally retarded and many, perhaps as many as 75%, who have autism have a cognitive disability (Wulff, 1985).

Seven months later, in July 1989, Biklen returned to Melbourne. He described his observation of 21 persons with autism or displaying autistic behavior who were either nonspeaking or echolalic and "were considered mentally retarded prior to being introduced to facilitated communication" (Biklen, 1993 p. 3). During facilitated communication Crossley's autistic students (henceforth I refer to all people who are being facilitated as students, partners, or clients) produced extraordinary written language—worlds away from any communication they had previously demonstrated. Biklen declared that prior to facilitated communication the students must have had difficulty in *expressing* their thoughts, not in *having* cognitively adequate thoughts. To describe their problem he used the word *praxis*, which my dictionary defines as the exercise of an art, science or skill.

A related word, *apraxia* (a-praxis, or loss of praxis), is a conventional diagnostic term for the impairment of complex motor skills.

Crossley's Predecessors

Rosalind Oppenheim used the word apraxia to characterize the communication difficulties characteristic of children with autism. In 1974 Ms. Oppenheim, a parent who worked with her own autistic child before she became a professional teacher, published a book on her method of teaching these children basic academic skills, including writing. Biklen maintained that Oppenheim's findings confirmed Goodwin and Goodwin's (1969) work with "talking typewriters," originally introduced by Omar Khayyam Moore.

---

[1]Prior and Cummins (1992), who from the beginning were involved in the controversy in Australia over facilitated communication's legitimacy, question Crossley's diagnostic accuracy: "Other cases did not appear to have a diagnosis of autism but were given this label during the process of enrollment into the facilitated communication program at the DEAL Centre in Melbourne" (p. 332).

According to Biklen, the accomplishments of Oppenheim, Moore, and Goodwin and Goodwin presaged facilitated communication, so we must interrupt our narrative very briefly to examine the work of these harbingers. Moore (1966) had made quite a splash with his talking typewriter and responsive environment (see Spitz, 1986, pp. 150–154 for a brief review). First, a child—whose fingernails were painted different colors to match the painted typewriter keys—entered a booth containing the typewriter. When the child struck any key the character was typed out and, to the child's surprise, a loudspeaker named the character (letter, number, or punctuation mark). In the next phase all typewriter keys were locked except the key for the character designated on a display screen. In the final two phases there were further interactions involving full words, sentences, and stories. Moore claimed that by using his typewriter 2- and 3-year-olds as well as retarded children learned to print and write. Controlled experiments failed to verify these claims, however, and for this and other reasons Omar Khayyam Moore and his expensive "responsive environments" soon faded into the night.

Before that denouement, however, Goodwin and Goodwin (1969) had purchased two or three (the number is unclear) of Moore's Edison Response Environments (E. R. E.)—units that consisted of a cubicle enclosing a typewriter, a projector, and audio and other equipment. Apparently anticipating criticisms, they forthrightly declared that their project would not be a scientific experiment. For half-hour periods one to five times weekly, this equipment was made available, at no charge, to 150 students who were autistic, learning disabled, or physically disabled. The students ranged in age from 3 to 16 years; many were neither retarded nor incapable of communicative speech. Unlike the procedure in facilitated communication, students entered the booth and worked in it alone because freely exploring the typewriter and experiencing the consequences of their actions were fundamental concepts in Moore's philosophy.

Instead of listing the general results for all 150 students, the Goodwins provided summary descriptions of only 12, some of whom (e.g., a 27-year-old man) were not among the original 150. For 2 of the 12 there is no evidence that they even used the talking typewriters! Of the remaining 10, a number wrote single words or phrases, such as those in television ads. Two, who apparently could read, speak, and write before they entered the program (descriptions of pre-program capacities are vague or absent), wrote stories. The Goodwins—more interested in speech development and reading ability than in writing—believed that Moore's techniques revealed abilities that standard psychological tests did not, but "In none [of the cases] did we attribute success, when it occurred, to the E.R.E. alone: maturation, school, and home experiences were also important. A large part, perhaps the largest, was due to the talents and ingenuity of the teachers who planned the curricula and originated programs for the E.R.E." (Goodwin & Goodwin, 1969, pp. 557–558).

In no instance did these students, *working alone*, type anything that remotely resembled what facilitated students are said to type. In contrast to the output of the Goodwins' students, Biklen's conversations with Crossley's autistic students via facilitated communication (and later protocols when he returned to the United States) were astonishingly sophisticated and centered on interpersonal relationships and personal feelings, especially feelings of being wrongly perceived as incompetent. Many messages also included accusations of sexual abuse. According to Biklen (1993) facilitated communication is able to elicit more than just imitative words and phrases: "By slowing down the person's typing, the facilitator allows the person to type what he or she wants" (p. 126), implying that people who were independently typing prior to facilitated communication were not typing what they wanted. The same tortured logic serves to avoid blindfolding the facilitator: "If blindfolded, the facilitator could actually misdirect and throw off the communication user's intended direction" (p. 126).

I have already mentioned Oppenheim, who varies her teaching techniques depending on what she is teaching. Biklen described her method of teaching writing as "hand-over-hand." In fact, however, teaching writing is just one facet of her general method for teaching any motor skill, which is to physically maneuver the child's limbs—arms, legs, hands, or feet—through the desired activity until the child performs it independently.

In the less than two pages that Oppenheim (1974) devoted to teaching cursive writing she described how, as a preliminary, the teacher manipulates the child's hand in drawing geometrical forms. Even after the pair progresses to writing letters, this manipulation continues for a considerable time until it is gradually faded "to a mere touch of a finger on the child's writing hand" (p. 54). Oppenheim went on to say that the quality of the writing deteriorates without a teacher's finger on the child's hand "despite the fact that the finger is in no way guiding the child's writing hand" (p. 54). Ultimately, "the finger-touching can be eliminated, and the child does write without it, although some children want the touch of a finger on some other bodily surface, such as the head, in order to write" (p. 55). She did not say what percentage of children required this contact or, for that matter, what percentage wrote completely independently and what their characteristics were.

Oppenheim's description corresponds with reports that most children who are autistic require continued contact when typing or pointing during facilitated communication, but this similarity should not obscure a number of differences: (a) For the most part, Oppenheim teaches cursive writing rather than typing on a keyboard or pointing to an alphabet board. (b) Oppenheim's students are taught to write as part of a total school program that includes reading and arithmetic, and presumably most of them learn to read before they learn to write. (c) Oppenheim does not give detailed descriptions of what her students write but—as with Goodwin and Goodwin—if they write the emotional, philosophical, and personal tracts presumed to have been written by almost all facilitated students we surely would have heard about it. Neither Oppenheim nor Goodwin and Goodwin mention the sexual abuse charges so frequently produced during facilitated communication.

Oppenheim (1974) does not ignore the typewriter.

> The typewriter, too, is a valuable teaching tool for a child whose eye–hand coordination is sufficiently developed. While the less severely afflicted child has little difficulty in learning the touch system and using the typewriter efficiently, it remains to be seen whether we can succeed in helping the more atypical child attain real speed and facility on the machine. (p. 58)

It is not unusual for some autistic students to use a keyboard. In fact the field of augmentative and alternative communication, within which facilitated communication falls, is by definition a search for better techniques and aids for promoting the communication of people who are disabled mentally and/or physically. Although there are many new and innovative techniques (Levine, Shane, & Wharton, 1994), the search continues on many fronts. What is atypical in facilitated communication is the percentage of children whose hand continues to be held by someone else, the claim that the success rate approaches 100%, and the startling nature of what is typed.

Biklen Starts the Movement

We return now to Biklen's epiphany in Australia. On his second trip there, in 1989, he was completely captivated by the performance of Crossley's students and, most significantly, was convinced that unwitting facilitator guidance was rare. In his judgment the students gave appropriate verbal and facial expressions as they typed, and the fact that some eventually typed either completely independently or with a facilitator's hand on the student's shoulder, leg, thread of a sweater, or other location convinced him that the facilitators were not directing the responses.

Returning to Syracuse, Biklen started a movement that grew quickly and continues to grow, spurred on particularly by speech and language therapists, whose job it is to improve communication. To experience such immense success after having struggled so long for small increments was, for them, especially exhilarating. Some psychologists, educators, and direct care workers also joined in. The movement was given impetus by Biklen's 1990 paper in the *Harvard Educational Review*—despite Cummins and Prior's (1992) critical commentary and Biklen's (1992) rejoinder—and a laudatory article in the Magazine Section of *The New York Times* in October 1991. Biklen established the Facilitated Communication Institute at Syracuse to generate grants, provide training for facilitators, and generally spread the word.

For Biklen, the success of facilitated communication tied in nicely with his active promotion of the normalization movement, which in its most radical form advocates total inclusion of all handicapped children in regular classes. In his book and in journal articles he documented the many successes of facilitated communication, and his cause was enthusiastically joined by many parents, teachers, and mental health workers. He conceded that facilitated communication does not cure autism; the many disturbing behaviors symptomatic of autism remain. Nevertheless, if the level of communication and understanding revealed by this method are valid there is justification for including autistic and retarded children in regular classes.

REACTIONS

Needless to say, there were many skeptics. A claim as revolutionary as the one made by supporters of facilitated communication requires the closest scrutiny. Had Biklen followed his initial skepticism with careful, objective tests of validity rather than generating a crusade, the stir that followed would have been dampened considerably. There is a relatively simple test to determine who is doing the typing: What happens when the student and the facilitator see or hear a different question and neither knows what the other was asked? This test, or variations of it, has now been used by many educators and psychologists in a number of different settings, with results so consistent that they leave no residue of doubt. In a typical experiment a picture or object is shown to both student and facilitator but, by the use of a dividing board, the facilitator cannot see what the student sees and vice versa. Sometimes the pictures are the same, sometimes different, and sometimes the facilitator is shown nothing. The student is then asked to type out the name of the picture while being facilitated. The same test has been done using earphones. Or the facilitator leaves the room and some object is displayed, topic discussed, or activity engaged in with the student, who is then asked by the returning facilitator to describe, via facilitated communication, what occurred while he or she was out.

Only a handful of the hundreds of people with developmental disabilities who have been tested under controlled conditions have shown any evidence that their responses are not driven by the facilitator. The few valid productions were single words and short phrases on occasional trials, but some of these people could already communicate at a higher level by other means, or could read before being introduced to facilitated communication (Green, 1992, 1994). In the overwhelming number of cases, what is typed is what the facilitator, not the student, sees or hears. When the facilitator is shown nothing, the response is unrelated to the question asked of the student.

In fact, objective tests showing negative results have been published at a rate and consistency unequaled in the history of education and psychology. Detailed reviews of this very convincing evidence can be found elsewhere and need not be duplicated here. Alan Hudson (1995) has described the history of facilitated communication in Australia. In the United States, John Jacobson and James Mulick (1994; see also Jacobson, Mulick, & Schwartz 1995), Gina Green (1992), and Howard Shane (see especially Shane's 1994 edited book) presented critical overviews, and have been very active, along with Travis Thompson (1994), Bernard Rimland (1992a), and many, many others—including investigative reporters of newspapers, news magazines and television feature programs—in alerting the professional and lay community to this extraordinarily unreliable technique and its perilous consequences.

Although massive evidence of facilitator direction during facilitated communication has been convincing for many, it has not slowed the movement (Dillon, Fenlason, & Vogel, 1944). Actually Biklen himself provided warning signs in his book, but chose to rationalize them. In one case a young boy accused his father of making him put his finger in his father's anus. However, the father was divorced and not living with his son, and, wrote Biklen (1993), "expressed outrage that his son might have been abused [but].... did not question that his son was communicating by typing, even though this was the first time his father had actually seen it" (p. 133). Biklen was pleased that the father accepted facilitated communication and did not raise the possibility of facilitator influence on his son's accusations. A week after his father's angry visit, the boy typed someone named Pete as his molester. To explain all this, Biklen concluded that the boy originally had named his father "perhaps because he felt his father was a 'safe' person to name or perhaps because he felt his father could protect him in a way that others had not" (p. 134). Then Biklen went on to say that "medical tests did reveal that he [the son] had been sexually assaulted" (p. 134). That is all we are told.

Biklen admitted the possibility that facilitators influence responses and described one instance in which a facilitator blatantly did just that. However, he implied that this was a rare event and suggested that facilitator influence might be impossible when the facilitator reached the point of holding the elbow or merely touching the shoulder. In this description he revealed his lack of familiarity with, or lack of respect for, the subtle influences that people can exert on each other and, in particular, the power of involuntary muscle movements. A facilitator's involuntary muscle movements can be felt or seen by the partner each time the partner's finger hovers over the desired letter of a keyboard or alphabet board.

Responses can be influenced by sounds of approval or nods of the head or very minute and subtle hand or body movements; there is no reason to touch the person being influenced. Even so, demonstrations of facilitated students attaining independent typing are difficult to find, whereas they should by now be commonplace. Biklen (1995) cited as evidence videotapes he had seen of independent typing by two clients whose sophisticated communicative level Thompson (1994) had doubted. In February 1995 Biklen generously sent me a videotape ("Toward Independent Typing," undated and with no author) of three people with autism who have been facilitated, two of whom are said to be typing independently. The first example, although not one of those said to be typing independently, is interesting nonetheless. The facilitator (apparently Rosemary Crossley) has her hand on the boy's head "partly to insure eye contact but more to insure he stays on task. He's not very keen on what I'm asking him to do." Typically, he types with an index finger, pressing the keys of a Canon Communicator placed on a table. The Canon, used frequently in facilitated communication, is described by Crossley (1994) as "a minitypewriter designed in Holland for people with dual sensory impairments" (p. 2). It is much smaller than a computer, and its smaller keyboard contains letter keys arranged, unlike the standard typewriter keyboard, in alphabetical order. The output is on a long, narrow paper tape, like a ticker tape.

The second scene of the second example shows a young autistic woman with autism typing, untouched, on a Canon held in her mother's outstretched hand. Handholding a keyboard raises the possibility of inadvertent movement that may influence the client's key selection. The third client appears to type independently while the male facilitator lends encouragement. However, I would feel more comfortable if I could see the facilitator's left hand, nearest the child, which, unlike his right, is out of sight as the client types on what appears to be a portable computer placed on a table.

Biklen (1995) also cited as evidence of independent typing a paper that A. J. Attwood presented at a professional meeting in 1953. I wrote to Australia requesting the paper from Attwood and he sent me instead a more recent paper that has nothing to do with facilitated communication. I wrote back telling him why I wanted the original paper but received no reply. Judging from his response to my first request, it seems that Attwood is no longer interested in facilitated communication.

If truly independent autistic and mentally retarded typists are presented as evidence for the validity of facilitated communication, evidence must be supplied that they could not type independently *before* being facilitated, or that they could not learn without being facilitated.

Extensive objective evidence that in almost all cases the facilitators rather than their autistic and retarded partners are doing the typing has not dissuaded the committed and dedicated, whose reputations and personal belief systems are so heavily invested. Even more distressing, the negative evidence has not been enough to deter school systems from mandating the use of facilitated communication for their special education students. "The General Assembly of Virginia has mandated F/C [facilitated communication] for use with the handicapped throughout the state" (Rimland, 1993b, p. 7).

CRIMINAL ACCUSATIONS

Perhaps the only way to fully understand the appalling consequences of unexamined premises is to read one mother's description of her family's experience:

> My husband and I were first introduced to facilitated communication (FC) by a Georgia police detective. The detective told us that allegations of the sexual abuse of our son by a family member had been made. He gave us typed transcripts our son was supposed to have spelled at school when "facilitated" by his teacher. At the time, we had no idea that FC was being used with Josh, our 13 year old son who is moderately mentally retarded. We were horrified, frightened, and confused! My heart was broken. Little did I realize then that this was all in preparation for months of heartbreak to come.
>
> We immediately contacted our pediatrician who advised us to take Josh to the local children's hospital for a physical examination. I sat in the hallway and listened to him scream and cry in protest as the doctor performed an anal exam. We experienced some measure of reassurance after the doctor reported no physical sign of sexual molestation. That reassurance, unfortunately, soon evaporated.
>
> Once home, I contacted the school personnel in my son's program that I had known for 10 years, and who knew my son well. "How could this be his writing?" I asked. "He can spell his first name, and that not very well. He can *talk* in complete sentences," I added, "but cannot read, write, or spell. How could this be?" Educators I trusted assured us repeatedly that they did not know how all this could be, but that FC was a miraculous new "thing" that unlocked hidden intelligence.
>
> As incredible as all this was, we trusted our school system. And for our son to be intelligent enough to have taught himself to read, write, spell, and punctuate was the fondest wish of any parent of a child with a disability. Although we were still doubtful, we went along with the recommendation of the school that FC was real, and that it continue to be used with Josh. As someone else has already said, we quickly became involved in a seductive and progressive entrapment.
>
> As months went on, the teacher/facilitator sent home FC-typed sheets each day. Even though we were watching our son literally every minute it continued to be facilitated, at various times, that he was being abused, was not protected by his family, or wanted to leave home to be safe. At one point, the police were called in again to investigate claims that he was making "plots and ploys to murder" his family!
>
> Hysteria reigned. We were dealing with a growing sense of paranoia every day. Suspicions and criticisms flared up over everyday matters. Actions were no longer considered innocent, but were immediately questioned and scrutinized.

The police asked permission to interview Josh this time and I agreed if it was videotaped and I received a copy of the tape. It was heart-rending to watch 43 minutes of my child struggling with the facilitator, repeatedly saying "Can I stop now? Can I go back to the room? No, no, no! I don't want to do this." He yanked his hand away from hers almost 50 times by my count, turned off the typewriter over and over and looked around the room while she concentrated on the keyboard. When the officer in charge suggested our son might not want to continue, the facilitator repeated part of the FC lore: what he says isn't valid, just pay attention to what is typed. Their investigation continued from that point.

A few weeks later, as his behavior in the classroom deteriorated while he struggled to keep his identity and his verbalizations valued, more accusations came. Now his grandfather was accused, and there were implications that I was involved. It was facilitated that everyone was underestimating the "ploy by my mother to appear normal."

We were more distraught than ever. If our son had been abused or neglected by anyone we certainly wanted to know the truth but none of this made any sense! He had been seeing a play therapist for several months and there was no sign of abuse. We were watching him every minute, he had endured an examination, he had never spoken about anything even remotely resembling sexual molestation. Yet his teacher claimed this was all originating from him.

A final interview by FC after the police were called to the school a third time resulted in specific, graphic descriptions of sex acts that directly accused me. I was hysterical after reading the single, typed sheet of sexual accusations. Despite their concerns which required the police interview, the school assured me that they were convinced that, although these were his words, Josh was lying. After deliberation, the detective in charge, thankfully, decided "not to pursue" and charges were never filed.

Then I discovered that he didn't do this. We experimented at home with our electric typewriter. I thought Josh's hand couldn't be pushed to keys he didn't want but I quickly discovered that I could spell out whatever I wanted while holding his hand and Josh didn't react any differently. If I looked away from the keyboard, the words turned to gibberish. FC could only be called a hoax, and it had nearly destroyed us!

A friend of mine with a son with autism who was "facilitating" gave me a copy of a newsletter from Dr. Rimland describing other situations like ours. A few phone calls and faxes later we discovered the scientific research on FC and made contact with fellow victims of this FC nightmare. A long process of coming back to reality began, which continues today. (C. Johnson, 1994, pp. 5–6. Reprinted by permission)

Ms. Johnson went on to write that although Josh discontinued facilitated communication at his family's insistence, the school continued to use it.

I know of no running total of the number of instances in which allegations of sexual abuse have been made via facilitated communication, but in 1994 Margolin wrote that there have been "at least 5 dozen reported to authorities" (p. 239), typically without any corroborating evidence. Two years earlier Rimland (1992a) had cited a newspaper article that mentioned 40 cases in the Syracuse, New York area alone. Even taking into account that Syracuse is the hub of facilitated communication, by now the number of worldwide instances of alleged sexual abuse must be rather large and continuing to rise. According to Biklen (1993), in the first year-and-a-half after facilitated communication was introduced to the Syracuse area, 10 of about 75 students asserted, while facilitating, that they had been sexually abused, and Biklen claimed that in at least 6 of the cases there was corroborating evidence. It is difficult to confirm this estimate.

Biklen (1995) cited a study by Botash, Babuts, Mitchell, O'Hara, Lynch, and Manuel (1994) as evidence that sexual allegations made through facilitated communication are similar to those made by nondisabled populations. The cited study took place at the State University of New York Health Science Center at Syracuse and was based on the Center's medical records (over a 3-year period) of all children who used facilitated communication to disclose sexual abuse. The major characteristics of the children and the resulting findings were presented in tables, which unfortunately provided limited information. There were 13 children, 2 diagnosed as mentally retarded, 1 as mentally retarded with delayed speech, 2 as presenting autistic behavior, and the rest multihandicapped, many with mental retardation plus autistic behavior. In 2 of the cases the medical records were said to be so limited that it was not possible to report the children's ability to use manual signs. All the other children used manual signs, some at a rudimentary level. Most used words, 2 spoke meaningful sentences, and 3 spoke meaningful phrases. Additionally, medical records were reviewed for evidence of suspicious physical findings.

Concerning the method of disclosure, 1 (a 7-year-old girl) facilitated the charge (typing partially independently) and was adjudicated to have been abused, another (a 5-year-old girl) gave a partial verbal disclosure and was adjudicated as suffering neglect (her grandmother, who was her legal guardian, violated an order of protection by allowing her and her siblings unsupervised contact with the perpetrator). Eleven of the cases were said to have given no disclosure other than by facilitated communication.

In addition to the summary tables, case reports of 3 of the cases were given. The first was the 7-year-old capable of independent typing. "Using FC with one instance of independent typing, she disclosed the abuse to law enforcement officials" (p. 1283). The second was a 5-year-old girl who made some partial verbal disclosures. The third was a 10-year-old girl who was said to have indicated only to her sister (via facilitated communication) that she was being grabbed by the babysitter's husband and that they touched each other sexually. (How old her sister was when she acted as facilitator is not given.) In this case there was no physical evidence of sexual abuse but there were "two brownish oval bruises on each upper arm" (p. 1285), which had prompted the alleged disclosure when her sister asked her how she got them. The parents changed babysitters and dropped charges. (In one other case where a sibling was the disabled child's facilitator the charges were dropped as unfounded.)

The Child Protective Services of the Department of Social Services believed that there was evidence for abuse of 7 of the children, but in the Family Court only 1 of the 13 cases was adjudicated as abuse. In 1 other case the perpetrator confessed, but we are not informed of the court action. One case was judged a misdemeanor, and 1 a case of neglect. In 1 the parents dropped the charges. About this, the authors commented that "In the present report, there is enough evidence to legally prove the allegations of sexual abuse of three children, and one additional child's perpetrator confessed" (Botash et al., 1994, p. 1287).

Unfortunately there were no attempts to validate by objective measures the source of the communications, and in their comments Botash et al. (1994) cautioned that

> The fact that [some] allegations of abuse rendered via FC were ultimately corroborated by physical evidence and/or confessions does not necessarily validate the technique of FC since the initial allegation may still have emanated from the facilitators. If any of the facilitators were adult survivors of abuse, it is possible that they may not have been as objective as nonabused facilitators. (p. 1286)

The abuse of children is so prevalent that a journal, *Child Abuse & Neglect*, is devoted to nothing else. Yet it is also known that some children, neither mentally disabled nor using facilitated communication, fabricate accusations of sexual abuse. The most dramatic such incidents, characteristic of what we might call the witch accusation syndrome, were false accusations made by groups of children in nursery schools (Eberle & Eberle, 1993; Nieves, 1993, 1994). Many times these false accusations are driven by presumably well-meaning professionals who plant suggestions, ask leading questions and coax the young children, sometimes using anatomically correct dolls. In facilitated communication—where the false accusations come directly, albeit unwittingly, from the facilitator—the mechanisms for producing false accusations are different, but no less reprehensible. Facilitated communication is, unfortunately, ready-made for this kind of injustice.

The case of 29-year-old Marc Warden, a live-in aide at the Institute of Logopedics (IOL, now called Heartspring) in Wichita, Kansas[2] (a case briefly examined most recently by Jacobson & Mulick, 1995), has been cited as evidence for the validity of facilitated communication (e.g., Donnellan,

---

[2]I Assume that Biklen (as did I) got much of his information on this case from the *Wichita Eagle*, which periodically published articles on it from July 10, 1992 to May 14, 1993. On October 15, 1994, a CBS television movie based on the case received a bitingly critical review in the *Eagle*. I also garnered much information from the review of the case in the decision of the Supreme Court of Kansas, graciously sent to me by Kenneth N. Margolin.

1996a. See also comment by Spitz, 1996, and reply by Donnellan, 1996b). Warden had traveled from Kansas to Oregon, where he turned himself in on an arrest warrant alleging one count of taking indecent liberties with a child in his care at the IOL, an 11-year-old boy who was mute and autistic. Initially Warden denied the charges.

Warden signed a waiver of his *Miranda* rights and after what his attorney described as the stress of a lengthy interrogation confessed to the investigating detective that when he (Warden) came out of the shower and saw the boy standing at the toilet he rubbed his penis against the boy's back and up to but not into his anus, because he knew how much that would hurt. Warden also allegedly told a co-worker he was accused of molesting the boy and admitted to the co-worker that he did it, adding that at one time he had fondled the boy.

To the interviewing detective's specific question of whether Warden himself had ever been touched inappropriately Warden responded that he had been sexually abused as a child but never told anyone and never received help. This admission was recorded on the tape during his 2-hour interrogation. At that point, at Warden's urging, the detective turned off the tape and it was then, the detective said, that he confessed to the crime. Consequently only his admission that he himself had been molested was on the tape played to the jury, not his confession of the crime. Warden later said that he was led to confess by the long interrogation (not a rare occurrence).

In court the boy, facilitated by his speech pathologist supporting his wrist, was permitted to respond to questions using a Canon Communicator that the facilitator held in her other hand. Also available was a clear plastic board with YES and NO panels. Proper controls, which would have insured that the responses were from the student and not his facilitator, were not permitted by the judge. Warden repudiated the confession he had given the police, saying he confessed to something he did not do because he was scared and wanted to leave, and maintaining that in his confession to his co-worker he was merely relating a story he had told the detective. No physical evidence was presented that the student was sexually abused.

The jury found Warden guilty of indecent liberties with a child and he was sentenced to 3 to 10 years. The verdict was upheld by the Kansas Supreme Court (*State v. Warden*, 1995), with two justices dissenting.

Attorney Kenneth Margolin, who has written on legal matters related to facilitated communication (Margolin, 1994), believes that the landmark standard set forth in *Frye v. United States* (1923) should have applied in the Warden case (K. N. Margolin, personal communication, June 22, 1995). The *Frye* test declares, in essence:

> Before expert opinion may be received in evidence, the basis of that opinion must be shown to be generally accepted as reliable within the expert's particular scientific field. If a new scientific technique's validity generally has

not been accepted as reliable or is only regarded as an experimental technique, then expert testimony based on its results should not be admitted into testimony. (*State v. Warden*, 1995, p. 1077)[3]

In the Warden case the courts ruled that *Frye* did not apply because the ability to transmit the testimony of a witness, for example by translating the signing of a deaf person, was not based on scientific theory. In their affirmation of the trial court's decision, the Kansas Supreme Court agreed with the trial court which had followed, instead of *Frye*, New York State's *Luz P* case (*Matter of Luz P.*, 1993). In that case the New York Court, the equivalent to the Kansas Court of Appeals, had ordered a hearing to determine the scientific reliability of facilitated communication, but after the Department of Social Services requested a continuance to send out of town for expert witnesses, the court simply dismissed the reliability hearing, so no outside experts were called to testify.

Statement Number 2 in the Kansas Supreme Court's Syllabus on the Warden case states in part:

> The test set forth in *Frye* ... does not apply to testimony by means of facilitated communication. As long as a facilitator is only assisting a witness in communicating responses in the court, scientific proof is not involved and the issue is whether the facilitator can reliably convey the witness' answers to the court. (*State v. Warden*, 1995, p. 1077)

That decision, they wrote, was to be made by the trial court judge.

After the trial the jury foreman said the jury's decision was not based solely on facilitated communication, and another member of the jury said the confessions weighed heavily on their minds. Whatever the jury's decision and whatever the actual facts in the case, we still have no proof that the student and not the facilitator typed the accusations and responses. The facilitator certainly had reason for suspicion. About three months after she had started facilitating the boy she received word that he had a tantrum when he saw his residential case manager (not Warden) with his pants off, and the tantrum did not stop until the pants were back on. She asked a psychologist at the facility to help interview the boy, which he did over the next two days while she facilitated. The initial accusations by the boy against Warden had been made during these interviews.

The Kansas Supreme Court decision (*State v. Warden*, 1995) recounted that in 1991 (the year before the molestation) the victim (JK):

> was able to select his name from a group of words, as long as there were no other words beginning with a 'J.' He was able to identify only 5 letters of the

---

[3]The *Frye* standard was relaxed somewhat by a more recent U. S. Supreme Court decision, *Daubert v. Dow* (1993), which abolished the *Frye* standard in federal court trials (Margolin, 1994).

alphabet. By 1992 JK still had no verbal skills but was able to sign some words, indicate yes and no, respond to commands, and use a picture book to identify his immediate needs and wants. (pp. 1078–1079)

The court also pointed out that although yes or no responses required only pointing to the words on the plastic board or simply shaking or nodding his head, the victim was facilitated to use the yes/no board. (If the boy independently pointed to or signed yes or no, the facilitator would obviously have lost control of the boy's responses.) Furthermore, the court rebuked the trial judge and expressed doubts "about the procedure by which the trial court determined that JK [the victim] was able to validly communicate through facilitation" (State v. Warden, 1995, p. 1093). The court described the many prudent steps that might have been taken to identify the author of the responses. Despite this understanding of the need for controls, the majority on the court refused to overturn the lower court's decision because the victim's disqualification as a witness depended solely on the trial judge, and he had ruled that the victim was qualified to respond via facilitated communication.

There was no acceptable, objective evidence that the boy did the typing—which, typically, was filled with errors and was sometimes unintelligible—but there also was no objective evidence that he did *not* do the typing. There were simply no tests performed that would have established the validity of the responses he made through facilitated communication. The defense attorney had in fact requested some obvious controls, including Biklen's suggestion of using another facilitator. Alternatively, the attorney suggested that the facilitator's eyes be averted or that she wear earphones so that music would mask the questions. But the trial judge pointed out that familiarity and predictability were essential for the boy to communicate (a frequent assertion by proponents of facilitated communication and apparently an argument made by the State). He remarked that because this field was so new he had "not permitted people who might otherwise be called experts to testify," and anyway, he really thought his jury might be as capable as were experts to determine what the victim means "because there isn't a consensus on this thing" (State vs. Warden, p. 1088).

Any suggestion that this case provides evidence that facilitated communication is a valid technique raises the larger issue of whether the courts can be vehicles for validity testing. In the view of most psychologists only carefully controlled studies provide an adequate test.

When considering the large number of sexual abuse accusations that occur during facilitated communication one must keep in mind the appalling fact that sexual abuse of developmentally disabled individuals is all too common (e.g., Baladarian, 1991). Reports in the literature often mention that people who are intellectually disabled and have limited ability to communicate may be seen as easy marks. Frequently they do not know what behavior is considered wrong and depend on others for that decision. Furthermore, many such abuses go unreported.

Still, although the literature contains many references to an increased risk of sexual abuse for people with intellectual disabilities, "there are few studies which assess either the actual levels of abuse compared to the general population or the way in which this sexual abuse is related to the knowledge and feelings of the victims" (McCabe, Cummins, & Reid, 1994, p. 298; see also Sobsey, Gray, Wells, Pyper, & Reimer-Heck, 1991). Many of the intellectually disabled participants in the McCabe et al. (1994) study did not know the meaning of the words rape or incest and did not know how to say no to unwanted advances. A significant proportion felt "neutral or good about incest, unwanted sexual contact, rape and sexual abuse" perhaps because "they are made to feel special and valued within these abusive relationships" (pp. 302–303). An informative report from Canada prepared by the G. Allan Roeher Institute (1988) not only emphasized the frequency of sexual abuse of persons with intellectual handicaps but also detailed the many factors that put these persons at risk.

The weight of the evidence is that sexual abuse of developmentally disabled people, primarily children, is widespread. This being the case it follows that at least some of the charges made by facilitators via facilitated communication must *by chance* be true. There is also the possibility that the presence of abuse is being conveyed by other means, some of them not consciously recognized by the facilitator. For many reasons, then, even the substantiation of charges made through facilitated communication does not by itself validate the technique. The only satisfactory resolution is to obtain, in each case, objective evidence that the facilitator is not the one who is responding.

The problems associated with the use of facilitated communication in the courts have been discussed by Meyers (1994). What is very clear is that despite a few aberrations, most judges believe that facilitators are indeed responding for their partners. In contrast to the Warden case, sexual abuse accusations made through facilitated communication have been routinely dismissed by the courts on the basis of the discrepancy between what the clients communicated and how they behaved, the tests that the judges conducted or observed being conducted, and failure to meet the *Frye* standard.

Frequently an objective test is requested before a case comes to trial or even to court. An Australian case provides an example of commendable precaution. Serious charges via facilitated communication had been made by a woman considered to be severely to profoundly mentally retarded. After proper controls were introduced it became evident that the woman "was not able to communicate using facilitated communication techniques" (Hudson, Melita, & Arnold, 1993, p. 171), and the case did not go to court.

Bligh and Kupperman (1993) described the case of a 10-year-old girl who was severely mentally retarded, had autistic characteristics, and was also legally blind. Her special education teacher, trained in facilitated communication, typed questions to her on a computer screen that was presumably read by the child. The same teacher facilitated the child's responses, which after several weeks included charges of sexual abuse against her mother's fiancé. The police were called and the child was removed to a foster home. The teacher "felt strongly that since she was not aware of physically assisting the child or consciously creating the messages, the source of the communication was from the child and the evaluation results would support this" (p. 555). They did not, and the lawyers—agreeing that the source of the communication was the facilitator—requested the court to dismiss the charges. The court granted the request and the child was returned to her family. "However, the teacher who was distraught and confused over the results remained convinced of the validity of the communication and continued to use facilitated communication with her students in her classroom" (p. 556).

Siegel (1995) described the case of a 14-year-old girl and an unrelated 15-year-old boy, both of whom were autistic and who alleged via facilitated communication that they had been sexually abused by their fathers. The boy had initially made his allegations while being facilitated by his teacher and then repeated them with an unfamiliar facilitator who had been asked by the police to try to get him to repeat his allegations. The girl's facilitator was a speech pathologist. After the accusation the girl received a physical examination that did not support the allegation. Nevertheless both children were removed from their homes by child protective service agencies.

In order to determine whether the evidence was sufficient to pursue the cases, two experienced facilitators who were unaware of the charges were recruited from a distant city and each child spent some time getting to know the facilitators and being facilitated by them. To summarize the results, both children usually responded to questions in a meaningful way, but the responses were unrelated to the facts of their family life and also different from one facilitator to the other. "Neither subject expressed any negative affect toward their fathers; no content impugned either father" (p. 324). Charges against both fathers were dropped.

Why so many facilitators are falsely asserting through their partners that abuse has taken place is among the more interesting questions raised by this entire unlikely phenomenon, and an attempt to answer it will be made in Chapter 6.

LITIGATION AGAINST FACILITATED COMMUNICATION

When accusations of abuse against a child's parents or caretakers are made, social agencies have no choice but to take the children from them until a determination can be made. As noted, usually the courts will ultimately return the children to their parents or caretakers. Although very often the parents are targeted, the accusations might target anyone, including other people with autism, professionals and paraprofessionals, peers, other family members, and even family friends. In a Massachusetts case a man who had no previous arrest was accused through facilitated communication of sexually abusing his girlfriend's autistic son. Because he violated the judge's order and allegedly visited his girlfriend before the trial was over he spent 8 months in jail before the judge determined that he had heard no evidence to convince him that facilitated communication was a valid technique (Margolin, 1994).

The pain and anguish experienced by anyone falsely accused, in particular the clients' parents, can never be undone, and many families spend large sums of money for legal help. Some families have begun to fight back; there are suits pending against Biklen, facilitators, social service agencies, schools, and other involved parties, thus far without success as far as I know. According to Gina Green (personal communication, September 12, 1995), two suits against Biklen have been dismissed by the courts, in one case because of "academic freedom" and in the other (which claimed that Biklen was practicing speech pathology without a license) because facilitated communication was ruled not to be speech and language intervention. Similar accusations and litigations are taking place in Australia and in Canada. These suits are not easily won, especially when they are against public employees. In the United States, "Public officials and employees have immunity against damages claimed for alleged civil rights violations, unless the person violated settled laws" (Margolin, 1994, p. 253). Facilitators working in private agencies do not have this mantle of protection. To protect themselves some agencies are preparing informed consent forms for their students. The parents' only protection is to win some of these suits, or better yet, not to allow their children to participate in facilitated communication.

There is money to be made. Manufacturers of simple typing devices and alphabet display boards, marketed through printed ads and videos, claim that using these devices during facilitated communication will assist mentally disabled individuals to communicate. A Federal Trade Commission (FTC) news release, dated December 15, 1994, announced that two companies marketing these communication devices have agreed to settle FTC charges of false and unsubstantiated claims.

DOES FACILITATED COMMUNICATION EVER WORK?

Occasionally there are individuals, generally referred to as *idiots savants* or autistic savants, who despite severe mental retardation and/or autism will display one or more special talent (Treffert, 1989). The most frequent island of exceptionality is in music, but numerical ability and calendar calculating—naming the day of the week of a given date in the past or future—are also relatively common. Extraordinary artistic, mechanical, and memory abilities have been demonstrated, as well as instances of very young autistic children suddenly reading without being taught, albeit with no understanding of what they are reading, a syndrome usually accompanied by severe language (speech) deficiencies (Goldberg, 1987).

Rimland (1990a) presented three such cases which he referred to as "autistic crypto-savants" because the savant skills were hidden by an inability or unwillingness to communicate. The first was a mute 10-year-old boy describe by Rimland as "a non-participating autistic pupil in a class for autistic children" (p. 3). His face and hands were bruised and scarred from hitting himself, which was his response to any request to participate in the classroom activity. Yet one day his teacher, a graduate student in psychology, discovered that the child could type and that she could communicate with him by means of the typewriter. Apparently he had taught himself and needed no one to touch him while he typed.

The second was an 18-year-old student who had never spoken. "He had run his tricycle into a corner, and was unable to figure out how to back it up to get it out, so he continued to try to pedal it forward, grunting" (p. 3). Yet when any book was taken from a shelf and a randomly chosen page was shown to him, he "glanced at it momentarily, then grunted" (p.3), after which he was able to answer correctly any multiple choice question about anything on the page by circling the correct answer.

The third, a 6-year-old boy, "communicates only by writing, and ... only when his teacher's hand is touching his" (Rimland, 1990a, p. 3). By leaving the room and later having the child accurately describe in writing the actions performed by his classmates while she was out, the teacher believed she had proven that she was not guiding the child's hand. We do not know whether a more objective assessment would have confirmed her claim, but these examples suggest that it is possible, in principle, for facilitated communication to work. The problem is that "writing" savants are extremely rare.

Advocates of facilitated communication contend that entombed behind the outer facade of most, if not all, people with autism there lies at least average cognitive competence waiting to be released. According to Crossley the only issue is whether "*most* non-speaking autistic people can communicate through spelling or whether it's really only one sub-category. Work at DEAL certainly supports the view that it's most, if not almost all" (quoted by Rimland, 1990b, p. 2. See also the epigraph at the beginning of this chapter, Makarushka, 1991). Nor do advocates hesitate to make the same claim for those who are severely and profoundly retarded but not autistic (but see Szempruch & Jacobson, 1993). In the face of serious opposition, Biklen (cited by Rimland, 1993a) appeared to have toned down these outlandish claims, but unfortunately they continue to be made.

Personal recollections of people with autism have been recorded and published (Bemporad, 1979; Cesaroni & Garber, 1991; Volkmar & Cohen,

1985), as have fuller autobiographies. Donna Williams (1992) followed her book about her autistic childhood with two subsequent books, but even as a child she could read, write and speak, athough she usually did not wish to do so. Ms. Williams apparently had a very troubled childhood and is emotionally disturbed, but the diagnosis of autism has been questioned. The facility with which she alters her behavior and changes roles has raised the possibility of deception, role playing, and even multiple personality (Gollan, 1996).

An earlier autobiography by Temple Grandin (Grandin & Scariano, 1986) was cited by Biklen (1993) as supporting Oppenheim's (1974) description of autism as communicative apraxia, as well as bolstering his own claim that in autism physical limitations prevent the expression of hidden cognitive competence (praxis). He quoted Grandin's statement that "Up to this time, communication had been a one-way street for me. I could understand what was being said, but was unable to respond. Screaming and flapping my hands was my only way to communicate" (p. 21). "Up to this time" meant up to the age of 3½ years, when she started to talk. Earlier in her book she wrote that she is living proof, "that the characteristics of autism can be modified and controlled.... And this seems to be especially true of autistic children who have meaningful language skills before the age of five" (p. 13).

Annabel Stehli (1991) described the events related to the rise in IQ, from 75 to 97, of her autistic daughter, Georgie. Considering her subsequent accomplishments her true IQ must be considerably higher than 97. She and her daughter attributed Georgie's recovery to a novel approach in which Georgie was assisted in self-adjusting her hearing to avoid hypersensitivity at certain frequencies and to compensate for deficits at others. When she emerged from autism she described to her mother the pain that certain sounds had caused her.

Neither Temple nor Georgie used facilitated communication so there was no danger of anyone speaking for them. In fact, only a minority of children with autism or severe mental retardation have the kind of motor problem that requires someone to hold their hand when they point or type.

A book by Birger Sellin (1993/1995), a young man with autism, contains the daily entries of his facilitated writings, many of them in the form of poems selected by journalist Michael Klonovsky. In his introduction to the book Klonovsky wrote that Birger had been a happy, outgoing child who talked at an early age. At 2 years of age he had a bout of recurrent middle ear infection and vomiting. When he recovered he was a different child, with all the symptoms of autism. Since then he has spoken only once, when he demanded that his father "Give me that ball back!" (Klonovsky's introduction in Sellin, p. 12). Otherwise, there was no communication until the Sellin family was introduced to facilitated communication in August 1990, when Birger was 17.

Klonovsky had heard about Birger in February 1992. He observed him for a while, read all his writings, wrote about him, and apparently encour-

aged publication of a book. Except for the early entries, which were unedited, typing errors and incomplete words were, "at Birger's request," cor-
rected by Klonovsky, even though "Birger has an excellent command of
spelling and grammar. As soon as he began writing for longer periods, he
made hardly any typing errors" (p. 32).

The entries pour out Birger's feelings about his life as a person with
autism, his loneliness, his anxiety, his despair, his lack of self-control, the
reasons for his stereotyped behavior, his triumphs, and his longing to be
normal. The book brought Birger to the attention of the media; indeed, a
French film company is making a film about him. His mother is his principal
facilitator, although his father and a "personal case helper" are also facilitators. His mother was described as a teacher of religious instruction who
studied psychology at the Free University of Berlin from 1977 to 1982. Since
her son's success she has been lecturing on facilitated communication
throughout Germany, presenting Birger's writings as illustrative material.

Here is the entry for October 5, 1991, which concerns facilitated
communication. During facilitation Birger uses one finger on the computer keyboard and consequently there are no capitals. The lack of
punctuation marks is true to the original. This is a translation, of course,
as is the entire book. The *it* referred to in the first line is facilitated
communication.

> not everyone is right for it working with support really
>   properly perseveringly so that i get the feeling i can
>   speak dependently but freely
> i dont think we will find the remnants of such a sure
>   persevering freedom of thought in very many lonely
>   autistic people
> collected thoughts totally dormant tremble with cold
>   when they make their way to the outside light of earth
> they are so sensitive and shy but they give other people an
>   impression of the unusual world of the lonely
> if i werent writing my lonely thoughts would die out so
>   would my very personal stories they would simply die
> but i can write it all down so that nothing can simply die
>   but will live on
> i will write properly as soon as the independent writing
>   looks like no one can think oh nonsense he isnt writing
>   alone at all it is the person supporting his arm
> they are trying to discourage me again the way they did
>   before discouraging me with vexatious doubts
> some of the teachers say these things in the school center. (p. 95)

Although Birger's parents and therapist believe his behavior has improved since he started typing, Klonovsky thinks it is essentially un-
changed.

The exact procedure used in facilitating Birger was never fully described.
Concerning facilitated communication in general, Klonovsky wrote in the

book's introduction that, in time, "Mechanical support can be withdrawn entirely or reduced to a hand laid on the writer's shoulder" (p. 21). He quoted Birger as writing in a letter, "i can write only with the help of another person which is very humiliating and i am ashamed of it" (p. 28). One of the book entries states, "i have noticed that we have the ability to speak but it is blocked somewhere and this is why it is impossible for us to behave properly or write alone" (p. 223). As best I can determine, the facilitators support Birger's lower arm, because that is how Klonovsky described external aid in general. Nowhere was there any statement that Birger can type independently. To determine whether Birger or his facilitators are writing these poignant accounts will take very careful evaluation, which to my knowledge has not yet been carried out.

The possibility is vanishingly small that people with severe and profound mental retardation unrelated to autism have hidden cognitive potential. Yet they too are facilitated, with the usual astonishing results that, alas, are subsequently proven to be the output of the faciliator (see especially Szempruch & Jacobson, 1993). On the other hand, that *some* autistic children have hidden cognitive potential is open to study. The question is how many, how to identify and reach them, and how to avoid the virulent dangers of facilitator direction if, despite everything, they are given facilitated communication.

It would be surprising if not one of the multitude of autistic children who have participated in facilitated communication benefited from it. But as we have seen, there are many potential snares in any assessment. Follow-ups should be routine. Even when a success is reported in an objective study there may be uncontrolled variables that the experimenter was unaware of and that readers, of course, cannot detect. For instance, one study reported dismal results except for one student. "One of the 7 students demonstrated validated facilitated communication on two trials" (Simon, Toll, & Whitehair, 1994, p. 647). The student typed "foritos" after he had just purchased a bag of Fritos, an activity the facilitator was presumably unaware of. However, a follow-up study with this individual—a rare but commendable procedure that would have been even more praiseworthy had it been carried out prior to the first publication—failed to replicate the original finding and suggested that in the first study the facilitator may have smelled the Fritos the student had just eaten (Simon, Whitehair, & Toll, 1995, 1996). This student, incidentally, was able to communicate by a picture exchange system that did not require holding his hand or otherwise supporting him.

But even a success, *properly verified according to accepted scientific standards*, would not change our revulsion over the reckless, unverified claims made for countless other children whose parents are destined for still another disappointment. It would not alter the fact that in the vast majority of instances the facilitators are—unknowingly to be sure—speaking for the students without the students' consent. In such cases proponents, facilitators and parents are living an illusion.

There have always been programs for assisting handicapped individuals to write or type, and there is much research and slow but persistent progress in understanding the communication problems of autistic individuals (Prizant, Wetherby, & Rydell, 1994). Unfortunately time, money, and effort are squandered when there is a useless grasping for chimerical solutions. One facilitated communication devotee has moderated her early enthusiasm and now advocates teaching autistic students to read before being facilitated to write one-word answers.[4] But this logical progression is bypassed by the leading proponents of facilitated communication, who have taken a cult-like rather than a scientifically cautious approach. They cite numerous instances in which severely retarded students, who had never displayed any ability to read, sit down at the keyboard with a facilitator's hand supporting theirs and type out sentences.

Teaching any person with a severe mental disability to type even a single word is a notable achievement, but the claims made by promoters of facilitated communication are far grander than that, making it the latest entry in a dossier filled with astonishing claims (see, e.g., Spitz, 1986; Wolfensberger, 1994). The question is no longer whether, in the overwhelming majority of cases, facilitated communication works. It doesn't. The question now is: How can the facilitators not know they are guiding their partners, and how can the professionals who direct these programs deny the clear objective evidence that this is so? These questions constitute one major theme of this book.

The other major theme, to which we now turn, is that facilitated communication has much in common with many other curiosities, from artful pendulums to clever horses. They are connected, in fact, by a single thread: dissociated involuntary muscle movements.

---

[4]I refer here to Dr. Carol Berger, New Breakthroughs, P.O. Box 25228, Eugene, OR 97402-0447. Note, however, that she is a firm believer in facilitated communication and has published a number of how-to books that can only advance a program unacceptable to responsible professionals and scientists.

2

Involuntary Muscle Movements, Clever Hans, and Lady

An essential element of facilitated communication that demands explanation is the fact that facilitators deny that they are directing the responses of their students. This denial is honest; most facilitators are unaware of their role in the responses, just as all humans are unaware of most of the motor movements they make. Physical movement without conscious control is such a pervasive part of our life that we rarely stop to examine its profound implications. Without thinking about it speakers use hand and arm movements to supplement an argument, drivers control their cars while thinking other thoughts, baseball pitchers reflexively catch line drives that are hit back at them at blinding speeds. Indeed, daily life would be impossible if we had to consciously plan our every movement, from simply walking to dodging cars or, in other circumstances, from escaping predators to tracking game.

Because it is impossible to attend to two events at the same time (although we can alternate rapidly between them), it is essential that motor movements be executed involuntarily while we attend to impinging events. No organism can survive without muscle movement that bypasses awareness and conscious control. For the simplest organisms, that is all there is. In evolutionary development, therefore, nonconscious movement must have preceded the development of consciousness. Consequently it remains a primitive, fundamental, often inaccessible component of the human organism.

Little wonder, then, that people make bodily movements they deny making, particularly when their attention is riveted elsewhere—the very circumstance that gave involuntary muscle movement its favored status in the course of human evolution. Many people are so convinced that they could not have been the source of such movements that they ascribe them to other worldly beings or to mysterious forces that have escaped scientific scrutiny. In psychology's relatively short history many interesting episodes, both in the laboratory and in the field, have illuminated the nature of involuntary muscle movements and their role in shaping belief systems.

COMMITTEE IS BAFFLED BY A CLEVER HORSE

In the September 22, 1904 issue of the British journal *Nature*, this paragraph appeared in the Notes section:

> Scientific critics in Berlin are now much exercised with regard to the remarkable performance of "Clever Hans," the thinking horse. According to the daily Press, a representative committee, which included the director of the Berlin Zoological Gardens, a veterinary surgeon, and a professor of the Physiological Institute of the Berlin University, witnessed these performances with the view of ascertaining whether they were the result of a trick, or whether they were due to the mental powers of the animal. Their verdict, it is reported, was unanimous in favor of the latter view. It is stated that when told that the day was Tuesday, and asked which day of the week this represented, the horse would give the correct answer by taps. Similarly he will tell not only the hour, but the minutes indicated by a watch; while he is reported to be able to record the number of men and of women among a row of visitors, and to indicate the tallest and the shortest members of the party. (Scientific critics, 1904, p. 510)

The description of the horse's performance was accurate, but the commission—"which, by the way, did not give itself this name, since it had been delegated by no one" (Stumpf's introduction in Pfungst, 1911/1965, p. 4)—did not conclude that the remarkable performance was due to the horse's mental powers; the press, as we know, is likely to add such embellishments for the diversion of its readers. In its report of September 12, 1904, the commission stated only that they could find no voluntary or involuntary movements on the part of those present that would have cued the horse. They noted that the horse's master, Herr Wilhelm von Osten, patterned his instruction after the teaching methods used in schools (he was, after all, a retired mathematics teacher), and they concluded that, "This is a case which appears in principle to differ from any hitherto discovered, and has nothing in common with training, in the usual sense of the word, and therefore is worthy of a serious and incisive investigation" (Pfungst, 1911/1965, p. 254). The report was signed by 13 distinguished gentlemen, among whom was Professor Carl Stumpf, director of the Psychological Institute of the University of Berlin.

Stumpf later pointed out that on September 22 (the same day as the infamous note in *Nature*) the newspaper *Frankfurter Zeitung* carried the report of an interview with him, from which the reporter concluded that the horse "learned to discover by purely sensory aids which are so near the threshold that they are imperceptible for us and even the teacher, when he is expected to tap with his foot and when he is to come to rest" (Stumpf, in Pfungst, 1911/1965, p. 5). Later Stumpf confessed that what he had suspected, without saying so, "was some sort of nasal whisper" (p. 7).

Stumpf reported that while he was away from Berlin from September 17 until October 3, "Mr. Schillings continued the investigation, and was assisted in part by Mr. Oskar Pfungst, one of my co-workers at the Psychological Institute" (in Pfungst, 1911/1965, p. 8). On October 13 an informal three-man committee—composed of Pfungst, Stumpf, and E. von Hornbostel—began a more detailed investigation, which they finished on November 29. Again according to Stumpf, "Dr. von Hornbostel had the important task of keeping the records, and Mr. Pfungst undertook the conduct of the experiment" (p. 9).

Stumpf's supplemental report of December 9 briefly summarized the studies carried out primarily by Pfungst. However, the professor was obviously still disturbed by the September 22 note in *Nature*, as well as by the press reports, and so he reiterated that the September 12 committee had

> in no wise declared itself to be convinced that the horse had the power of rational thinking. The committee [had] restricted itself entirely to the question whether or not tricks were involved, and, intentionally and rightly referred the positive investigation to a purely scientific court. (Stumpf's report in Pfungst, 1911/1965, pp. 264–265)

Perhaps Stumpf now wished in retrospect that the commission had expressed some skepticism in their September 12 Report, but they were mystified by the horse's performance. In fact, until Pfungst's brilliant analysis (and in spite of what he had told the reporter) Stumpf had been prepared to change his views "with regard to the nature of animal consciousness, as soon as careful examination would show that nothing else would explain the facts, except the assumption of the presence of conceptual thinking" (Stumpf's introduction in Pfungst, 1911/1965, p. 3).

Stumpf could not have been pleased by the rather derisive article that Meehan (1904) published in *Nature* a month after the September 12 report. Twelve or 13 years ago, wrote Mr. Meehan, he had witnessed similar feats performed by a horse named Mahomet at the Royal Aquarium in London. Mahomet's American master described to Mr. Meehan the extent of the training that was required, and how the horse "had been taught to begin pawing the ground when the trainer looked straight at him, and to cease when the trainer turned his gaze to the floor.... Similarly, he had been drilled into bowing his head at one tone of his trainer's voice, and shaking it on hearing another" (p. 602).

Later, the trainer and Meehan remained to watch another animal act, a clever dog who answered questions and spelled words by moving past the letters of the alphabet strung on a line at the back of the stage. He would pick out the required letters one by one and lay them out in front of the footlights. The feat was wondrous to Meehan until his companion pointed out that the dog's master carried gloves in his hand and that a slight twitch of the gloves, the very barest stir, cued the dog to retrieve the letter he was passing at that moment. After a few further comments about other animal acts that had been reported since at least 1658, Meehan (1904) concluded:

> I am open to conviction, but I am greatly afraid the "German representative committee," including the "professor of the Physiological Institute of the Berlin University," that have reported, according to the daily press, on "Clever Hans" have written themselves down as at least not ungullible. (p. 603)

There were other doubters. Edmund C. Sanford (1914b, footnote 3) credited Emilio Rendich with demonstrating to several members of the committee, and perhaps also to Oskar Pfungst, that Rendich's dog, properly trained, could duplicate the performance of Clever Hans.

But the members of the commission were not naive. Its 13 members, including a circus manager, knew very well that signals were used in animal acts, yet not one of its members—each of whom had been assigned to watch different parts of von Osten's body—found any evidence that von Osten was intentionally or unintentionally influencing the horse's responses. It puzzled them that the horse performed successfully when his master was absent as well as when the person asking the question did not know the answer. When the correct answer was a large number Hans started tapping at a faster rate than he did for smaller numbers, as though recognizing that he had a long way to go. Despite the doubters a mystery remained, and it was a mystery that could not be easily solved because, unlike the animal acts observed by Meehan, Clever Hans, as we shall see, *had trained himself and his master.*

A word first about the horse and its master. Pfungst (1911/1965) described the horse as "a stately animal, a Russian trotting horse," and von Osten as "a man between sixty and seventy.... [whose] white head was covered with a black, slouch hat" (p. 18). As were most of the educated population of Berlin, von Osten was an adherent of Darwin's theory of evolution (Fernald, 1993). If it is true, he reasoned, that humans evolved from lower animals, then horses must have similarly evolved; therefore they must also be advanced intellectually, a thesis he set out to prove by "teaching" (not training) a horse as he would teach a child. In 1888 he began his experiment with the first Hans who, unfortunately, died after 3 years of hard work. But von Osten was persistent and in 1900 bought a second Hans, with whom he had some success. Nevertheless, after a couple of years, at a time when von Osten was ill and had tired of the training he had undertaken (Pfungst, 1911/1965, p. 228), he advertised for sale "a seven-year-old stallion who could distinguish ten colors and knew the four rules of arithmetic"

(Sanford, 1914b, p. 1). Either he had no takers or took renewed heart, because more than a year later there was a very different advertisement, this time inviting readers to a free demonstration of experiments that were being carried out to determine the mental powers of horses.

Using a method that is very familiar to us now, von Osten had spent 4 years teaching this horse to display its mental powers. To teach Hans to point to something with his head von Osten gave a command, pushed the horse's head, and rewarded him with a carrot or a piece of bread. After some time the horse responded to the command and to a mere touch to the head, and then to the command alone. In this way he taught the horse to respond to other commands, such as tapping the ground (lightly) with his hoof. First von Osten guided the horse's leg while simultaneously giving a command (for example, when two wooden pins were placed before Hans, "Raise the foot!—One, two"). Eventually it was no longer necessary for von Osten to physically raise the horse's foot; the horse simply complied with his master's request. The teacher used this hoof-tapping command to teach Hans to count, for example, the number of wooden pins on a table. For correct responses Hans was rewarded with snacks, most welcome because as a sedentary horse he was kept on short rations (Pfungst, 1911/1956, p. 213).

Hans would respond to a request from anyone, even without his master present. He nodded his head if he understood a question and shook it if he did not. He not only counted correctly but added fractions (by tapping first the numerator then the denominator), factored numbers and calculated primes. When wrong he almost always responded correctly when asked how many units he was off. He discriminated colors by indicating, and even retrieving in his muzzle, the cloth of a requested color among many strung on a line. Given a means of communication, the horse now had the ability to express its latent mental powers.

Hans could not only pick out a requested word among a series of printed words, but he could also spell. Von Osten had written the letters of the alphabet in rows and columns on an upright board that was placed in front of the horse. When asked, for example, what a woman in the crowd of observers was holding, Hans would tap out the number of the row and then the column, in this way specifying each letter until he had spelled the word *Schirm* ("parasol"). By similar means, playing cards and musical tones could be indicated by hoof taps. He demonstrated his understanding of musical harmony by tapping out the components of a chord and choosing the tones that must be changed for improved harmony. He could give the date of any day of the current year, could tell time, and could answer questions about the position of the hands of a watch. He recalled correctly an entire sentence from the previous day and recognized persons he had seen but once, or had seen only in old photographs. Needless to say he was not always successful, but he was more successful with his master and (later) with Herr Schillings than with strangers, with some questioners more than with others, and with some people not at all.

He had other powers as well. One day Schillings—the zoologist whom Sanford (1914b) described as "an African explorer and a man of scientific standing" (p. 6)—and a companion approached Hans in his stall. Schillings asked his companion to think to himself of a number between 1 and 20. Schillings then asked Hans to tap out the number, after which Schillings became very still. "On several occasions Hans played his part as mind-reader with astounding success" (p. 6).

Herr von Osten displayed his horse's ability in the courtyard beneath his residence. These demonstrations were intended to provide evidence that he had proved his thesis, and were given in the name of science, not for financial gain. He never charged admission and the horse was no longer for sale, even for the princely offers that were now made.

THE INVESTIGATION BY PFUNGST

Over the 2 months of his investigation, Pfungst did something others did not or could not do: He introduced careful controls.[5] In order to avoid distraction, a large tent was erected in the courtyard. The questioner stood to the right of the horse, as von Osten routinely did, and bits of bread, carrots and sometimes sugar were given for correct responses.

Problems were presented to Hans, but this time the answers were unknown not only to the questioner *but to anyone else who was present*, and results were compared to results obtained when the questioner knew the answer. A series of cards with numbers on them was shown in such a way that nobody but the horse could see them. When the questioner (von Osten, in this case) knew the number, the horse was correct 98% of the time; when no one knew which number was exposed, the horse was 8% correct (chance level). Words were written on cards and hung in a row in front of Hans. When asked which card held a particular word, all his responses were correct when the questioner knew the answer, none when he did not. Similarly, when Pfungst knew the placement of only two letters on the alphabet board in front of Hans, then whispered a word in the horse's ear, every letter Hans tapped out was incorrect except the two that Pfungst knew. When Hans was asked to add the number von Osten whispered in his ear (so no one else could hear it) to the number that Pfungst then whispered to him, Hans got 3 of 31 correct, compared with 29 of 31 correct when both numbers were known to the whisperers.

---

[5]In 1907 Pfungst recorded the entire episode in a book that included the September 12 and December 9 reports, two other supplements, and an introduction by Stumpf. The heart of the book was Pfungst's experimental investigation. An English translation by Carl L. Rahn was published in 1911 by Henry Holt & Company and included a prefatory note by Professor James R. Angell. In 1965 the 1911 book was reissued under the editorship of Robert Rosenthal, who also provided an introduction. I used the 1965 edition.

And so it went. The mystery, then, was the nature of the cues. Were they auditory or visual? Blinders were placed on Hans and he was asked questions by someone standing next to him but beyond his view and then again when the questioner moved forward to the horse's field of vision. Tellingly, in the former case Hans tried very hard to see the questioner, but when it was certain that he could not he performed only at a chance level (6% correct), compared to 89% correct when he could. The cues were visual. But what were they?

Here is what Pfungst (1911/1965) wrote:

> Investigations of the other senses became needless, for I had, in the meantime, succeeded in discovering the essential and effective signs in the course of my observations of Mr. von Osten. These signs are minimal movements of the head on the part of the experimenter. As soon as the experimenter had given a problem to the horse, he [the experimenter], involuntarily, bent his head and trunk slightly forward.... As soon as the desired number of taps had been given, the questioner would make a slight upward jerk of the head. (p. 47)

In sum, a slight bend forward (or just lowering one's head a bit) was a signal to Hans to start tapping, whether he had been asked a question or not. A slight upward movement told him to stop, after which one could return to a normal position. As proof, purposely making these movements produced the expected responses in the horse.

But why hadn't these involuntary movements been picked up by any of the sharp-eyed observers? For one thing, the movements were, in Pfungst's word, extremely minute. For another, von Osten was at the same time constantly walking back and forth and making many other movements. In a word, the critical cues were camouflaged. Schillings—to whom Hans responded very well—was serendipitously helpful because he was less restless and the crucial movements were more distinct.

In fact, the cues were generally more obvious in others than they were in von Osten, but for questioners who did not make the key movements, or who made different movements, the horse performed poorly or failed entirely. When the "stop" signal (given without awareness, of course) was slightly premature or delayed, Hans would be incorrect by a single tap. Pfungst noted that von Osten usually wore a wide-brimmed hat that "made the movements appear on a larger scale.... But observation was successful, even at a distance of 1½ meters, when he worked with head uncovered. And even if head and forehead were covered entirely, it was still possible to note the movements by watching the eye-brows" (Pfungst, 1911/1956, p. 49). Indeed, although not as reliable as an upward head movement, almost any upward movement served as a stop signal, including not only raised eyebrows but also "the dilation of the nostrils—as in a sneer" (p. 63), or raising the arm or elbow nearest the horse. Hand movements were ineffective, as were all horizontal movements. Anybody could get Hans started but—with exceptions—unless the questioner was a person with whom he had worked for some time, Hans uniformly looked to the most significant person in view (von Osten, if he was there) in order to get his stop signal.

Furthermore, if Hans seemed to be stopping too soon, a slight bend forward by whomever Hans was watching prolonged the response. In fact, "the greater the angle at which the body inclined forward, the greater the horse's rate of tapping" (Pfungst, 1911/1965, p. 64). Consequently, when Hans was given a problem requiring a large number of taps von Osten would unwittingly "bend forward somewhat more, owing to his desire to observe the tapping more carefully" (p. 220). Hans's increased rate of tapping had nothing to do with a prescient equine intelligence concerning the length of the response.

There was another interesting finding. When a series of numbers was repeated, the horse improved his performance the second time around. It is likely, therefore, that the questioners, without awareness, were improving their signaling skills (were training themselves).

Pfungst noted that even after he had solved the mystery there were times when he made involuntary movements that cued the horse, especially when he concentrated strongly on the desired number. He determined, by introspection, that an important element was *the questioner's wish that the horse should succeed*. This wish initiated muscular tension in the head and neck, which increased as Hans approached the correct number. When the correct number was reached the questioner relaxed, signaling the horse to stop tapping. Too much or too little tension caused a premature or delayed release, respectively, and consequently an incorrect response.

As a rule, the horse failed when the questioner did not know the answer even when the spectators did. There were important exceptions, however. When Hans was accustomed to responding to someone among the spectators, or when someone was around who regularly fed him, the horse would succeed in his tapping responses. One time when Hans's groom (stablehand) happened to be among the observers, Hans responded correctly when only his groom knew the answer (Pfungst, 1911/1965, p. 38). Another exception occurred when a single unfamiliar observer was present in addition to the questioner (in Hans's stall, for example). In such a case the horse read the signals unwittingly given by the observer, even though the observer was a stranger.

But the horse also nodded "yes" and shook his head "no" and in other ways used his head to respond. How did he know when to tap and when to use his head? Experiments indicated that when the questioner stood very straight and *raised* his head almost imperceptibly, Hans began to nod and would continue to nod until the questioner lowered his head. These head movements were in the opposite direction of the start and stop signals for tapping. Another cue separated tapping from head movement. "Hans responded with a nod of the head whenever the experimenter, while bending forward, chanced to stand in front of, or to the side of the horse's head, but … he would begin to tap in response to the same signal, as soon as the experimenter stood farther back. The difference in the two signals, therefore, was very slight" (Pfungst, 1911/1965, pp. 75–76). Presumably the stop signal could be given from anywhere.

A somewhat higher than usual upward or downward movement of von Osten's head caused Hans to throw his head upward or downward, as if pointing. A minuscule turn of von Osten's head to the right or left was mirrored by a turn of Hans's head to the left or right. When von Osten turned his head ever so slightly first to the right then to the left, Hans followed with a left to right shake of the head, thereby giving a "no" response. In one experiment the questioner—standing erect in front of Hans—did not know that he was holding a card with a zero on it. Without being aware he was doing so,[6] he leaned forward expecting Hans to indicate the number on the card (usually a number larger than zero), but instead of shaking his head to indicate a zero, Hans started tapping. This "error" would not have happened had the questioner known what was on the card.

To maneuver (unwittingly) Hans to a series of cards or colors hanging on a line or placed along the ground, the questioner merely, and naturally, turned in their direction. As Hans proceeded there the questioner, by turning slightly left or right, could delicately (and unknowingly) control Hans's movement, thereby leading him toward the correct response. As might be expected, however, errors were frequent in this task, especially when there were many items or when they were placed close together. His performance improved when he also received auditory signals. If he was about to pick up the wrong cloth and von Osten shouted at him ("wrong" or "blue" or some other exclamation), Hans would move on. "If he was approaching a series from the right, then a call would cause him to turn to the left, if he was coming from the left, he would turn to the right" (Pfungst, 1911/1965, p. 84).

Over the 4 years in which von Osten thought he was teaching Hans to read, spell, and cipher, it was Hans who was doing all the teaching. In order to receive his edible rewards, Clever Hans had not only trained himself, he had also—with exquisite precision—trained his master. In the year of B. F. Skinner's birth, Hans and von Osten had unknowingly followed, and Pfungst had artfully uncovered, the principles that were to form the basis of behaviorism some 30 years later.

---

[6]We might simply call these involuntary movements "unconscious," but there is much disagreement about the use of that term. Pfungst (1911/1965) wondered whether these involuntary movements, when not noted, were truly unconscious or merely "at the fringe." His own inclination was "to believe that these movements are not unconscious, but merely unattended to" (p. 203). More on this subject later.

BACK TO THE LABORATORY

After the preliminary December report, which revealed some of Pfungst's findings, von Osten withdrew his permission for further investigations. But even before then, in November 1904, Pfungst had begun related experiments with humans in the laboratory at the Psychological Institute of the University of Berlin. In these, Pfungst took the role of Hans. He would have a questioner stand to his right and concentrate strongly on a number or a simple addition while Pfungst would tap with his right hand until he detected an involuntary stop signal. He tested 25 people, including 5-year-old children, none of whom knew the purpose of the experiment. All but 2 of the 25 made some kind of involuntary movement, primarily the slight upward head movement when the final number was reached. Pfungst not only correctly guessed the number, but even the addends of an addition problem a subject had silently improvised. Subjects were also asked to think of one of the directional words (up, down, left, right, yes, or no) when given the command "Now," and Pfungst determined which word the subject was thinking of by observing the slight directional head and eye movements. Pfungst's subjects were unable to figure out how he did it and were "thoroughly astonished" when he told them.

In an interesting variation he asked subjects to stand with their heads back while he tapped out the number they were thinking. When the number was reached, the subjects would usually move their head *forward* as an involuntary stop signal—in contrast to the typical upward head movement that usually served as a stop signal. Analogously, left or right stop signals could be induced by having the subjects bend their heads slightly right or left as Pfungst started to tap. From these tests Pfungst deduced a general principle: "The release of muscular tension which occurs with the cessation of psychic tension tends to bring about that position of the head (and body) which, at the time, represents the slightest amount of muscular strain" (Pfungst, 1911/1965, p. 104).

However, this principle did not apply to the choosing of an item in a series. When five sheets of paper were laid out on the floor, Pfungst correctly determined about 80% of the time which sheet a subject was thinking of. He succeeded by observing the subject's inadvertent eye glance and, at times, head and body movement in the direction of the chosen sheet. When the distances between the sheets of paper were greatly reduced, success decreased, as it had with Hans. In this and other experiments, the greater the subject's attention and concentration—up to a point—the easier the perception of the signs. With the tapping responses, for example, a questioner's concentration induced tension (the greater the concentration, the greater the tension), and the subsequent release of tension produced the involuntary body movement (signal). However, there was an ideal concentration level: Whereas too much concentration could lead to a premature release, too little concentration could produce either premature or delayed release.

More precise studies were undertaken with Schillings and three university students, two of whom (Schillings and one of the students) knew something of the movements involved. An instrument was attached to a subject's head to record head movements and at the same time a pneumograph recorded the subject's respiration while Pfungst tapped out the number that a subject was silently contemplating. As might be expected, best results were obtained from the two subjects who had no knowledge of the expected movements. Astonishingly, although there was much variation in the extent of the head movements that unwittingly gave the stop signal, the average was 1 *millimeter* (0.039 inches) with a range of 0.1 to 2.3 millimeters. Invariably this stop signal corresponded with a deep inhalation (although the stop signal occurred even when subjects were requested to hold their breath). Based on the curves obtained in the laboratory, Pfungst estimated the magnitude of von Osten's signaling head movement as less than 0.2 millimeters—or 0.3 millimeters when measurements were made of the distance traveled by the brim of von Osten's wide-brimmed hat. No wonder members of the committee had failed to find any cues despite their determined efforts.

THE AFTERMATH

In his review of the 1911 publication of Pfungst's book, Harry Miles Johnson (1911) commented on von Osten's reaction:

> A pathetic incident of the investigation was the grief and indignation of Mr. von Osten when the facts were laid before him. He felt, despite the expressions of confidence in his good faith published by the experimenters, that his character had been questioned and his years of work wrongfully discredited, for he never could bring himself to accept their conclusions. At his death, which occurred not many months later, he was doubtless yet unaware of the service which he had unwittingly rendered to a young science. (p. 665)

He spent his remaining time (which, contrary to Johnson's assertion, apparently was many months, perhaps closer to a year) trying to rid Hans "of the habit of responding to signals, into which the scientific experimenters had stupidly trained him" (Sanford, 1914b, p. 16). As far as von Osten was concerned, it was all the fault of the scientific investigation.

For Pfungst, the juxtaposition of his own interests and abilities with the celebrity of Clever Hans was a happy match that gave him a sliver of immortality at the same time that it provided psychology with increased leverage in its search for scientific status. His talents were called on again shortly thereafter to investigate Don, the talking dog, who was said to have a vocabulary of eight words. Pfungst's brief report, summarized in English by H. M. Johnson (1912), displayed his typical thoroughness. According to Johnson, Pfungst described Don's voice as "a high tenor, ranging from F [sic] on the bass clef to the octave above middle c, usually pitched in talking near d above middle c" (p. 750). After further meticulous analysis, "Mr. Pfungst concludes that the speech of Don is...to be regarded properly as the production of vocal sounds which produce illusions in the hearer" (p. 750).

The Clever Hans investigation was the apex of Pfungst's career; he died in 1932 at the age of 57. After his publication on the talking dog I can find no record of his subsequent work. In fact, the only mention given him in Boring's (1950) *A History of Experimental Psychology* occurs in a list of influential psychologists who were Stumpf's students, but there is no mention of Pfungst's work with Clever Hans—a regrettable omission, in my opinion. Pfungst's work was a landmark in psychology. It later formed the basis of an extensive literature on how experimenters inadvertently influence their subjects (Rosenthal, 1966), and it is still indispensable in tempering overly zealous claims that we can teach sign language to other primates and then converse with them, syntax and all (e.g., Sebeok & Rosenthal, 1981; Sebeok & Umiker-Sebeok, 1979). The general mechanism of unconsciously influencing other organisms became an instrument for self-fulfilling prophecies.

Stumpf, who was 56 in 1904 and lived another 32 years, had a distinguished academic career and published profusely, primarily "on the problems of tone and of music" (Boring, 1950, p. 366).

But Hans was not finished. A wealthy jeweler from Elberfeld, Karl Krall, continued to believe in Hans and persuaded von Osten to cooperate with him on new experiments with Hans. When von Osten died, Krall acquired Hans and continued his experiments. He purchased two other horses, and later others (collectively known as the Elberfeld horses, one of whom was blind) and introduced improved training techniques that produced in a matter of months achievements that "soon surpassed those of Hans at his best" (Sanford, 1914b p. 17). Their performances were applauded appreciatively.

Krall believed that human and animal minds were identical, a fact obscured from science because there was no means of communicating. This barrier, said Krall, was breached by von Osten, to his everlasting glory. "Krall's own function had been to save von Osten's great discovery from oblivion (impending on account of the blunders of Pfungst and the bigotry of science)" (Sanford, 1914b, p. 19).

Having reviewed, in 1908, Pfungst's book in the original German edition, Sanford (1914a) reviewed the 1911 English translation along with Krall's lengthy book and four related papers on the Elberfeld horses. Two of the papers were by the Swiss psychologist, Edouard Claparède. The first, in 1912, described his observations of the Elberfeld horses and his conviction that correct answers were given "under conditions which exclude absolutely the hypothesis of voluntary or involuntary signs" (p. 133). He believed it was logically possible for horses to have this kind of intellectual power, although he pointed out the necessity for more rigorous experiments. Claparède's second paper recounted another series of observations a couple of years later, when he and two colleagues had an opportunity to work with the horses when Krall was present as well as when he was absent. This time the results were negative, particularly on tests where the questioner had no knowledge of the answer. He nevertheless defended Krall by countering the protests "by opponents of Krall's views among German zoologists and comparative psychologists" (p. 134).

One of Sanford's (1914a) remaining two reviews was of a paper by William Mackenzie presented to a meeting of the Italian Society for the Progress of Science, where Mackenzie defended Krall and expressed his belief that the Elberfeld horses thought independently. The final paper, by Max Ettlinger—described by Sanford as "a literary man and magazine editor of Munich, a student and writer of some years' standing in animal psychology" (p. 135)—was the only truly critical one.

LADY THE WONDER HORSE

Belief in learned animals was documented at least 3 centuries before Clever Hans (Mountjoy & Lewandowski, 1984), and neither Pfungst's revelations nor the advance of science has dulled its enduring attraction. In 1952 *Life* magazine revisited Lady, a 27-year-old horse whose psychic powers were first suspected by her owner in 1925, not long after the horse was born. By 1927 her fame had spread, but in 1940 Lady's powers had abandoned her and she was put out to pasture. Surprisingly, in 1950 it was discovered that her psychic powers (and more prosaic ability to read and cipher) had returned (Truitt, 1952). A sign near the road declared that LADY WONDER HORSE WILL SPELL AND SUBTRACT MULTIPLY DIVIDE TELL TIME ANSWER QUESTIONS, open to the public for a nominal fee. What the customer saw was a swaybacked 27-year-old mare standing in front of an array of levers on which she typed out her responses by pressing her nose on the required lever, causing the letter or number to pop up. Not exactly touch typing but not too shabby for a horse.

Like Hans, Lady responded to people who were not her trainer and who could not have known they were giving cues. It was reported in *This Week* that a Mr. Les Leiber went unexpectedly to Lady's barn, clutching in his hand a paper on which he had written his name. When Lady spelled out LES, Mr. Leiber said it gave him the willies (Christopher, 1970).

Among those impressed with Lady's wondrous abilities were Joseph B. Rhine, his wife Louisa E. Rhine, and William McDougall, all of whom, incidentally, were also convinced that the Lamarckian theory of the inheritance of acquired characteristics was valid. McDougall, an important figure in psychology's relatively short history, had been at Oxford from 1904 to 1920, when he moved to Harvard University where the Chair of Psychology had been vacant since Münsterberg's death during the war. Having served on the council and as president of England's Society for Psychical Research (founded in 1882), he joined its counterpart in the United States, the American Society for Psychical Research, founded in 1884 by a committee that included William James and G. Stanley Hall.[7] In his contribution to Murchison's *A History of Psychology in Autobiography* McDougall said of his limited work in psychical research, "If I had not found it necessary to earn some income, I should perhaps have chosen to give all my time and energy to work in this field" (McDougall, 1930/1961, p. 220). In 1927, when he was 56 and had achieved prominence as an experimental and theoretical psychologist (for work unconnected to his interest in psychical research), he left Harvard to develop a psychology department at Duke University, where he remained until his death in 1938.

Some 24 years McDougall's junior, Joseph Rhine, along with his wife Louisa, had earned a University of Chicago doctorate in biology (botany), which he subsequently taught at West Virginia University. But botany was soon to be a spurned love. Early in the 1920s the Rhines attended a lecture on spiritualism given by Arthur Conan Doyle and were so impressed that they decided that spiritualism and mental telepathy were subjects worthy of exploration. Obviously aware that McDougall—himself influenced by the psychical research of William James—would be a sympathetic mentor, they went to Harvard in 1926 just as McDougall was leaving for a journey round the world that was to terminate at Duke (McDougall, 1935). The Rhines were assigned (by James, no doubt) to work under Walter Franklin Prince (not to be confused with Morton Prince) of the Boston Society for Psychical Research. The following year Joseph Rhine became a research assistant to McDougall at Duke, doing research on psychic forces. He became a faculty member in 1928 and director of the parapsychology lab in 1940 (Boring, 1950; Christopher, 1970; Gardner, 1957).

---

[7]Hall left the society before his term on the Council was completed, disenchanted, as were many others, with the direction the society was taking. Only 4 years younger than James, they had formed a friendship on Hall's earlier visit to Cambridge, Massachusetts. They renewed the friendship when Hall returned and in 1878 earned his doctorate at Harvard, where James was on the faculty and "took great interest in the experiments connected with my thesis" (G. S. Hall, 1923, p. 219). However, Hall's subsequent interests took a decidedly different turn from James's (Boring, 1950). More on this in Chapter 4, and see Rosenzweig (1994).

The American Society for Psychical Research was dissolved as an independent organization in 1890, discontinuing the publication of its *Proceedings* and becoming the American Branch of the Society for Psychical Research; that is, a branch of England's society, which frequently published its minutes. In 1906 even the branch was dissolved. That same year the American Institute for Scientific Research was formed in New York, one section of which became the present American Society for Psychical Research (Burkhardt & Bowers, 1986).

Mrs. Claudia Fonda acquired Lady when she was 2 weeks old. According to Rhine and Rhine (1929a) she "reared her on the bottle" (p. 452), and according to Christopher (1970) she "raised Lady as she would a child.... [and] taught her how to count, master the alphabet, then perform simple feats of mathematics" (p. 40). During this period of training, Lady responded by touching wooden blocks of numbers and letters. Mrs. Fonda was surprised that Lady learned so quickly and even more surprised that she would often respond before her trainer had asked her the question, which indicated to Mrs. Fonda that the horse could read minds. She decided to exhibit Lady's accomplishments and word soon spread not only about Lady's school learning but also, and of even greater interest to the public, about Lady's ability to express opinions, give personal advice and, most marvelous of all, read people's minds and predict the future. There was no need to question the horse; a person need only write down a question and show it to Mrs. Fonda and without a word being said the mind-reading horse responded.

Duke University in Durham, North Carolina is not far from the outskirts of Richmond, Virginia where Lady, in 1927 a 3-year-old filly, performed. In December of that year the Rhines, occasionally accompanied by McDougall, traveled to Richmond to study Lady's telepathic ability (more precisely labeled, in the name of science, extra sensory perception or ESP).

They knew all about Pfungst's experiments but were not convinced by them. In the introduction of a subsequent paper describing their study—published in *The Journal of Abnormal and Social Psychology*—the Rhines commented on a study by Yerkes, who "compared the case to that of Clever Hans, at that time famous among psychologists as a study of *supposed* [italics added] unconscious indication" (Rhine & Rhine, 1929a, p. 450). Unlike many others, they wrote, they were open-minded. The attitude of "curious skepticism" about telepathic abilities in animals was unwarranted, they warned, and only hard facts should decide the issue.

Obviously, then, the horse's telepathic ability could not be validated if there was any evidence of conscious or unconscious signaling, so the Rhines set out to discover any cues that Lady might be picking up. Just like Pfungst, but without Pfungst's perspicacity and patience. They carried out their experiments on 6 different days over a 6-week period, from December 3, 1927 to January 15, 1928, in a 9 x12 foot demonstration tent. The filly's stall was in one corner of the tent, and on a table in the center was the material Lady used to indicate her answers. McDougall participated on 2 of the 6 testing days, and John Thomas, Assistant Superintendent of the Detroit schools, participated on 1. Mrs. Fonda's husband was occasionally present.

Mrs. Fonda stood to the left of the horse's head, holding a whip in the hand that was away from the horse. Initially, Lady's abilities in unrestricted conditions were established. She correctly spelled a word or chose a number or design written or drawn on a pad by an experimenter and shown to Mrs.

Fonda. She indicated the time, did arithmetic problems, spelled out answers to questions, and found the appropriate picture blocks.

Following this the critical tests began. For purposes of the experiment only 10 or fewer letter blocks (each with a letter on one side only) or 10 or fewer number plates (0 to 9) were used at a time, and the order of the letters or numbers was frequently changed. The 10 number plates were placed in two rows of 5. Sometimes only 5 numbers or letters were used, and on one test only 2 letters. Less frequently used were picture blocks and cards with unnameable designs drawn on them. Lady responded by touching the blocks or plates with her nose.

In a typical test, experimenters picked a letter, number, or position and informed Mrs. Fonda of their choice. Then they gradually eliminated possible cues. First Mrs. Fonda was requested to remain silent, then told to remain motionless. All or most of the horse's responses were nevertheless correct, even when the letter blocks were turned face down and the selected position was indicated to Mrs. Fonda on a diagram drawn on a pad. Furthermore, the horse correctly picked the chosen unnameable design. The conclusion was that Lady did not have superior intelligence and did not know her letters; knowledge of location alone was sufficient.

An attempt was then made to restrict Mrs. Fonda's head and eye movements. Unfortunately, "she glanced back at Lady several times" (Rhine & Rhine, 1929a, p. 456). On this test Lady was correct half the time on numbers and entirely correct on position. During the position test Mrs. Fonda "glanced around momentarily at about the time Lady touched. During the last five [tests] both she and R [J. B. Rhine] were motionless and silent. No one else knew the number" (p. 456). On these and related tests, Lady was quite successful. But why didn't J. B. Rhine leave the room? He must have known that Clever Hans had been cued by questioners from the audience.

A failure occurred when Mrs. Fonda was requested to keep her eyes closed so Lady could not see them. Only two letters were used. McDougall mixed the blocks and Mrs. Fonda and J. B. Rhine did not see them after they were mixed. This was the *only* test in which only Mrs. Fonda and J. B. Rhine knew the letter chosen *but in which neither knew its location.* Under these conditions, "The horse's movements lacked their usual definiteness.... [and she] touched or nodded ... in an apparently random fashion" (p. 457). As far as the experimenters were concerned, this proved that the horse was using location only. Presumably telepathy was not ruled out because *someone* had to know the location of the chosen letter in order to send it to the horse!

A folded woolen scarf was used to cover Mrs. Fonda's face from her forehead to her nose (which, however, would allow Mrs. Fonda to see by looking downward under the scarf). J. B. Rhine "looked away during the tests.... [and] gave the location [to Mrs. Fonda] by description only, speaking in low tones to F. Numbers were changed around so that F would not know the number at a given location" (p. 457). Lady correctly identified five different locations. Unfortunately, we don't know how low the whisper was or who else in the tent might have heard it, nor how much Mrs. Fonda saw from beneath her blindfold.

The evidence thus far indicated to the experimenters that "Some unusual transfer of thought, whether by signaling or by telepathy, is involved. Either explanation is theoretically adequate to explain the results without the assumption of superior intelligence" (Rhine & Rhine, 1929a, p. 457). Because some of the test results indicated that Lady's responses were based on location, not on a knowledge of letters or numbers, the experimenters no longer felt subject to the criticism that they entertained assumptions of superior equine intelligence. The horse really couldn't spell or do arithmetic but "was somehow directed to a given location" (p. 458). Intelligence was eliminated but not telepathy. The possibility that thoughts in the human brain were somehow carried through the air and then reintegrated and interpreted by a horse continued to merit thoughtful scientific interest.

It was difficult to separate Mrs. Fonda from her horse because as soon as Lady discovered her absence she stopped working. A few tests were managed, however. In one, L. E. Rhine interposed herself between the horse and her trainer, and Mrs. Fonda gradually withdrew. In another, an 18 x 18 inch board was used to partially screen Mrs. Fonda. Lady continued to perform quite well. On one test, with Mrs. Fonda blindfolded and outside the tent, McDougall audibly requested the horse to compute ½ of 68. Lady responded with a 32 on her first trial and a 34 on her second. But here again the researchers forgot or ignored Pfungst's findings that other people in addition to the trainer could cue the horse.

In the final series of tests Mrs. Fonda was to be kept entirely ignorant of the chosen number, but there always was someone in Lady's view who knew the answer. In spite of all they had read, the experimenters were convinced that they could control their own movements. Here are typical comments (Rhine & Rhine, 1929a):

F [Mrs. Fonda] ignorant of number. Precautions against unconscious signalling. T [Mr. Thomas] and R [J. B. Rhine] alone knew number. (p. 460)

R alone knew the block, which he chose mentally. He stood motionless except for his eyes, which were shaded by his hat from the vision of F and Lady. He was consciously non-communicative and held his head straight ahead throughout. His hands were clasped in front against the body. (p. 460)

Group C demonstrated that others could act as agents [senders], instead of F [Mrs. Fonda]. Though not as successful as F, they still succeeded well above the allowance for chance, *even when under conscious control over unconscious indications* [italics added]. (p. 461)

In the one instance in which they took precautions against anyone in the tent knowing the answer, the horse failed. Pfungst had taken that precaution almost at once (although he experimented to see whether Hans could spell, not whether Hans was telepathic).

In their discussion, Rhine and Rhine (1929a) ruled out two of three possible explanations of Lady's behavior: that the horse was using consciously given signals or unconsciously given cues. "There is left, then, only the telepathic explanation, the transference of mental influence by an unknown process. Nothing was discovered that failed to accord with it, and no other hypothesis proposed seems tenable in view of the results" (p. 463).

In a supplement at the end of the paper they described unexpectedly dropping in on Mrs. Fonda 3 months later when the Fondas were preparing to move for the summer. Mrs. Fonda had not been well and she was impatient with Lady, who was misbehaving. "As would be expected on a theory of telepathy, the horse did not work well and made many mistakes, even for Mrs. Fonda herself.... It seemed probable that Mrs. F. was not calm and self-controlled enough on this occasion to keep her own mind blank" (p. 463). Thus are failures turned into support for a favorite theory.

Also in 1929 the Rhines published the results of a further study of Lady, which had taken place about 8 months after previously described incident. This time they found that the horse was clearly responding to cues. As a result, "We were forced to conclude that the telepathic ability we earlier found the horse to possess has been now almost if not entirely lost.... Unfortunate to science as this change in Lady is, at least the negative results of our final week of experimentation may be taken as a check upon our earlier conclusion that the horse was then telepathic" (Rhine & Rhine, 1929b, p. 291).

Four years after the *Life* article a professional magician, Milbourne Christopher (1970), accompanied a friend from the *Saturday Evening Post* to a private audience with Lady. Under an assumed name, Christopher played the role of photographer. As part of the demonstration he and his friend were each given a pad and a pencil and told to stand far away from the stall and write numbers on the pad. Neither Lady nor Mrs. Fonda could see what they wrote. Lady showed her clairvoyance by correctly typing each number after it was written. She was correct, that is, until Christopher went through the motion of writing a 9, but only touched the pencil to the pad to produce a 1. Lady incorrectly typed 9. Christopher concluded that Mrs. Fonda was reading the path of the top part of the pencil, a ploy that is familiar to magicians because it is a staple of mediums. Mrs. Fonda had simplified her task by giving them unusually narrow (2½-inch) pads and long pencils. Here was another source of Lady's success that the Rhines and McDougall were unlikely to spot.

In fact psychologists (and other scientists) have no special talent for detecting duplicity and would do well to take a professional magician with them when they explore the source of extraordinary demonstrations. "Most people assume that if a man has a brilliant mind he is qualified to detect fraud. This is untrue. Unless he has been thoroughly trained in the underground art of magic, and knows its peculiar principles, he is easier to deceive than a child" (Gardner, 1981, p. 92). We should now add that misperceptions and missed perceptions can occur even when there is no intentional fraud, because few people have a thorough understanding of the power of involuntary muscle movements.

3

Clever Hans and Facilitated Communication

Herr von Osten, understandably, could not accept Pfungst's findings, for he had expended all the energies of his waning years on proving the advanced mentality of horses. He had wasted time and effort on a horse that died, but gamely started anew with a second horse. He must have been overwhelmingly proud of Hans's performance. Under such circumstances, who could accept the verdict that Hans was not performing arithmetic, was not spelling words, was not choosing colors, was not analyzing chords, but in every instance was responding only to exquisitely small bodily movements? Whether the problem was mathematics or spelling was totally irrelevant to the horse, who couldn't have cared less whether wooden pins or an alphabet board was set before him.

And so it is in facilitated communication. In typical cases, whether facilitated students are asked to tell a story, spell a word, answer a question or name a picture couldn't matter less. In the minds of facilitators their students are responding to questions by spelling out words. In the students' minds their hands are being directed across a keyboard until their finger presses a key. Or their hands wander across the keyboard until they receive a signal—perhaps pressure on a shoulder or a slight touch—to push a key. Nor is direct contact necessary for a signal to be given, as Pfungst demonstrated.

Even the founder of facilitated communication, Rosemary Crossley (1994), conceded that "subtle physical signals" (p. 111) could be given by the facilitator, although she believes it is rare and does not invalidate the method. In one of her examples she contended that the client was consciously doing the manipulating:

Jill was attending a regular secondary school when some of the facilitators who worked with her in class said she was "getting into their thoughts." Jill's mother also thought she [Jill] was telepathic and gave examples of situations in which Jill had typed information known only to her [mother]. At this stage Jill was receiving only minimal facilitation from her mother, generally typing just with her mother's hand on her knee. When I asked Jill and her mother to demonstrate Jill's "telepathy" it became clear that Jill was picking up physical cues from her mother. (p. 110)

Jill's mother, continued Crossley, was unconsciously moving her hand (her own hand, presumably) "toward the next letter she expected Jill to hit in an effort to speed up her typing, in the same way as a passenger may press a nonexistent accelerator or brake to speed up or slow down an incompetent driver. As she thought Jill was telepathic she expected Jill to type what she was thinking, so the process became self-reinforcing" (p. 110). Crossley went on to say that Jill admitted to picking up cues from her school facilitators "so she could get answers to her school work, and then, once she discovered it was possible, for fun" (p. 110). It was all a game on Jill's part, you see. "She would introduce a likely topic into her typing—if they [the facilitators] jumped to attention she would continue exploring it, if not she would erase the typing and it would just seem like a loss of attention" (p. 110). Jill was allowing the facilitators to reveal themselves by typing without awareness. This is a succinct description of the technique used by "mind-readers," a subject included in the next chapter.

No doubt Jill's mother would have been a firm believer in Lady's clairvoyant powers, as would advocates who use telepathy as an explanation for the performance of students being facilitated. According to Haskew and Donnellan (1993):

> Shortly after facilitation begins ... facilitators often report that their communicators have an uncanny ability to know thoughts in their facilitators' minds. Exploration usually reveals that communicators have a well developed "sixth sense" that allows them both to understand what others think, feel, or know, and to transmit their own thoughts to other nonverbal acquaintances, and sometimes to their facilitators.... Reports that facilitated communicators seem to be able to read their facilitators' and other people's minds surface wherever facilitation is attempted. We have reports from dozens of sources in several countries, and the numbers continue to grow. (p. 13)

Haskew and Donnellan denied that facilitators can be the source of the communication because "facilitators themselves say this is nonsense" (p. 13). So committed are Haskew and Donnellan that they are unable to accept a more reasonable explanation: The communications contain information that only the facilitators know because the facilitators themselves are, without awareness, directing the typing. Naturally the facilitators deny this, just as those who questioned Clever Hans and Lady denied their roles in the horses' responses.

After giving three illustrations of students knowing intimate details of their facilitators' lives—e.g., "A mother told us about the adjustments she has made knowing that she can have no secrets from her teenage daughter" (p. 14)—Haskew and Donnellan (1993) reported that "among experienced facilitators" the occurrence of this sixth sense "is no longer controversial; and that it has enormous utility for speech is self-evident" (p. 14). If people without speech could communicate by a sixth sense it would indeed be useful, but these assertions are nothing less than bizarre. They are followed by speculations about "vestigial psychic abilities" that are even more preposterous.

Haskew and Donnellan, among many others, should take note of the fact that Crossley (1994) found no evidence of telepathy, and warned that in cases "where paranormal abilities are suggested ... the first step should be to examine the facilitation process closely" (p. 111). But the fact that so many facilitators (and "the numbers continue to grow") resort to extra sensory perception (ESP) to explain how their partners know so much about them should be a sobering message to those who deny that facilitators control what is being typed.

Facilitated communication has many other parallels with the Clever Hans phenomenon. The proponents of facilitated communication keep promising to produce proof of their claims, but the proof proves to be insubstantial or nonexistent. Independent typing is one bit of evidence they repeatedly invoke (although even this can be cued), but in his 1993 book Biklen said of the students facilitated during the first 1½ years of his project at Syracuse: "For none of the students has physical support yet been faded completely" (p. 75). And so it was with Clever Hans (Pfungst, 1911/1965).

> Mr. Grabow, a member of the school board and an enthusiastic follower of Mr. von Osten ... mentions a large number of successful tests, which were supposedly made in accordance with the method of procedure without knowledge. A thorough analysis of his experiments was not possible, because the conditions under which they were conducted were not adequately specified. But I have no doubt that the successful responses of the horse were due solely to the absence of precautionary measures. I, too, could cite a number of seemingly correct responses which demonstrably were due to the absence of adequate precautionary measures. (p. 40)

ADDITIONAL COMPARISONS WITH CLEVER HORSES

Clever Hans

> Mr. von Osten was aware of the grosser movements, and talked quite freely concerning them, but in so doing, showed he was quite unaware of their true function. He undertook to show us what we already knew—that, when he remained standing perfectly erect, he could elicit no sort of response from Hans. Furthermore, that whenever he continued to bend forward, Hans would always respond incorrectly with very high numbers. He knew, also,

that Hans was distracted [halted] in his operation every time the questioner resumed the erect posture while the tapping was in progress.... Mr. von Osten, however, believed this to be a caprice of the horse and at first declared that he would yet be able to eliminate it, but later became resigned to it as an irremediable evil. Mr. von Osten was also aware that the questioner ought not move while the horse was approaching a colored cloth.... And, finally, he also knew what influence his calls had while the horse was selecting the cloth, and he told me it was of great assistance to Hans to be admonished frequently, since thus his attention was brought to bear upon the proper cloth. (Pfungst, 1911/1965, p. 230)

Facilitated Communication. The following two quotes are from Biklen (1993):

[Pull back the client's hand while] reminding the person of the question or request whenever an incorrect or nonsensical choice is about to be made.... In other words, help the person to avoid errors. (p. 22)

While it is possible in any instance of facilitation involving the forearm, wrist, or hand for the person's communication to be influenced by a facilitator, presumably such instances, if they were particularly important, could be double-checked at another time by withholding support. (p. 27)

Clever Hans

Different questioners who worked with the horse required different lengths of time to obtain proper responses.... I, myself, found that in the degree in which I learned to control my attention, in that degree did this phenomenon tend to disappear, but would reappear the moment I became indisposed. A massing of errors toward the end of a long series occured only when the questioner was fatigued. There was nothing which had to be interpreted as fatigue or indisposition on the part of the horse.... To be sure, Mr. von Osten always offered these two excuses. That they were without warrant is shown by the fact that Hans, after appearing indisposed or fatigued while working with one questioner, would nevertheless react promptly and correctly a moment later for some other experimenter. (Pfungst, 1907/1965, pp. 150–151)

Facilitated Communication. The following three passages are quoted from Biklen (1993):

Of course the fact that a student does not communicate with certain facilitators does not explain why the person does not communicate. Some students have typed words to the effect that "so-and-so doesn't believe I am smart." (p. 120)

Students are fluent with some facilitators but *not* with others, although this problem seems to be resolvable if new facilitators are persistent and willing to suspend disbelief. (p. 128)

Hardly anyone has observed certain facilitators without commenting, "She (or he) is really good." (p. 131)

Clever Hans

They [Mr. Schillings and the Count zu Castell] had noticed, independently of each other, that the horse would often fail to react when for any length of time he was given problems dealing with abstract numbers, even though they were of the simplest kind, but that he would immediately improve whenever the question had to do with concrete objects. They believed that Hans found applied mathematics more interesting, and that abstract problems, or those which were altogether too elementary, bored him.... Quite in accord with this is the statement to be found in the report of the September-Commission, in which we find this note in the discussion of the arithmetical problems.... "The horse responded with less and less attentiveness and appeared to play with the questioner." (Pfungst, 1911/1965, p. 151)

About this situation Pfungst (1911/1965) commented:

Mr. Schillings was capable of intense, but not continued concentration and it was he who was bored, and not the horse. And it was Count zu Castell and not the horse that found it necessary to invoke the aid of perceptual objects to bring his attention to the proper height of concentration. (p. 151)

Mr. Schillings, owing to his great impressionability, remained long under the spell of Mr. von Osten's point of view.... For a long time ... he could receive no response to questions put in French until one day he made the discovery that, curiously enough, the animal never responded adequately unless he [Schillings] firmly believed in the possibility of success. It is noteworthy that Count zu Castell, independently of Mr. Schillings, made the same discovery. (p. 158)

The Elberfeld Horses

One of the papers reviewed by Sanford (1914a) was by Claparède, who was unsuccessful with the Elberfeld horses. Krall suggested that those failures were due to the fact that the horses were shedding their coats, a trying time for them. Apparently that was not the problem, however, because the next day two of the horses performed well for a major, whom Krall described as elderly and very friendly. "You see," said Krall (according to Claparède), "everything depends on the visitors, especially if they are, or are not, on good terms ... with the horses." Bemused by this response, Sanford (1914a) wrote: "We fear that this is the handwriting on the wall for Prof. Claparède at Elberfeld and indeed for any visitor who cherishes scientific reserves" (p. 134). Later he added that there would be no crucial experiment "unless Herr

Krall is willing to offer more facilities than he has yet been ready to offer to those whom he knows to be hostile to his views" (p. 136).

Facilitated Communication

A test with blindfolds [on the facilitator] would convey to students that the facilitators are questioning their [the students'] competence. This could undermine students' confidence in themselves and in their facilitators.... Unless the particular test is one used with all students or is normative for the setting … any tests designed to validate or invalidate communicative ability will almost certainly convey to the student that the facilitator is questioning the student's competence or at the very least is not "with" the student.... The effects of this message may be to make a student excessively nervous, to undermine the student's confidence, or to anger the student enough … to refuse to participate in the test. (Biklen, 1993, pp. 124–125)

The effect on an individual of having long-term, unremedied communication impairment needs to be taken into account in any assessment.... They may have negative attitudes to assessment as the result of past experience with inappropriate testing strategies.... Without a great deal of encouragement they may be unwilling even to try at the test and may just answer at random in order to get the procedure over with. (Crossley, 1994, pp. 80–81)

The Elberfeld Horses

According to Sanford (1914b):

[Krall] finds still clearer evidence for [Hans's] independent thought in the peculiar and erratic spelling of his own horses, arguing that, as no one can foresee the particular one of several ways which they will use on any given occasion, each case of their spelling becomes in fact an experiment "without knowledge." (pp. 26–27)

Facilitated Communication.   One of the ways Biklen and his colleagues know that students' words are their own is "their unique phonetic and creative spelling" (Biklen, 1993, p. 115).

The Elberfeld Horses

Another paper that Sanford (1914a) reviewed was by Max Ettlinger. Ettlinger pointed out that a veterinarian noticed that the eyeblink of the horse's groom coincided with Muhamed's starting and stopping taps. Others noted that "the horses seem to pay little or no attention to the blackboard from which they are supposed to be reading" (p. 136).

Facilitated Communication.   During facilitation, many students do not look at the keyboard. Biklen (1993) gave these descriptions: "When she types ... she frequently appears to be looking off into space, to the side rather than forward" (p. 13). "As she types, Lyrica often looks away" (p. 88). But unless Lyrica looks completely away she can still type validly, according to Biklen, because she "may use peripheral vision effectively" (p. 88).[8]

The Elberfeld Horses

After describing the cues given through the bridle attached to one horse who was blind and another who wore blinders, as well as the pinching of the horse on the flanks to make it turn its head, Sanford (1914b) made this comment: "The use of these means of control is not denied by Kralls [sic] partizans, but they explain that such means are used only in the early stages of the training and later become unnecessary" (p. 20).

Facilitated Communication.   Following is a comment from Crossley (1994):

> Communication aid users may initially need physical assistance from the communication partners while they develop specific skills such as index finger isolation.... As the users' skills increase the amount of physical assistance they receive should diminish. The ultimate aim is for the user to access their communication aids with no physical contact from their communication partner. (p. 57)

MECHANISMS CONTROLLING FACILITATORS

Smith and Belcher (1994) reasoned that two learning processes must be at work in facilitated communication: one on the part of the students and one on the part of the facilitators. In steadying a partner's hand and in preventing errors—as facilitators are told to do with new students in the initial sessions—the facilitator must have a relatively firm grip on the student's hand until they approach the desired key. The students learn that when facilitators relax their grip, they (the students) are rewarded by praise for striking downward on that key. "Over time, differences in the amount of pressure used to hold the hand back and prompt release of the finger become increasingly less and are finally imperceptible to the facilitator" (p. 71). On the other hand, this cue need not remain imperceptible to the students, who are rewarded for knowingly following it.

---

[8]Crossley, on the other hand, insists that the student must make "eye contact with the target before making a selection" (1994, p. 19).

In sum, for remaining *unaware* of the cue they are giving, the facilitators are rewarded by the gratitude of parents and colleagues and by the satisfaction of liberating an autistic or retarded child from the bondage of cognitive inadequacy. For *consciously* picking up the facilitator's minute cues, the autistic or retarded client is rewarded by praise and attention.

It is likely that the cues differ for different facilitators. Some may tighten rather than loosen their grip when passing over the correct letter; many may guide a client's finger to the key. Some may give vocal cues. The mechanism for each facilitator and partner needs to be determined, but the underlying principle is the same: The aware Hans and his unaware master are reinvented.

There are still other possibilities. Some facilitators may consciously guide their partner's hand and simply lie about it. No mystery there. In some instances, students may be unaware of the cues to which they are reacting; that is, *both* partners may be unaware of the subtle cues guiding their behavior.

The precise way in which facilitators guide their partner's hand to prevent errors in the early sessions, as prescribed in their training, may indicate the cues they unwittingly provide in later sessions when they mistakenly believe that all cues have been eliminated. Again we find a parallel in the clever animals. Christopher (1970) and Mountjoy and Lewandowski (1984) mentioned a book written by William Frederick Pinchbeck and published by him in 1805. It included a detailed description of how he trained his pig to spell words by picking up letter cards. Most interesting for our inquiry was Pinchbeck's assertion that after he faded out the consciously given cue (a nasal sniffle) by which he controlled the pig's responses, he really did not know what cue he was giving.

> Hath none detected the secret communication by which he [the pig] is actuated? What will you conclude, when I inform you that communication is unnecessary? You may relinquish it by degrees; for the animal is so sagacious, that he will appear to read your thoughts. The position you stand in, not meaning any stipulated place, or certain gesture, but what will naturally arise from your anxiety, will determine the card to your pupil. (As quoted by Mountjoy & Lewandowski, 1984, p. 34)

As with Clever Hans, the animal was training the master as much as the master was training the animal.

Needless to say, even in instances when the facilitator's hand is moved to the partner's arm, then to the shoulder, then off the partner entirely, there is always a possibility, or more likely probability, that an unrecognized cue is guiding the response. Produced when an individual merely thinks of the correct response, involuntary muscle movements require no learning. Consequently new facilitators, probably the more suggestible ones, can achieve almost instant success. Telling facilitators during training what to expect when they are assigned a student sets in motion the entire process, for knowledge of what to expect is all that is necessary to produce the appropriate involuntary muscle movements. During training, novice facilitators are told that success is expected and failure indicates a lack of trust or insufficient belief, exerting powerful pressure on the facilitator to succeed. Finally, what the students "type" frequently reflects the philosophy of the directors that the facilitators incorporate during their training.

Although individual differences between facilitators are affected by differences in the will and the need to believe, it is likely that these differences are due largely to differences in suggestibility. In fact, a fortunate few fail as facilitators because they are not very suggestible. That such differences exist was demonstrated by Eysenck and Furneaux (1945), who found stable individual differences on 6 of 12 tests of suggestibility given to 60 army-hospital patients. Significantly, in each of these 6 tests the suggestions induced involuntary muscle movements (in the other 6 the suggestions involved what was seen, smelled, or felt). In other words, the individual members of the group maintained their general position—in terms of suggestiblity level—relative to the rest of the group on each of the 6 tests in which involuntary muscle movements were induced by suggestion.

To unravel the precise cues in each case of facilitated communication will take controlled studies ingenious enough to do justice to the elegant work of Oskar Pfungst. But a general study of facilitators could be very revealing. As a starter, one might use tests of suggestibility to compare individuals who fail as facilitators with those who succeed. Further studies (if permitted) might compare facilitators whose partners make sexual abuse charges with facilitators whose partners do not. And finally, some interesting data on individual differences might emerge if facilitators are recruited to observe the results of objective tests of facilitated communication, and follow-up assessments are made to determine the effects of these results on the facilitators' attitudes.

In facilitated communication as with clever horses, involuntary muscle movements are the irreplaceable core without which there would be no "miracle." We now examine other phenomena that are driven by this ubiquitous human characteristic.

4

Involuntary Muscle Movements in Other Phenomena

Thus did a great chemist [Chevreul] and a great physicist [Faraday] serve the cause of science by recognizing a psychological principle.

—Jastrow (1937, p. 487)

People frequently attribute the information communicated by involuntary muscle movements to a range of other phenomena that are based on the belief that exterior forces move handheld objects—including the pencil in a person's hand that appears to write by itself—or that one person's mind can read the mind of another. I do not attempt to trace each belief to its inception or to cover the huge literature comprehensively. Rather, tribute is paid to some of the pioneer investigators and illustrative studies are provided to convey some idea of the subject. I hope to illustrate that facilitators' misguided conviction that they are not moving their client's hand is merely one more expression of the conjunction of involuntary muscle movements with fixed ideas, suggestion, and wishful thinking that has been recorded for hundreds of years.

Pfungst (1911/1965) believed that individuals were unaware of their own involuntary muscle movements when their concentration was intense and they were absorbed in some small content-area. The same principle explained the fact that when questioners' concentration diminished, their early success with Clever Hans also diminished. He repeatedly illustrated the generality of this principle in his references to what people referred to as "psychic" phenomena.

He also pointed out that involuntary movements were more easily elicited if the arm or leg that manifested the involuntary movement was in an unstable state:

In the case of table-rapping there are movements of the hands, in our case
there are those of the head [particularly susceptible because of its instability].
... But I could induce not only movements of the head but also of the arms
and legs, and this by having the subject assume a posture which enabled him
to hold arms and legs in as unstable a position as possible. (Pfungst,
1911/1965, p. 206)

Scientific confrontations with spiritism had already taken place at the
beginning of the 19th century (Eysenck, 1947), but a pivotal event was the
publication in 1833 of an objective investigation of the mysterious swaying
pendulum.

THE PENDULUM

In 1833 Professor Michel-Eugène Chevreul, a distinguished French chemist
(who, outside of France at least, has not received the credit due him,
according to Costa, 1962), published an open letter to his close friend, the
eminent physicist André M. Ampère.[9] Chevreul was acquiescing to Ampère's request that it was important that Chevreul publish the experiments
he had performed in 1812 on the oscillation of a pendulum, composed of
thread with an iron ring at its end.

In his open letter Chevreul wrote that he had observed a pendulum
oscillate when someone held it above water, although as far as Chevreul
could tell the person's arm was immobile. Urged to try it, Chevreul held it
above mercury, an anvil, and numerous other things, and was surprised to
see that it indeed oscillated although he had no sensation of moving it.
Furthermore, when the professor interposed a pane of glass between the
object and the pendulum he was amazed that the oscillations slowed and
finally stopped, only to reappear when the glass was removed. All this
seemed to be convincing evidence that somehow the pendulum was being
moved by its relationship with the material below it. When the interaction
between the material and the pendulum was prevented by the pane of glass,
quite naturally the pendulum stopped moving.

To examine whether these effects were independent of muscle movements, Chevreul leaned his arm on a wooden rest which he gradually slid
forward from his shoulder to his hand. The oscillations decreased progres-

---

[9]Ampère was renowned for having developed a mathematical theory of the relationship
between electricity and magnetism. His name is now used as the practical unit of electric
current and for the ampere meter, or ammeter, which measures the strength of an electric
current. Chevreul was not only a pioneer in organic chemistry (Costa, 1962) but also produced
a substantial body of work on color theory, among the many interests and contributions of this
gifted Renaissance man. Following Jastrow (1937), I have hyphenated Michel-Eugène although
I have often seen them printed as separate words.

sively as the rest was moved down his arm and stopped entirely when it reached the fingers holding the pendulum. The opposite effect was obtained when he moved the wooden rest back. Furthermore, he recalled that watching the pendulum produced in him a peculiar effect, which "caused me to think that quite probably a muscular movement ... was taking place quite unbeknownst to me" (Chevreul, 1833, pp. 250–251).[10] Consequently, he took away the wooden rest and while the pendulum was oscillating had someone blindfold him. The oscillations diminished and the weak oscillations that remained were unaffected by interposition of the glass pane. The pendulum finally stopped altogether, and even though Chevreul—still blindfolded—continued to hold it above the mercury for another 15 minutes it never resumed its movement.

His interpretation of these results was that unfelt and unwilled muscular movements start the pendulum in motion, after which observation of the movement produces a tendency for even more movement. The same disposition, however, slows and stops the movement when one thinks that something (e.g, interposition of a pane of glass) will stop it. For Chevreul, his experiments demonstrated that thoughts regarding certain movements, even thoughts that are not deliberate, can produce unfelt muscle movements. This should be of interest, he wrote, not only for psychology but for the history of science as well, for it demonstrates how easily we can believe in illusions.

Although removed from us by more than 160 years, Chevreul has important things to say to proponents of facilitated communication. Despite his initial experiences he did not become wildly enthusiastic and proclaim that the pendulum's movement could not be coming from him. Instead, he systematically tried to disprove that theory, as good scientists do even with a theory they favor. If he couldn't disprove it then its validity would be strengthened. Interestingly, once Chevreul was convinced that there was no unnatural cause for pendulum movements, he was no longer able to produce them.

Though a chemist of great renown, Chevreul's interests were very broad and his investigations extended to many other disciplines, including psychology (Jastrow, 1937). In 1853 the Académie des Sciences appointed him chairman of a three-man committee to study the pendulum, séances and other popular delusions such as the divining rod and table turning, the results of which were published in 1854 (see Costa, 1962, who also described the national celebration of Chevreul's 100th birthday in August 1886, 19 months before he died).

The pendulum is among the oldest of all the phenomena that, although muscle generated, have been ascribed to enigmatic forces. In his 1854 book,

---

[10]Chevreul's paper was translated for me by Yves Marcuard, to whom I am most grateful. An English translation of all but the last 2½ pages can be found in Binet (1891/1896, pp. 222–227).

Chevreul included a description of the pendulum given "by the Latin historian Ammianus Marcellinus, who died in A.D. 390" (Vogt & Hyman, 1979, p. 106). A ring suspended on a thread and held by a priest over a circle of alphabet letters pointed in turn to the first four letters of the name of the emperor's successor. Used in that way, it presaged what we refer to now as the Ouija board.

Although the Chevreul pendulum, as it is sometimes called, has become one of many expressions of involuntary muscle movements used to measure an individual's suggestibility (e.g., Eysenck & Furneaux, 1945; Weitzenhoffer, 1989), it has also continued to be used as it was in the past: as an arcane tool of mysticism, for making decisions, for locating underground water and minerals, for determining the sex of a fetus, for diagnosing physical maladies, for receiving messages from the great beyond, and for innunerable other purposes. The direction of the rotation (clockwise or counterclockwise) or the course of the oscillations (north–south or east–west) are presumed to be discriminative signs; the pendulum can also be held above a chart. An article about the testing of alternative medicine at a prominent New York City research hospital, which appeared in the Magazine section of the July 30, 1995 edition of *The New York Times*, included a photo of a woman holding a pendulum over a patient's chest. Below the photo was this caption: "Julia Motz dangles a pendulum to test Ron Aiossa's chakras, or vortexes of energy" (Brown, 1995).

MIND-READING

> I began my investigations by seeking to determine the range of muscle-reading, and I found that—apart from all other modes of contact—a gentle touching of the shoulder sufficed for definite guidance. (Dessoir, 1886, p. 111)

Although Clever Hans is by far the most famous and most thoroughly examined early example of the existence and influence of involuntary muscle movements, earlier analyses of alleged mind-readers had provided very relevant information. These mind-readers, although blindfolded, were able to find a hidden object and perform a variety of other feats merely by being in physical contact (and sometimes even without direct physical contact) with someone who knew where the object was hidden. Pfungst (1911/1965, p. 113) did some mind-reading of his own in one of his laboratory studies during the Clever Hans investigation, for it was obviously related to his work with the clever horse. He commented (on p. 108) on the mind-reading literature and noted that although mind-readers depend primarily on physically sensing the involuntary movements of the subject's hand, some of them perform without touching the subject. They do so, he wrote, by using auditory cues, such as footsteps, involuntary whisperings, changes in breathing, and the murmuring of spectators, as well as, to a lesser degree, visual signals of the type that Hans had picked up. He referred to the American neuropathologist George M. Beard who, in 1877, "first explained the phenomenon of thought-reading, on the basis of the perception of very minute muscular jerks, and therefore called it 'muscle-reading' or 'body-reading'" (p. 183).

In his paper, Beard (1877) discussed the brilliant success of a Mr. Brown, who performed by firmly placing the back of the subject's hand against his (Brown's) forehead. At the same time, Brown lightly pressed his other hand against the palm and fingers of the subject's hand. He asked the subject to concentrate on some part of the room or some hidden object or a letter of the alphabet hung along the wall. Beard then explains that when together they approach the target area, "A slight impulse or movement is communicated to his hand by the hand of the subject. This impulse is both involuntary and unconscious on the part of the subject. He is not aware, and is unwilling at first, to believe that he gives any such impulse" (p. 460). Mr. Brown was especially convincing when he picked out very small objects that a subject was thinking of, such as a particular key grouped with many other keys, or—in a large room where any object could be thought of—correctly picked one capital letter in the title of a newspaper pinned on the wall.

Apparently muscular tension indicates direction whereas relaxation indicates that the object is being closely approached, but Beard emphasized that unless the subject concentrated on the location there would be no unconscious muscular tension and relaxation, and the mind-reading would fail. He and subsequent investigators noted individual differences in the production of unwitting muscle cues; consequently, with some subjects mind-readers failed or took a long time to succeed. However, "Credulous, wonder-loving subjects are sometimes partially entranced through the emotions of reverence and expectation; with subjects in this state, operators are quite sure to succeed" (Beard, 1877, p. 467).

Beard (1877) also experimented with others, many of whom were naive, and satisfied himself that successful mind-reading was independent of knowledge about the true cause of the effect. Some mind-readers, particularly amateurs, were convinced that the source of their success was magnetism, mesmerism, electricity or "thrills or vibrations which they feel, auras and all sorts of indefinable sensations" (p. 466).

The following year Beard (1878) published in *Popular Science Monthly* a letter to the editor which included the full text of a letter he in turn had received from "an expert in the art of mind-reading by the eye or by the touch" (p. 362). This expert was very much aware of the true source of his powers but requested anonymity. As a prologue to the letter, Beard pointed out that mind-reading can be performed not only by touch, as described in his article of the previous year, but also by sight and hearing, thereby agreeing with his correspondent, who had taken issue with Beard's assertion that a physical connection between the mind-reader and the subject was essential. In fact, Beard's correspondent said he regularly performed mind-reading when blindfolded and unattached to the subject. All he required, he wrote, was that the subject follow him by a distance of 3 or 4 feet and concentrate on the object. By focusing on how readily or hesitantly he was followed, the mind-reader developed an idea of the direction he should take. When not blindfolded his indicator was not simply "muscular contractions or relaxations from the arm, but it is a sympathetic movement of the whole body" (as quoted in Beard, 1878, p. 362). Nor does revelation of the method affect the results, for "you may assure them that every *correct* movement you make is only a translation of their own, and they will declare positively that they are trying to move in the *opposite* direction, and, in fact, they often do hold back with their feet, while giving the most positive indications with their arms" (p. 362). He noted that most well-educated people would rather ascribe these phenomena to such enigmas as animal magnetism or psychic forces than to the more rational explanation of unconscious movement.

A few years later and an ocean away, George J. Romanes (1881) published a paper in *Nature* expressing regret that the eminent physiologist William B. Carpenter, a "great opponent of humbug," had recommended for scientific investigation the mind-reading performance of the famous Washington Irving Bishop. In Romanes' opinion, Carpenter's proposal conferred on Bishop's powers "a fictitious degree of importance in the eyes of the public" (p. 171). Nevertheless Romanes was joined by several distinguished scientists, including Francis Galton (28 years before he was knighted), for two meetings with Mr. Bishop, who professed ignorance about how he succeeded and wanted his performance investigated and explained—quite likely a deceptive ploy from this clever professional conjuror. In July of 1881 he was appearing at the Brighton Pavilion performing muscle reading and other tricks, and, to his credit, revealing to the audience how spiritualists performed their feats. In 1880 he had published a small book on the codes used by spiritualists during what are called "second sight" acts, thereby exposing those who claimed their performances had some paranormal source (T. H. Hall, 1964). In this he was a progenitor of Houdini and those magicians who refuse to let their audience believe that their mystifying performance is anything other than clever deception, talent and hard work.

During the investigations Mr. Bishop was taken from the room and blindfolded with a handkerchief. Pieces of cotton-wool were stuffed below the eyes, eliminating the possibility of looking down along the nose, a favorite trick of blindfolded performers. One member of the group, Henry Sidgwick, hid a small object somewhere in the room, after which Mr. Bishop was led back to the room and handed over to Sidgwick. He took Sidgwick's left hand and placed it on his (Bishop's) forehead, requesting Sidgwick to think continuously of where the object was hidden. He continued to hold Sidgwick's hand to his forehead. "After standing motionless for about 10 seconds Mr. Bishop suddenly faced round, walked briskly with Professor

Sidgwick in a direct line to the rug, stooped down, raised the corner of the rug, and picked up the object" (Romanes, 1881, p. 171).

The other members of the group each took a turn, and Mr. Bishop succeeded far better with some than with others. In fact with some he failed completely. Nevertheless, some of his successes were extraordinary, such as putting his finger exactly on the spot of a table being thought of by his subject or finding an object on a chandelier. He also localized any spot on one's body that a person concentrated on.

Romanes (1881) then explained the source of this remarkable power:

> Of course the hypothesis which immediately suggests itself to explain the *modus operandi* is that Mr. Bishop is guided by the indications unconsciously given through the muscles of his subject—differential pressure playing the part of the words "hot" and "cold" in the childish game which these words signify. Mr. Bishop is not himself averse to this hypothesis but insists that if it is true he does not act upon it consciously. (p. 172)

As evidence that this hypothesis was correct, Romanes pointed out that when the *subject* was blindfolded and lost his bearings (but nevertheless still remembered where an object was hidden), Mr. Bishop could not find it (a point that had also been made by Beard's anonymous correspondent). Furthermore, the blindfolded Mr. Bishop failed when he was connected to the subject by a loose strap, whereas he succeeded when he was connected by a solid walking stick, a firmer conveyer of muscle movement. And when an object was hidden by Sidgwick without Romanes' knowledge, and Sidgwick held Romanes' *left wrist*, Mr. Bishop could find the object by holding Romanes' *left hand* (the muscle tension thereby passing from Sidgwick's hand to Romanes' wrist and then to Romane's hand, which was held by Bishop). However, Bishop could not pick up any muscle tension that crossed Romanes' body: Bishop failed when Sidgwick held Romanes' left wrist, as above, but this time Bishop held Romanes' *right* hand.

Muscle readers have also duplicated actions that are merely thought about. Max Dessoir (1886)—whose statement that guidance stemmed from a mere gentle touching of the shoulder introduced this section on mind-reading—used a student not to hide objects but to *think* of some activity. The student told no one that he thought of going through several rooms, taking a bronze figure down from a cupboard, stroking it, and then putting it down and moving to a chair to sit down. Dessoir, blindfolded and with the student's hand on his shoulder, was able to duplicate in actuality the student's imagery and then described how he did it. When, for example, the pressure on his shoulder diminished Dessoir deduced that the student's hand had risen slightly, indicating an upward direction (the raised shelf). That he could duplicate the imagined stroking of the figure, which

> at first sight seems remarkable, is explained by the fact that every agent [the student, in this case] has, as it were, a code of [involuntary] confirmatory

> muscular movements expressive of satisfaction. When I let my hands slip
> down the figure—entirely by accident—I was clearly sensible of this approv-
> ing pressure; this induced me to repeat the movement until a cessation of the
> pressure indicated to me that this part of my task was accomplished. (p. 111)

After being unwittingly guided to the chair, involuntary downward pressure of the student's hand was enough to induce him to sit.

In 1908 Professor June E. Downey of the University of Wyoming discussed the controversy among philosophers and psychologists "relative to
the interpretation of so-called unconscious phenomena" (p. 650), a controversy that Downey would be surprised to know is still far from settled (e.g.,
Loftus & Klinger, 1992; Shevrin & Dickman, 1980; Spitz, 1993). In earlier
years many academic experimental psychologists were—as now—uneasy
about the possibility of a resourceful mental system operating outside
conscious control. As Downey (1908) phrased it, they granted only that the
unconscious can control "sundry routine acts, but if otherwise it runs on its
own account, we expect it to do trivial and rather stupid things.... Little
wonder, then," she continued, "that we are startled if it takes to presenting
us ... with solutions to difficult problems," or if subconscious phenomena
"actually exhibit intelligence, as we usually rate intelligence" (p. 651).

Different people used slightly different methods to pick up involuntary
cues by contact (to say nothing of picking up auditory or visual cues). In a
later paper, Downey described her method. (She used the term *guide* for the
person who had placed the object, exposed or hidden, somewhere in the
room while the experimenter was absent.) The blindfolded experimenter
returned and "with her right hand touched lightly either the wrist or
finger-tips of the right hand of the guide, or clasped the guide's right wrist
with her right hand and touched the guide's right finger-tips with her own
left hand" (Downey, 1909, p. 265). By this method she read the variations in
the unconscious muscle tensions that occurred as the guide looked at,
approached or receded from the object.

She gave a number of examples of muscle-reading (mind-reading), in
which she was very experienced, having played the role of mind-reader in
her laboratory (Downey, 1909). One interesting phenomenon, also mentioned by Beard (1877), occurred in almost 25% of her subjects. Instead of
unconsciously leading the experimenter *directly* to the object, as usually
happened, some subjects retraced the idiosyncratic paths they had taken in
placing the article (as recorded by a third person), "a retracing which often
involved a circuitous route and often reproduced all [their] original hesita-
tions" (Downey, 1908, p. 652). Needless to say, subjects disclaimed all
knowledge that they were leading the experimenter on the same meander-
ing routes they (the subjects) had originally taken.

For Downey, the uselessness and even absurdity of these actions gave
credence to their automatic and involuntary origin and raised doubts that
the unconscious performs only routine acts induced by repetition. Even

mental detours were occasionally registered. With the experimenter out of the room a subject "may, for instance, mentally hesitate whether to place an article on a radiator or on a table several feet to the right of the radiator, [then] decide upon the table and place the object there." When the blind-folded experimenter returns and holds the subject's wrist while atempting to locate the article, "the experimenter may go first to the radiator and then point to the table" (pp. 653–654). When this happened the subject could accept the explanation of how the experimenter found the object, but could not understand how the experimenter reproduced movements that, al-though previously considered, *were not thought of during the test*. In such instances thoughts that were not in the subject's consciousness during the test were nevertheless expressed by involuntary muscle movements. Note that the paths taken to place the object were certainly not the center of the subject's attention.

In a test of the ability to traverse an unknown pathway, a blindfolded experimenter and her subject had wandered some distance away when the experimenter suddenly returned to the exact beginning of the pathway, an action that the subject thought was a sensible thing for the experimenter to do. But of course it was the variations in the subject's *own* unconscious muscle tensions that were sensible, not the experimenter who was sensing them. In another instance this same subject left her purse on an apparatus case and returned for it the next day. A few days later, when she again served as a subject, she frequently guided the experimenter to the apparatus case before guiding her to the hidden article. Downey commented (1908): "In such cases … the automatic or subconscious seems to be approaching our idea of intelligence. It is acting 'sensibly,' to quote the guide again" (pp. 655–656). We repeatedly encounter this characterization of involuntary motor movements as expressing acts that are more than simply routine.

Also relevant is Downey's (1909) statement that one of the surprises of her study was

> the refusal of many subjects to accept the writer's explanation of her success. One guide (H) insists that she finds by actual experiment that when blind-folded she [the guide] is unable to move as directly and accurately to the object as the [mind] reader does, therefore, the reader must be responsible for the guidance. What is emphasized by such facts is the extraordinary difficulty of bringing such involuntary movements to attention. Only a few of the subjects … have ever succeeded in observing them even when warned to be on the watch. (p. 275)

Not only is the guide unaware of sending cues, but readers can also be unaware of picking them up. Downey commented that "the reader is often as unconscious of his method of reading as the guide is of his movements, although an intelligent reader usually grows sophisticated in time" (p. 259).

Downey described occasional "verbal automatisms" in which a subject would say something in a whisper or even aloud without being aware of having done so. With "fit" subjects Downey was able to duplicate all the feats of experts, including the ability to find objects without contact with the subject, cued by movements of the subject's body or even by the sound of their footsteps as she moved with them. She was also able to find an object when several persons, ignorant of where the object had been placed, intervened between a subject and her. Presumably they held hands, but nevertheless this was a feat that Mr. Bishop was unable to perform.

Downey (1909) concluded her paper by remarking how impressed she was "with the exceeding delicacy of the expressive side of mental life and, above all, … with the minimal awareness of the subject as to the nature of such expression" (p. 301). She would be pleased to know how applicable her impression is today, when facilitators consistently deny that they are guiding the responses of their students.

More than a decade later, G. M. Stratton (1921) of the University of California described experiments with an international performer, recently arrived in San Francisco. The performer was able to locate hidden objects when connected with his subject by a loose watch chain, as well as with no contact at all, but he was unwilling to be blindfolded. Stratton concluded that "this may be taken as an indication that he depends to some appreciable extent, even though subconsciously, upon visual cues" (p. 309). After the first series of experiments established the performer's level of proficiency with and without contact (by means of a watch chain), a second series introduced some precautions to reduce possible auditory cues. These changes had no effect. The performer's success rate for these first two series combined was about 1½ times the results predicted by chance and only slightly better with contact than without it. In the final series there was no contact between the performer and his guide, and Stratton and his associates took additional precautions to limit the performer's visual field (including the use of blinders, à la Clever Hans). This reduced his performance to chance level.

Still, unlike Pfungst, Stratton (1921) was unable to determine what visual cues the performer was using. "These signs were exceedingly obscure, [and] rarely evident to the experimenters watching the guide." Stratton was willing only to conjecture that the cues were "from fleeting glimpses of the guide's change of place and posture caught in the very margin of vision and perhaps without any conscious intention by the subject [performer] to notice or use them. Yet upon these, when touch was excluded, his truly remarkable power seems to depend" (p. 314).

After reviewing these and many other phenomena explored by psychologists in the past, I suggest without stretching the point that even when touching only their students' shoulder, or when not touching them at all, facilitators unwittingly send cues and students unwittingly pick them up. The experimental psychologist Clark L. Hull (1933) wrote of his own experience as a mind-reader (muscle reader) and proposed, as have others, that ideo-motor actions—a term William Carpenter (1852) introduced to describe involuntary muscle movements based on a dominant idea—are basic not only for mind-reading and similar phenomena but also for our understanding of hypnosis.

TABLE MOVING AND TABLE RAPPING

Pfungst (1911/1965), remember, was well aware of the relationship of his findings with Clever Hans to many other "mysterious" processes:

> It has been scientifically proven that the number of supposed mystical phenomena, table-moving, table-rapping, and divination by means of the rod, all are the result of involuntary movements made unawares by those concerned, just as in this work with Hans. (We must of course except those not infrequent instances in which the phenomena in question are purposely and fraudulently simulated). (p. 159)

> Just as the spiritualists ascribe the "messages" which are revealed to them through table-rapping, to certain rational spirits, so Mr. von Osten credited the intelligence of the horse with the result produced by his own involuntary signs. (p. 222)

In the mid-19th century, France and England received a curious import from the United States, a plague of table turning and table rapping that William Carpenter admirably described in the course of reviewing 12 books (Electro-biology, 1853):[11]

> Go where we would, we heard of the intimations which our friends had received from departed souls; or of the agility of some sprightly table under the hands of dignitaries of the Church, and … of Privy-councillors and cabinet Ministers.... We had supposed its "run" to be suspended for a time, but the epidemic has broke out in a new form, and is spreading through a class which may be seriously endangered by it. The farce becomes tragical when we find clergymen of undoubted honesty, deluding themselves into the belief that "Satanic Wonders and Prophetic Signs" are disclosed by the movements of

---

[11] All reviews in the *Quarterly Review* were unsigned, but this review (Electro-Biology, 1853) and an anonymous review in the same journal 18 years later (Spiritualism, 1871), must have been by William B. Carpenter, for the following reason. In 1878 Carpenter published a paper in the *Popular Science Monthly* in which he referred to the paper he had published in the *Quarterly Review* of October 1853 (actually September 1853). The anonymous author of the 1871 review paper "Spiritualism and its recent Converts" referred to himself as the author of the account of these oddities published in the *Quarterly Review* in 1853, so all three papers must have been by Carpenter. As further evidence, Pfungst (1911/1965) cited Carpenter as the author of the unsigned "Spiritualism and Its Recent Converts." Unquestionably Carpenter would have been a logical choice to review books on these subjects. Note that in the 1853 review 1 of the 12 books he reviewed was the latest edition of his own highly regarded *Principles of Human Physiology*. From a contemporary perspective, reviewing one's own work is something of an oddity.

their tables. If they have still ears to listen to a rational explanation, they will find that the turning of tables, and the supposed communications made by spirits through their agency, are due ... to the mental state of the performers themselves. (p. 505)

Rather than serving the simple utilitarian functions for which it was made, the table became an instrument of the devil or a channel for communicating with the dead. All kinds of strange phenomena were produced by people sitting at, then rising to stand around the table with their hands upon it. The table moved, the table turned, the table became agitated. The tapping by a table leg in response to questions was even more clever, considering its source, than the tapping of Clever Hans.

I have mentioned Chevreul's (1833) letter to Ampère, the scientist responsible for opening up scientific inquiry into electromagnetism. Another great scientist, Michael Faraday, born 15 years after Ampère, extended greatly Ampère's studies of electromagnetism. He was, like Ampère, interested in *natural* forces and consequently set up a scientific experiment to test the claims attributing table turning "to electricity, to magnetism, to attraction, to some unknown or hitherto unrecognized physical power to affect inanimate bodies, to the revolution of the earth, and even to diabolical or supernatural agency" (introduction to Faraday, 1853, p. 801). He first mentioned his experiments in *The Times of London*, followed by a more complete description in the *Athenæum* of July 2, 1853.[12]

Faraday (1853) performed a number of experiments after he had established that the table turners were, although "very desirous of ... establishing the existence of a peculiar power," absolutely honest when they said "the table draws their hands; that it moves first, and they have to follow it,—and sometimes it even moves from under their hands" (p. 801). Working with these firm believers, Faraday first removed any question that the substances he might use in his apparatus would somehow affect the movement of the table. He tied sandpaper, tinfoil, cardboard, glue, vulcanized rubber, wood, and so on into a bundle and placed the bundle on the table. The group of believers placed their hands on the table. The table turned. He then established a number of points: There was no evidence of any electrical or magnetic effects; a single individual could produce the effect; the motion of the table was not necessarily circular but could be straight; no experiment that he devised gave any indication of a peculiar natural force—not attraction or repulsion or any "tangential" power. All that was left was the "mere mechanical pressure exerted inadvertently by the turner" (p. 801).

He set about measuring the horizontally directed hand pressure required to move the table. For his first apparatus he prepared a soft cement made

---

[12] Almost 20 years later a digest of Faraday's experiment was given by Carpenter because "it is not now generally accessible" (Spiritualism, 1871, p. 311).

of wax and turpentine, or wax and pomatum, which he rolled into pellets that were used to separate four or five pieces of smooth, slippery cardboard, one above the other. The lowest piece was joined to the back of a piece of sandpaper which rested on the table. The edges of the sheets overlapped a bit, and on the underneath surface of each he made a pencil mark on the overlap to indicate each cardboard's relative position. The topmost cardboard was larger than the others and shielded them from view. Note that the cement pellets were strong enough to temporarily hold the cardboard pack together; they gave way slowly only to continued force but held the cards in their new positions. When a table turner placed his or her hands on the top cardboard, eventually the hands, cardboard pack, and table all moved to the left.

Faraday then lifted up the pack and examined it. By looking at the indicator lines he had drawn underneath each cardboard, he observed that the hand had moved earlier and farther than the table; the upper card moved first and the lowest two cards and the table followed behind. Even when the table had not moved, the upper card did, indicating that the table turner was inadvertently pressing the hands not simply straight downward but in the direction in which he or she expected the table to move.

I will not describe the second apparatus, which provided a still more visible index of movement. A third, even more sophisticated apparatus consisted of an arrangement of two thin 9½ x 7-inch boards and one 9 x 5-inch board. The 9 x 5-inch board was centered and glued beneath one of the two larger boards so as to raise the larger board slightly above the table. When placed on the table this assemblage served as the "lower" board. An upright pin was fixed into the top side of the raised board. The pin acted as a fulcrum for a cardboard piece which could swivel around it. Attached to the long arm of this cardboard piece was a 15-inch hay-stalk "indicator." The other 9½ x 7-inch board, placed on top, became the "upper board." A pin was inserted into this upper board and bent so that it extended downward into the short (back) arm of the of the cardboard.

Four glass rods, 7 inches long and with a ¼-inch diameter, were placed between the boards to serve as rollers. When the upper board moved, the bent pin moved the small arm of the cardboard whose longer arm (on the other side of the fulcrum) carried the hay-stalk indicator. The greater the movement of the upper board, the greater the movement of the hay-stalk indicator that extended from between the boards.[13] The entire apparatus was held together by two vulcanized rubber rings encircling the boards near their ends, where the lower board was raised above the table. These acted also as springs which, "whilst they allowed the first feeblest tendency to motion to be seen by the index [hay-stalk]" (Faraday, 1853, p. 802), exerted sufficient restraining power to resist strong lateral pressure.

---

[13]The indicator moved in the opposite direction from the top board because the pin from the top board was attached to the short arm of the cardboard that extended *behind* the fulcrum.

First Faraday introduced a control condition in which the indicator was removed and the boards were tied firmly together and placed on the table. In this condition, when hands were placed upon the upper board the table turner induced the table to move. When Faraday untied the boards so the upper board was free to move, and returned the indicator but hid it from sight, the results were very revealing. When a table turner willed the table to move in either direction, the indicator—hidden from the table mover but visible to Faraday—showed that the hands were gradually pushed in the desired direction "though the party certainly thought they were pressing downwards only. When shown that it was so, they were truly surprised; but when they lifted up their hands and immediately saw the index return to its normal position, they were convinced" (Faraday, 1853, p, 803). When they could see the indicator from the start and know when they were pressing downward (no movement of the index) or obliquely (index moved), the table never turned, though several tried for long periods of time. When they could no longer deceive themselves the effect evaporated. (Faraday constructed still another version of the index apparatus, but I will spare the reader.)

Faraday also noted that hand pressure tended to occur when continued downward pressure made the fingers and hands stiff and numb, as anyone can experience by pressing steadily against a flat surface. This pressure dulls sensitivity and can easily cause people to believe that they are pressing straight down when they are in fact exerting lateral pressure.

In these experiments Faraday clearly demonstrated that the source of the movement was the hands laid upon the table. I have gone into this in some detail not only because Faraday's experiments are not readily accessible, but also because they demonstrate, as had Chevreul's (1833) experiments, the scientific approach to events whose explanations are dominated by wishful thinking without any real attempt at objective assessment.

> Faraday mentions that he called on Chevreul at his laboratory in 1812 and again in 1845, but their interests were diverse.... Both distinguished scientists regarded it as an interruption to their scientific labors to devote time to correcting popular opinion; but the occupation was far more congenial to Chevreul than to Faraday. (Jastrow, 1937, p. 496)

Sadly, Faraday's study did not impress those who were committed, any more than did Chevreul's experiments. Carpenter recorded this reaction of two clerics, N. S. Godfrey and E. Gillson, whose books were among those Carpenter was reviewing and who were certain that the actions of the table revealed the hand of Satan:

> Both these clerical seers assert that Professor Faraday's physical proof that the table never moves, unless the performers make it move by their own pressure, has not the slightest bearing upon *their* experiments; inasmuch as, naively observes Mr. Godfrey, "those who tried it in his (Professor Faraday's)

presence imparted the motion, he tells us, *which we did not:*" whilst Mr. Gillson assures us that "the most violent movements were often performed *without the slightest pressure.*" But they must have read Professor Faraday's letter to very little purpose, if they did not see that *his* table-turners were at first as fully convinced as *theirs* that the table could not have derived its motion from them; they repudiated the idea as stoutly when it was suggested to them; but the infallible indicator showed that they always *did* press before the table moved, and that *until* they pressed, the table was stationary. (Electro-biology, 1853, p. 555)

So it was with Krall and his horses and so it is with Biklen and Crossley and their facilitated communication. *Objective proof that challenges the validity of a belief system rarely persuades committed believers to relinquish their beliefs.* Chevreul's demonstration of the origins of swaying pendulums and Faraday's of the moving tables have done nothing to dissuade the committed. The *Encyclopedia of Occultism & Parapsychology* (Shepard, 1978), written by and for the faithful, says of Chevreul's work:

It seems likely that Chevreul is correct in his investigation of some of the mechanism [sic] of pendulum divining, and also in his assumption that mental processes may effect the pendulum movement, but there is equal evidence of paranormal information obtained by the pendulum or divining rod when suggestive factors are not operating. (p. 161)

The torch raised by Godfrey and Gillson in defense of table moving has been passed through the ages to others.

However, the pressure of the hands [on the table] was trifling and was practically neutralised by the absence of unanimity in the direction. The sitters never desired the same movement at the same moment.

For this reason, and the still weightier one that tables moved without contact as well, his [Faraday's] theory soon went overboard.

In a series of seances between 1888–1910 in Spring Hall, Kansas, the presiding spirit claimed to be Faraday. His communications were published in four books. (L. Shepard, 1978, pp. 324–325)

Poor Professor Faraday. He had to go dabble with the spirits and *now* look what happened!

THE DIVINING ROD (DOWSING)

Various explanations of the movement of the rod had been proposed; for example, a seventeenth century Cartesian, Saint-Roman, explained the phenomenon in terms of the emission of corpuscles from the object to the rod. Chevreul's observations and experiments [published in 1854] proved to him that the movements of the rod were the results of subconscious reflexes governed by preconceived notions or by the appearance of the surroundings. (Costa, 1962, p. 14)

Some 70 years after Chevreul's experiments, Pfungst (1911/1965) wrote, "It has been a common custom of man to posit some extraneous cause for movements resulting from certain involuntary motions of his own, of which he is not aware, (witness the divining rod)" (p. 221). Indeed, "the untenability of this theory [of the divining-rod] comes home to us most forcibly when we recall how various are the kinds of things which have been discovered by means of the branch" (p. 222).

When a Y-shaped branch (or some other object) is held with a hand on each extension the pointer is said to dip when the holder passes not only over water and gold but also, observed Pfungst (1911/1965), over "coal, gypsum, ochre, red-chalk, sulphur and petroleum,—according to the desire of the one searching." It also "will point out a murderer or the place where a murder has been committed, [and] it will discover the thief or his trail, as well as the things stolen or merely touched by him" (p. 222), and much, much more. That was in 1907. The pendulum had served a similar purpose 75 years earlier, as we know from Chevreul's (1833) letter to Ampère.

According to an article by Haines in a 1926 issue of the *Journal of the American Society for Psychical Research*, water divining (water witching, dowsing) goes back at least to the 7th century A.D. (cf. Vogt & Hyman, 1979). In explaining how water divining works, Haines agreed with W. F. Barrett that the evidence

> points to the good dowser's unconsciously possessing the faculty of clairvoyance, in fact, a supersensory perceptive power.... As in cases of hypnotism, the dowser has to leave his mind absolutely vacant, so that it may receive any impression, however faint, and have it recorded at once in the form of motor-automatism. (Haines, 1926, pp. 616–617)

Haines acknowledged involuntary motor movement as the source of the rod's actions, but invoked a supernormal perceptive faculty as the true source of the dowser's power to find water.

Dowsers use different intruments and have different ways of holding them. Many hold the two ends of a forked twig, one end in each hand, with palms up and thumbs facing out (which, incidentally, brings their elbows in against their bodies). This position is unnatural and unstable. As Pfungst (1911/1965, p. 206) pointed out, when the head, arm, or leg is in an unstable position it is susceptible to involuntary motor movements that induce it to return to a more natural position. If readers try holding a y-shaped object in this manner they will observe that very little effort is required to snap the hands back to a more natural position, bringing the stick sharply downward in the process. Time and again instances of involuntary muscle movements occur under these circumstances.

In 1923 William Foster of the Psychological Laboratory of the University of Minnesota was contacted by a 70-year-old man who asked that experiments be conducted to explain his ability to locate materials by means of divining rods. For the past 45 years he had successfully located not only water but also oil, natural gas, iron, gold and silver, as well as such mundane (hidden) objects as coins and watches. Foster agreed. He moved a large table into the main laboratory and chalked on its top fourteen 20 x 20-inch squares, parallel with identical squares chalked on the floor beneath it. A small cardboard box that held silver coins, one silver watch and two gold watches, was placed on the floor in the center of the square *chosen by the diviner*. Sure enough, when the diviner mounted the table top and stepped on the corresponding square, his divining rod—a piece of piano wire looped in the middle into a small e-shaped pointer with the ends held by the dowser—"rotated definitely and strongly" (Foster, 1923, p. 304).

Next, in a series of random trials, the box was placed under the table *while the diviner was out of the room*. When he returned he walked slowly over the table top until the rod in his hand rotated. Out of 28 trials (on an additional 4 trials the box was not placed at all), the correct square was chosen only once, equivalent to chance. On the 4 trials in which the box was not placed, the diviner unhesitatingly chose four squares. In other experiments, including the divining of water mains, the occasional above-chance performance occurred only in instances where there was the possibility of picking up cues such as the sound of running water, a visible hydrant, or a cue inadvertently provided by a knowledgeable person who accompanied the diviner as a "checker." Foster was adamant in his belief that diviners are sincere believers in their powers and unaware that they are picking up cues. Furthermore, "The movements of the rod appear to the diviner to be automatic, and often not even to be subject to his voluntary control. ... The form of the rod and the mechanics of its movement are such as to favor the suggestion that it 'moves of itself' and sometimes moves in spite of voluntary efforts to restrain it" (p. 310). Foster (1923) concluded by emphasizing:

> the importance of cues and suggestions often given by the knower's unconscious and involuntary actions and accepted by the "sensitive" without clear realization of the fact. To become convinced in the latter regard, one has only to compare the conditions and results of divining with those of mind-reading, muscle-reading, table-turning and of thinking animals like Clever Hans. (p. 311)

In 1952 Thomas Riddick, a consulting engineer and chemist, found it necessary to discuss dowsing in the pages of the *Proceedings of the American Philosophical Society* because of the support it had recently received from no less a celebrity than the popular writer Kenneth Roberts, who had written a book extolling the dowsing ability of Henry Gross. The book was enthusiastically reviewed in the *Atlantic Review*, *Harper's*, *The New York Times* and elsewhere, but Riddick was less enthralled:

> From the standpoint of a waterworks engineer, this ready severing of the Gordian knot of geology, hydraulics, physics, and hydrology by a forked twig

seems amazing. If factual, it constitutes a heretofore unsuspected short cut on the royal road to learning, and an astounding metamorphosis of science into intuitive art. (p. 526)

Henry Gross had, since his youth, spent many hours in the woods and fields (which was to be a crucial element in his success). One day, when he was 12 years old, Henry was in the woods with an 80-year-old stone mason who suddenly cut a Y-shaped stick from a wild apple tree, explaining that this looked like a good place to find a spring. As they walked along the stick suddenly jerked strongly downward. The stone mason marked the ground and said there was a vein of water under there. Henry took the stick and when he walked over the marked spot, sure enough the stick turned downward. Henry was impressed.

Gross later moved to Biddeford, Maine, where where his vocation as game warden was supplemented by his avocation as a dowser. But when he met Kenneth Roberts his powers multiplied. Roberts taught him how to determine the depth and amount of water that flowed through a water vein, and Gross was soon "predicting the depths of veins to the nearest foot and sometimes the inch, and rate of flow to the nearest gallon and oftentimes the quart" (Riddick, 1952, p. 532). With Roberts urging him on—a clear case of folie à deux if there ever was one—reality deteriorated even further. Soon Gross was predicting the chemical and bacteriological content of the hidden water. Nor did he have to walk over the vein to find it; the rod responded to questions such as, "Is it 100 yards away?" and so on. And lo and behold, he could even dowse long distances. While sitting in Mr. Roberts's bar and holding his rod over a map of North Africa, he was able to dowse in the Sahara Desert!

Like Foster, Riddick (1952) did not argue that dowsers did not have successes, even at above-chance levels (although controls for random guesses would be useful). Dowsers were, however,

> generally successful where a yield of only a few gallons per minute is required, such as for household or small estate usage; though no more or less so than any person with a reasonable knowledge of the flow of underground water. When dowsers attempt to locate water supplies where requirements are hundreds to thousands of gallons per minute, however, the story is quite different. (p. 529)

Riddick supported this assertion with several examples. He also noted that when Gross had been a simple dowser he succeeded when he stuck to areas of grass that "remained verdant, even during drought periods; and to the sand, gravel and shell formations which are pervious and water-bearing if fed by a drainage area of appreciable size" (p. 531). A precise spot need not be chosen, because "most water that is obtained by means of wells and so forth is in pools and reservoirs underground" (Randi, 1982, p. 316). In other words, good dowsers don't need a rod; they are capable of picking up cues on the surface (although Vogt and Hyman, 1979, think this unlikely for amateurs). In any case, these surface cues are not enough to pick up large flows. But don't expect dowsers to search without their divining rods, which allow involuntary muscle movements to provide the necessary aura of mystery.

Vogt and Hyman (1979), in their outstanding book on water witching, presented a fictional account—based on the evidence garnered over the years—of what must be happening when a novice is recruited into the world of water divining. A fictional rookie, Jim Brooks, has been observing in wonder as a seasoned diviner works.

> The diviner notices Jim Brooks's incredulous gaze. He walks up to Jim and hands him the rod, telling him it will also work for him. As a result of this direct suggestion, Jim's forearm muscles again make microscopic contractions as the idea of duplicating the diviner's performance leads to this imperceptible acting-out. This time we might theorize, on the basis of what we know, that the action potentials in the arm are greater than before and that the initial reaction to witnessing the performance has facilitated the response to the direct suggestion.
>
> Jim grasps the rod in the same grip that he saw the diviner use. His arms tense, his eyes fixed upon the rod's point, he becomes oblivious of the surrounding spectators as he concentrates upon the dominant theme of the rod's actions. The increased tension in his arms and body facilitates muscular response. An impulse that might not lead to overt muscular action in a relaxed muscle may be sufficient to trigger off such action in a tense one. This heightened and prolonged tension, furthermore, masks the neural feedback from his arms and hands. The focusing of his attention on the dominant idea further enhances the effectiveness of the expectation that the rod will move.
>
> Now Jim is nearing the site over which the diviner's rod had dipped. The image of the rod's movements becomes much stronger in the face of the expectancy that it will move. The contractions in the forearm spread to the adjoining fibers; the minute contractions begin rallying together. Suddenly the minute contractions—in a great wave of union—produce a larger muscular contraction. With an almost imperceptible spasm the hands suddenly come closer together and the wrists turn slightly inward. This action upsets the delicate balance of forces existing between Jim's grip and the tensions in the rod. The rod suddenly springs forward with such force that the bark peels off and Jim's hands become painfully scratched. (Vogt & Hyman, 1979, pp. 150–151)

Jim cannot explain it, but he insists to the onlookers that he did not make the rod move and that, indeed, he tried to hold it back. The proof, after all, is the peeled bark and the painful effect on his hands.

A fictional account, certainly, but one based on the experiences of dowsers and drawing on all we have learned about involuntary muscle movements and the ideas that drive them. The peeled bark, incidentally, is not unusual because green sticks with slippery bark, such as willow, are said to be ideal for dowsing (Randi, 1982). Note how in this sketch the minuscule movements typical of von Osten's signals to Hans can, when driven by suggestion and a dominant idea, build into the kind of gross movement required to suddenly jerk a stick. As we shall see, this phenomenon is also consistent with physiological evidence. Recall Chevreul's suggestion that simply observing the small movements of the pendulum had induced progressively larger movements. Furthermore, the prolonged muscle tension built up while holding the rod, like the prolonged pressure on the table by table movers, reduces sensitivity and muscular feedback, thereby screening diviners from realizing that it is they who snap the stick. In short, from barely observable movements that defy discovery to the sharp deflection of a forked twig to the gross maneuvering of another person's hand, involuntary muscle movements have few constraints.

Vogt and Hyman (1979) reviewed several carefully controlled scientific investigations of dowsing, and since 1979 there have been additional studies, one of which was carried out not by a psychologist but by a magician and debunker, James Randi (1982), following in the grand tradition of Houdini. In 1964 Randi had offered $10,000 to anyone who could demonstrate a paranormal power under controlled conditions. No one has yet won the money. Because there are so many paranormal phenomena, Randi has been kept busy. For dowsers he set up an experiment in Italy, in the town of Formello, 30 miles from Rome. A network of plastic pipes 3 centimeters in diameter was buried at a depth of 50 centimeters in a 9 x 10-meter area. Three pipe paths were laid, but only one pipe at a time had water in it, flowing at the rate of at least 5 liters per second. The entry control valves were visible and the dowsers could see the water gushing out after its journey under the prescribed area, so the dowsers could assure themselves that water was indeed flowing somewhere beneath them. The exact location of the pipes were shown to each contestant after the test so it could be compared with the dowsers' markings.

Four claimants were tested, one at a time. All were reputed to be successful dowsers. The first started with a straight willow rod, then switched to a pendulum, all to no avail. The second used two hinged sticks that spun about and were very sensitive to changes in wrist placement or in tension. Although the sticks rotated impressively, their splendid display of rapid motion was unrelated to the flow of water. They whirled about even when the water was depleted and nothing was flowing beneath the dowser. The third contestant also failed. Randi (1982) described the final contestant as the most dramatic of all. "He used a piece of cane, broken almost in two at the center to provide a flexible joint." In his hands the cane became a dangerous weapon, forcing the spectators to stand back. "It continually flew out of his hands; once it hit a cameraman, and it was replaced five times after breaking" (p. 322). Despite the pyrotechnics, he too failed. These failures, produced under objective, controlled conditions, discouraged none of the contestants, who declared before the camera that they were entirely successful.

Objective evidence is powerless against the uncritical wish to believe and the magic of involuntary muscle movements. Use of the divining rod continues to flourish. An article in *The New York Times* of June 26, 1994, described the exploits of a dowser who works with two L-shaped brass rods, one in each hand. The rods signaled *no* by moving apart and *yes* by crossing over each other. "No one knows why the practice works," according to the the article, which described another dowser who "says he believes that he can move a vein of water to a desired location" (Logan, 1994, p. 41).

In the cemetery of a church in a small township in Pennsylvania, on the back of a tombstone for a man and his wife, is etched the official trademark of the American Society of Dowsers (headquartered in Danville, VT). The trademark consists of a circle containing a pair of hands, one on each end of a forked stick. One word on the left and one on the right of the stick extension spell out the Latin phrase INDAGO FELIX, loosely translated, according to the society, as The Fruitful Search. Below this logo is the official prayer for dowsers.

The Dowser's Prayer

Lord guide my hands, enhance my sensitivity, and bless my purpose, that I may be an instrument of Your power and glory in locating what is searched for.

THE OUIJA BOARD

A special education teacher in Tucson, Arizona had her students communicate by handwriting instead of by typing. She sent this personal communication to Biklen, who quoted it appreciatively:

I got a little perturbed with him when he wouldn't point to the ABC's for me. I slapped my hand on my side and said, "Garrett, you know the ABC's as well as I do. Now point to the W." That he did. He pointed to each one of them. I turned the page over and said, "now, we're going to write the ABC's and I'll help you." All I did, I put my hand on his and my god, he wrote them all. (Quoted in Biklen, 1993, p. 96)

Then, according to Biklen (1993), "She asked Garrett how he felt about being mainstreamed in regular classes. At that point she turned over the paper and he began to write in sentences" (p. 96). Presumably he wrote in sentences with her hand still on his. Biklen calls this phenomenon "facilitated handwriting" (p. 96) but of course it is no different in principle from facilitated communication, and neither are different in principle from the

Ouija board, which requires the involuntary movement of a planchette.[14] When two or more people simultaneously place one hand on the planchette it mysteriously moves across a board to the words *yes* or *no* (on some boards there are also *maybe* or *don't know*), or to numbers, or to the letters of the alphabet to spell out words.

Of all the phenomena induced by involuntary motor movement and erroneously attributed to some other source, the Ouija board comes closest to facilitated communication because there are usually two people involved in spelling out words. There is, however, one major difference: Although during facilitated communication the facilitators believe the clients are doing the writing, it is reasonable to assume that most clients know they are being guided by their partners. So we have the unlikely situation of one person, the facilitator, believing the partner is writing whereas the partner probably knows otherwise. On the Ouija board, on the other hand, neither partner believes the other is guiding the planchette and consequently they both believe that the movement comes from some external source (unless, of course, they are willing to acknowledge that unconscious processes are at work).

The similarities with the Ouija board are especially striking when, during facilitated communication, the facilitator and student use an alphabet board and point to the desired response. Kathleen Dillon (1993) has documented the many parallels. For example, during facilitated communication there are instances of grammatical errors, lack of punctuation, run-on words, and phonetic spelling, which proponents brandish as proof that the facilitator cannot be doing the typing. But the same thing occurs on the Ouija board even when both participants are well educated or are professional writers. After a time the errors disappear as they do also in facilitated communication. In fact this description applies to any automatic writing.

For his books of poems the late James Merrill won the Pulitzer Prize, The Bolingen Prize in Poetry, two National Book Awards, a National Book Critics Circle Award, and the first Bobbitt National Prize for Poetry awarded by the Library of Congress. Many parts of his books were products of sessions on a homemade Ouija board with his friend David Jackson. These

---

[14]Ouija is a combination of yes in French and German, oui-ja, and the Ouija board is a registered trademark of Parker Brothers. The French *planchette* ("small plank") was originally a miniature table, which was derived from table rapping. As someone recited the alphabet the little table tilted when the desired letter was spoken (Christopher, 1970). A lot of time was saved when the little table was placed on an alphabet board so that it could move to the letters, and *planchette* became the general term for any object used in automatic pointing or writing. When used on a Ouija board it is typically triangular or heart shaped and supported by casters or otherwise made to slide easily across a board or paper. Either the apex of the triangle, a pointer, or a glass window designates the letter, number or word. When used for automatic writing it has a pencil placed vertically in it, attached to it, or serving as the third leg. Divination using mysteriously moving objects (which we now know are moved by involuntary muscle movements) is very ancient, going back at least to Pythagoras and his sect in the 6th century B.C. (L. Shepard, 1978).

sessions were initiated at a time when Mr. Jackson was an unpublished novelist because, according to Merrill, he was disinclined to revise or plan ahead and consequently had stopped writing. This "fueled our séances at the Ouija board. Here the problem of shaping the material into an intricate, balanced whole was out of conscious hands" (Merrill, 1993, p. 77). Initially their setup consisted of a heavy piece of cardboard on which the alphabet was spread in an arc along with the words *yes* and *no*, and a cup was used as a planchette. Here is Merrill's (1983) description of their first use of the board, when they contacted the spirit of someone named Ephraim:

> But he had not yet found us. Who was there?
> The cup twitched in its sleep. "Is someone there?"
> We whispered, fingers light on Willowware,
> When the thing moved. Our breathing stopped. The cup,
> Glazed zombie of itself, was on the prowl
> Moving, but dully, incoherently,
> Possessed, as we should soon enough be told,
> By one or another of the myriads
> Who hardly understand, through the compulsive
> Reliving of their deaths, that they have died
> —By fire in this case, when a warehouse burned.
> HELLP O SAV ME scrawled the cup. (p. 6)

Soon the cup was moving swiftly with Merrill taking down the letters "blind," as he described it, with his free hand. Later, to please Ephraim, they propped a mirror in the chair facing them. Other spirits came to them: dead relatives and friends, dead poets and living poets such as William Butler Yeats and W. H. Auden, ancient luminaries including Homer, Nefertiti and Montezuma, and even Jesus and Mohammed (Merrill's spelling). Merrill revised the product into a poem or, as he called it, a play of voices. The words of these spirits, in capital letters, contribute substantially to many of his poems.

Merrill moved from the Ouija board to the keyboard but maintained that his writing was no less automatic.

> Low on public spirit, without "ideas" in … [my brother's] sense of the word, or should I say ever leerier of their frontal presentation, in writing I have resorted, after the first scrawled phrases, to keyboards of increasing complexity, moving from Olivetti to Selectric III, from Ouija to this season's electronic wizard. (p. 202)

Then he divulged, in the expressive language of a poet, that in "the arcane glow of a little screen," he writes in a dreamlike aura "until a length of text is at last woven tightly enough to resist unmaking. Then only do I see what I had to say" (p. 202).

The Ouija board game is only one of many manifestation of automatic writing. Usually, however, automatic *hand*writing springs to mind when automatic writing is mentioned, and it is automatic handwriting that has received the most attention and for which there is the most extensive literature, dating back many centuries. We turn to it now with the understanding that all forms of automatic writing are subject to the same dynamics.

AUTOMATIC HANDWRITING

Compared with the Ouija board, automatic handwriting (henceforth I bow to convention and use the term *automatic writing*) using a pen or pencil is a simpler, faster and more direct outlet for involuntary muscle movements. Occasionally the two partially merge: a planchette with a pencil in it becomes the medium for writing because of the ease with which the pencil is moved.

Because automatic writing (with either a planchette on a Ouija board or a pencil on a paper) is an outlet for thoughts that are consciously unexpressed, it is a valuable tool not only for poets such as Merrill but also for researchers and therapists. It is repeatedly mentioned in cases of multiple personality (a fuller discussion of which is reserved for Chapter 6). At the same time, the implausible nature of automatic writing—that people can be unaware of what they are writing or even that they are writing—has made it an ideal instrument for alleged supernormal phenomena such as telepathy, and for paranormal processes such as communications from the spirit world.

In England in the 1880s Frederic W. H. Myers published a series of four articles on automatic writing in the second through the fifth volumes of the newly published *Proceedings of the Society for Psychical Research*. References to the first three can be found in the fourth article (Myers, 1889). Myers was a knowledgeable observer:

> But we know that a great deal more than this [conscious thoughts and voluntary movements] is in fact going on within us. Multitudes of involuntary movements, both peripheral and internal—multitudes of spontaneously arising images, during both sleep and waking—testify to cerebral activities of which we are never consciously the originators.

> All that we can say of these cerebral activities is that if it had been of much practical use to our ancestors to be conscious of them, they, and consequently we, would probably have become conscious of them. (Myers, 1886a, p. 259)

In that same article he briefly reviewed previous articles in which he had

> tried to show that an automatic impulse, arising, so far as we can tell, wholly within the writer's brain, may sometimes prompt him to write words or sentences whose meaning he does not discern while writing them,—nay, whose meaning he does not discern till after a tedious process of decipherment. (p. 210)

He contrasted acts such as automatic writing, which he labeled *primarily* automatic (by which he meant a primary process) and therefore instinctual (inborn, unlearned, evolved), with acts that are *secondarily* automatic, such as playing the piano, which have become automatic only with practice. Touching on alternate personality, he astutely raised the possibility of a secondary chain of memories "linking together those periods of altered consciousness into a series of their own. And when once a second mnemonic chain is woven, the emergence of a second personality is only a matter of degree" (p. 225). He discussed dreams, hypnotism, possession, and other related phenomena and included some important communications from, among others, Pierre Janet.

In the first article Myers (1884) had quoted extensively a friend's description of automatic writing that sounds very similar to Merrill's Ouija board experience. In addition, alluding to instances of more than one person putting their hands on a planchette and writing automatically, Myers suggested that "two minds are acting on each other, and the writing is a resultant of their unconscious mental play" (p. 233). But Myers went astray. By unconscious mental play he meant that the unconscious interaction was telepathic, for Myers was not simply a believer in unconscious processes; he believed that the unconscious is assisted by telepathy, which "seems sometimes to reveal our unconscious to our conscious selves" (p. 219).

Telepathy was only a first step. Personal problems apparently drove Myers to prove the existence of survival after death (T. H. Hall, 1964). Even though he had suggested that his explanations of certain instances of automatic writing precluded their use as evidence of spiritualism, he nevertheless pointed out that in other instances the revelations from automatic writing and other automatisms go beyond unconscious productions or even telepathy. In the fourth article he specifically asserted that some automatic messages provide evidence of influences from departed souls or, as he put it, supernormal processes that "transcend human powers, as known to us at the present stage of evolution" (Myers, 1889, p. 525). To buttress this belief he had to accept some of the descriptions he received from "reputable" acquaintances and strangers. He appealed to spiritualists to send him any evidence, based on the content of automatic messages, that might provide proof "that the mind of some departed friend has in truth inspired them.... [because] actual proofs—or even attempts at proof—are hardly ever forthcoming" (p. 546). The proof he wrote of was the information received during automatic writing or during other automatisms, information presumably unknown to the automatic writer or to anyone else who was present.

A trusting nature was a common trait in the group of eminent men who formed and contributed to England's Society for Psychical Research. There is, for example, the case of Edmund Gurney, who after many years of disinterest was finally persuaded by Myers and Henry Sidgwick (whom we met during the investigation of Mr. Bishop's mind-reading skills) to devote himself to psychical research. Gurney joined them and others (notably William Fletcher Barrett) in founding the society in 1882, and he became its secretary, the editor of its *Journal* and *Proceedings* and an admired contributor to their pages (Hall, 1964; James, 1892). With Myers and others he conducted many "experiments." An early one was a follow-up of Barrett's investigations of the Reverend Andrew Creery's family and the family's servant girl, who in 1881 convinced Barrett and then the society's Committee on Thought Transference (Myers, Gurney, Barrett, and later Frank Podmore) of their telepathic powers.

Barrett published his preliminary findings in *Nature* (1881):

> A clergyman in Derbyshire [the Reverend Creery] has five young children, four girls and one boy, aged from nine to fourteen years, all of whom are able to go through the ordinary performances of the "willing game" rapidly and successfully.... More than this, letters and words, or names and places, of persons and of cards, can be guessed with promptness and accuracy.... [Even] more curious, the maid-servant was equally sensitive. This led me to try other experiments ... and the father was found to be pre-eminently the best willer, and to be in fact almost as necessary for success as the sensitive "guesser"; further experiments showed that a battery of minds, all intently fixed on the same word, was far more successful than one or two alone. Apparently a *nervous induction* of the dominant idea in our minds took place on the passive mind of the child, and the experiments recalled the somewhat analogous phenomena of electric and magnetic induction. There seemed to be a veritable exoneural action of the mind. (p. 212)

In the two-volume *Phantasms of the Living*—published in 1886 by Gurney, Myers, and Podmore but written almost entirely by Gurney—the powers of Creery's daughters were credited with contributing to the conviction by Gurney and his colleagues that thought transference in normal states was indeed possible. That convincing finding—convincing to them, that is—was the final inducement to the founding of the society (Hall, 1964).

Unfortunately in later card experiments two of the girls were detected signaling to each other, and the unhappy task of recanting fell to Gurney. "Two of the sisters, acting as 'agent' and 'percipient,' were detected in the use of a code of signals; and a third has confessed to a certain amount of signalling in the earlier series," wrote Gurney (1888, p. 269), and he went on to describe the codes they used.

Meanwhile Gurney and his colleagues pursued other psychics, including two young men, George Smith, a mesmerist, and Douglas Blackburn, a journalist who was performing with Smith in a "second sight" act in the entertainment halls of Brighton. *Second sight* simply means that the person on stage, in this case Smith, who was the medium or percipient sitting blindfolded with his back to the audience, saw not only with his own eyes but had a second means of sight through the eyes of a telepathic agent, in this case Blackburn. The agent was given or shown any object by a member of the audience, and to the audience's amazement the medium identified and described the object, sometimes in great detail.

This is an old act in which the agent uses codes to cue the percipient, and it is a skill that, as noted earlier, had been explained in detail in the book by Mr. Bishop, the mind-reader. But not many people read Bishop's book (or believed it) and as far as the Brighton audience was concerned the percipient was capable of reading minds, thereby proving the existence of thought transference. Unfortunately, he could read only the mind of his partner.

Astonishingly, when Myers and Gurney privately tested Smith and Blackburn they allowed (even encouraged) Blackburn to hold Smith's hand while Smith was asked the colors and names written down by Myers or Gurney and shown only to Blackburn. In later "experiments" the young men were separated, and in one experiment Smith reproduced drawings of animals and objects. The two men obviously used codes (e.g., the Morse code) because the experiments failed when skeptical observers introduced proper controls. This fact was ignored in the published reports, where the results were touted as providing convincing evidence for the existence of telepathy. One of the members of an outside investigative committee later recalled that Myers attributed failures to the presence of nonbelievers (Hall, 1964, p. 114), a ploy often seized upon to protect a cherished belief.

Young Smith (only 18 when he performed at Brighton entertainment halls) later became Gurney's private secretary (and when Gurney died, Myers's secretary) and was employed by the society to do clerical work and assist in their investigations. But his most significant job was as a hypnotist for Gurney and others in "experiments" using young acquaintances from Brighton to demonstrate thought transference during hypnotism (Hall, 1964).

There was more disillusionment in store for the faithful. Starting in 1908, in a series of publications about his association with Smith, Blackburn confessed "that the 'experiments' were simple trickery," explained how they were performed, and noted "that the S.P.R. [Society for Psychical Research] investigators had been as easy to deceive as children" (Campbell & Hall, 1968, p. 186).

This admission, denied by Smith, came 20 years after Gurney's sudden death at the age of 41 in June 1888, in a hotel room in Brighton. The previous day Gurney had received a letter, postmarked Brighton, whose contents have never been revealed. Hall (1964) makes a case for suicide, reasoning that Gurney had been summoned to Brighton by someone (other than Smith, who was away at the time) to be told that Smith had deceived him. Hall presents evidence that the person who summoned Gurney was one of Smith's sisters, Alice, who had been briefly involved some time earlier in demonstrations before the society's committees on mesmerism and thought transference. She admired Gurney and may have wanted to end the deception for his sake, or for her brother's own good, or because she had some disagreement with her brother. Hall speculates that Gurney had known for some time about the Smith–Blackburn hoax but had received a promise from Smith to reform. For Gurney, a revelation by Alice that the "telepathy during hypnotism" experiments were also fraudulent must have been catastrophic, following as it did his painful public revelation of the Creery sisters' deception (Gurney, 1888), which in turn was only one of several humiliating revelations. The major pillars supporting his public claims for the reality of telepathy were crumbling, to say nothing of his well-known trust in human goodness and morality. The criticisms being made of *Phantasms* and the evidence brought against the ghost stories that comprised most of that book would only have added to his burden. For these reasons, the case for suicide is substantial.

I have gone into some detail here to emphasize that eminent, respected and highly achieving professionals can become deeply enmeshed in obvious fraud and nonsense; not long ago several psychologists and physicists believed that a young Israeli, Uri Geller, was bending spoons by thought control (Gardner, 1981; Randi, 1982). As I will periodically repeat, eminence in another discipline is no match for the wish to believe. For some of the faithful it was not simply that they were inept at picking up the tricks used by spiritualists; some went so far as to believe that some people had prostituted their supernormal powers in order to pose as magicians, and therefore it was psychic power, not clever deception, that was the actual source of their wizardry!

So it was with Arthur Conan Doyle, creator of the keenly observant, highly analytical Sherlock Holmes. Doyle was a dedicated spitualist who was frequently requested to give public lectures on the subject; one of his talks, remember, had enchanted Louisa and Joseph Rhine. Despite his friend Harry Houdini's disclaimers, Doyle insisted that Houdini performed his magic tricks and unique escapes by using hidden psychic powers. In a book exposing spiritualists, toward the end of a chapter he had devoted to Doyle's beliefs, Houdini (1924) wrote: "Sir Arthur thinks that I have great mediumistic powers and that some of my feats are done with the aid of spirits. Everything I do is accomplished by material means, humanly possible, no matter how baffling it is to the layman" (p. 165).

But Doyle was not convinced. Here are excerpts from a chapter, "The Riddle of Houdini," in a book by Doyle (1930) defending spiritualism, published 4 years after Houdini died:

> As an example it was said, and is said again and again, "How absurd to attribute possible psychic powers to a man who himself denies them!" Is it not perfectly evident that if he did not deny them his occupation would have been gone for ever? What would his brother-magicians have to say to a man who admitted that half his tricks were done by what they would regard as illicit powers? It would be "exit Houdini." (p. 35)

> There is one thing certain, and that is that the fate of the Davenports must have been a perpetual warning to Houdini. They had been ruined and hunted off the stage because it was thought that their claim was psychic. If his powers were to be drawn from the same source, and if he were to avoid a similar fate,

then his first and fundamental law must be that it be camouflaged in every possible way, and that no one at all should know his secret. (p. 50)

From personal observation I have assured myself that mediums in sealed bonds can cast those bonds, walk about the room, and be found later with the sealed bonds as before. If they could get out by a trick I see no way in which they could get back. I am forced, therefore, to predicate the existence of such a dematerializing and reconstructing force, which would amply cover most of the phenomena of the Davenports and of Houdini. (p. 54).

In other words Houdini escaped from boxes and prison cells and even handcuffs by dematerializing and then rematerializing after his escape, and the same process could be used to return to bondage. The two Davenport brothers were performers who, like Houdini, escaped from restraints and confinement; in fact Houdini had been a pupil of one of them, Ira Erastus Davenport. Doyle was explaining that the Davenports' refusal to deny that they were actually spiritualists had angered the public, and he made the elementary deduction that Houdini denied his psychic powers in order to avoid a similar fate.

Doyle had lost a son in the war, and the possibility that he could communicate with him must surely have influenced his journey into spiritualism. Houdini had lost his beloved mother, to whom he was deeply attached, and for this reason he was willing to attend séances and explore spiritualism, hoping he could communicate with her. But unlike Doyle's, Houdini's wish to believe—the most potent driving force of false beliefs—did not cloud his critical faculties. As Houdini (1924) wrote in the beginning of his chapter on Doyle, "Spiritualism has claimed among its followers numbers of brilliant minds—scientists, philosophers, professionals and authors" (p. 138). Substitute any pseudoscience for "Spiritualism": This statement has universal application.

The illustrious American psychologist and philosopher William James (1892, 1901) was a great admirer and friend of Gurney and Myers and very sympathetic to the aims of England's Society for Psychical Research, which he served as president from 1894 to 1895, and after which The American Society for Psychical Research was modeled. James, as did his colleagues in these societies, demanded a scientific approach, but considering the nature of the experiments in this strange field the term *scientific* was very loosely defined. When he could find no indication of fraud—which he was careful (but not careful enough) to look for (see especially James, 1886)—he was persuaded that telepathy or clairvoyance was the only explanation.[15]

At about the same time that Myers published the last of his four articles on automatic writing, James published his own notes on the subject, in which he slipped gradually from a discussion of altered states of conscious-

---

[15]For a complete collection of James's writings on psychical research, along with informative notes, see Burkhardt and Bowers (1986).

ness to a consideration of telepathic communication. "But there are other cases harder so to treat," he wrote, "cases where some sort of telepathy appears to be involved" (1889, p. 559). In fact he believed that in some cases of automatic writing even more than telepathy was involved.

Of all the mediums and seers James was acquainted with it was the Boston medium, Mrs. Leonora E. Piper, who had the greatest impact on him because of the details she knew about his family's affairs (James, 1886). For James she was the single "white crow" who proved that white crows (supernormal phenomena) existed, a metaphor introduced in his valedictory address as President of the (English) Society for Psychical Research and read before that Society in London by F. W. H. Myers. James himself delivered this address to the American Branch in Boston as well as in New York, and it was later published in the *Proceedings of the American Society for Psychical Research* as well as in *Science*. In it he discussed the proof for supernormal phenomena such as psychic and telepathic performances.

> But it is a miserable thing for a question of truth to be confined to mere presumption and counter-presumption, with no decisive thunderbolt of fact to clear the baffling darkness.... For me the thunderbolt *has* fallen.... If you will let me use the language of the professional logic-shop, a universal proposition can be made untrue by a particular instance. If you wish to upset the law that all crows are black, you mustn't seek to prove that no crows are; it is enough to prove one single crow to be white. My own white crow is Mrs. Piper. In the trances of this medium, I cannot resist the conviction that knowledge appears which she has never gained by the ordinary waking use of her eyes and ears and wits. (James, 1896a, p. 884)

Cattell (1896) briefly criticized James's address. "The discovery of a great many gray crows would not prove that any crows were white, rather the more crows we examine and find to be black or gray, the less expectation have we of finding one that is white.... One white crow is enough, but its skin should be deposited in a museum" (pp. 582–583). One issue later James (1896b) responded, in part, "But our reports are not of gray crows; at the very worst they are of white crows without the skins brought home" (p. 650; see also Moore, 1977).

Mrs. Piper held sittings in her home and spoke or wrote in a trance for, among others, the spirits of Bach and Longfellow. One of the spirits who communicated through Mrs. Piper was a deceased French physician named Phinuit, who acted primarily as an intermediary for other spirits (see, e.g., Gauld, 1968, who was sympathetic to psychical research). In his famous *The Principles of Psychology*, James (1890/1950) discussed Mrs. Piper (without naming her) as a case he had in mind of a medium through whom spirits made contact with the living. One such spirit professed to be a dead French doctor (also unnamed). James wrote that he was convinced that this departed French doctor's spirit, speaking through the medium (Mrs. Piper), is "acquainted with facts about the circumstances, and the living and dead relatives and acquaintances, of numberless sitters whom the medium never met before, and of whom she has never heard the names" (p. 396).

What James did not tell readers of the *Principles* is that the spirit of the French Dr. Phinuit (who, incidentally, has never been traced) could not, except for a few words of greeting, either speak or understand French (Burkhardt & Bowers, 1986; James, 1890). James (1890) easily rationalized this: "Phinuit himself, however, bears every resemblance of being a fictitious being" (p. 655). But that doesn't mean he isn't a spirit, *somebody's* spirit. "The crumbs of information which he [Phinuit] gives about his earthly career are, as you know, so few, vague, and unlikely sounding, as to suggest the romancing of one whose stock of materials for invention is excessively reduced. He is, however, as he actually shows himself, a definite human individual, with immense tact and patience, and great desire to please and be regarded as infallible" (p. 655). In other words, the spirit of Phinuit is attempting to romanticize his prosaic earthly career by claiming to have been a French doctor.

When Mrs. Piper, whether hypnotized or in a medium-trance, failed the controlled test in which James used cards unknown to her, James simply concluded that there was no sign of thought transference and went on to report Mrs. Piper's similar failures in the waking state, inferring that "her medium-trance seems an isolated feature in her psychology" (1886, p. 105).

Four years later James (1890) wrote a more complete report on Mrs. Piper in the form of a letter to Myers, which was read by his brother, the author Henry James, to a meeting of the English society. In it he related that a friend had reported Mrs. Piper's talents to James's mother- and sister-in-law, each of whom then obtained a sitting, after which they told James about Mrs. Piper's extraordinary knowledge of their family and its affairs even though each had seen her anonymously. James then accompanied his wife to a sitting with Mrs. Piper, saw her frequently after that and collected the testimony of others. In the published letter to Myers he conveyed his conviction that Mrs. Piper had supernormal powers.

As he did when Mrs. Piper failed his card test, James (1889) rationalized other negative findings. About a medium who was touted for her powers but failed when James tested her, he wrote, "These negative results are, of course, not incompatible with the positive ones previously obtained, for if telepathy exist, it is certainly a fitful occurrence, even in a given individual" (p. 562). So loose a standard of scientific objectivity makes it impossible to disprove telepathy or anything else.

James's descriptions of Mrs. Piper's powers can be found among his papers on psychical research collected by Burkhardt and Bowers (1986; see also Murphy & Ballou, 1960). Included are descriptions not only of Phinuit's successes and failures but also of James's complaint about Phinuit's frequent banality: "I confess that the human being in me was so much stronger than the man of science that I was too disgusted with Phinuit's tiresome twaddle even to note it down" (James, 1890, p. 656).

In working with Mrs. Piper sporadically over a period of 25 years, James wrote that he could find no evidence of fraud. Despite all the evidence, nothing could persuade this eminent psychologist that Phinuit was Mrs. Piper and not a spirit contact from the great beyond. If William James could believe this nonsense despite the contrary evidence we should not be surprised that parents of retarded and autistic children believe that facilitated communication really works, nor that its defenders use every kind of rationalization to preserve their belief.

The wish to believe is more powerful than we can ever imagine. Rosenzweig (1994) noted that James's mother and father both died in 1882, and his son Herman, not yet 2 years old, died in 1885, just months before James's first visit to Mrs. Piper. Perhaps James, like Conan Doyle, was ripe for belief. On James's first visit Mrs. Piper mentioned several spirits in her trance state, including Herrin, which she apparently spelled out and which James took as a misspelling of his son's name (James, 1890). She also mispronounced his deceased father-in-law's name but on a second try got closer to his true name. These errors would impress the impressionable. On the other hand, the reason James gave for his beliefs, revealed in a letter to his lifelong friend Thomas Davidson, was that Christianity was in ruins and physical evidence of an afterlife might be the only path to a new era of faith and a new popular religion (Coon, 1992)

From the way in which James met Mrs. Piper to the way in which she dropped in at his house and the kinds of information she produced in her séances, it appears that she had a conduit through the servants in the James household (Burkhardt & Bowers, 1986, p. 397). In the October 20, 1901 issue of the *New York Herald* Mrs. Piper published a statement (reprinted in Bell, 1902) in which she said that she did not believe in spiritualism or that dead spirits spoke through her. Rather, she believed that the best explanation of her powers was telepathy, including unconscious telepathy and the "unconscious expression of my subliminal self" (p. 145). Her description of how she met James was quite different from James's. "My maid of all work told a friend who was a servant in the household of Professor James, of Harvard, that I went into 'queer sleeps,' ... [He] recognized that I was what is called a psychic, and took steps to make my acquaintance" (quoted in Bell, 1902, p. 143). Having a maid who was friends with a servant in the James household would have been very convenient for gathering information.

In 1889 Mrs. Piper was sent to England for 15 months, where she impressed the members of the Society for Psychical Research before returning to the United States for additional triumphs. In 1906 and 1909 she again traveled to England at the society's expense. Books and articles have been written about her for she was, and is, a favorite of believers and consequently a target of debunkers (Gauld, 1968). Of particular interest is the psychologist Amy Tanner's (1910/1994) book on spiritism, which includes six séances Mrs. Piper gave for her and G. Stanley Hall, one of the pioneers of American psychology. Mrs. Piper went into a trance and the spirits responded primarily through Mrs. Piper's automatic writing, unlike the voice communications she apparently used quite often with James. Transcripts of the six séances with Mrs. Piper were reproduced in Tanner's book, with frequent spaces representing illegible script.

The primary spirit allegedly communicating with G. S. Hall was Richard Hodgson, who until his recent sudden death had been an very active member of, and contributor to, the Society for Psychical Research in England. Hodgson had come to the United States to assist the financially troubled American branch of the society, and he served as its salaried secretary and executive agent (Burkhardt & Bowers, 1986). He had been Mrs. Piper's manager for 18 years.[16]

Hall wrote extensive comments in Tanner's book and also contributed the introduction. During the séances with Mrs. Piper, Hall asked the questions and Tanner read the written responses and took notes. Hall surreptitiously tested Mrs. Piper by introducing fictitious people and events that were readily accepted and discussed by the spirit of Dr. Hodgson, who also recollected a nonexistent friendship with Hall.

> Although I [Hall] never met him [Hodgson] in the flesh, yet in these sessions he always addressed me in the most familiar manner, had many totally false memories of former interviews with me and of discussions which never took place, and in a word seemed to feel just as intimate with me as Mrs. Piper in her normal state thought he used to. He recollected also everything that I pretended had passed between us.... Perhaps when living he meant to have made my acquaintance, and as a ghost mistook the will for the deed. (Tanner, 1910/1994, p. xxi)

Hall asked Hodgson's spirit whether he knew the late Dr. Borst (fictitious) and whether he (Hall) could speak with him. Hodgson said he did know him, and shortly thereafter Hall was communicating with the spirit of a person who never existed. Hodgson also assured Hall that Hall's (fictitious) deceased niece, Bessie Beals, was doing well, and soon Hall was communicating with her also. Tests such as these could easily have been made by James, but he simply would have rationalized the responses.

Tanner's book evolved from a study of the Psychical Research Society (presumably the English society) that Tanner was doing as Hall's special assistant. Hall, as well as James, had helped found the American Society for Psychical Research in 1884 and 1885, and Hall, then at Johns Hopkins, was one of five distinguished people who served as vice presidents at the Society's inaugural. "One of the purposes of the Society was to record,

---

[16]According to Tanner (1910/1994), "Dr. Hodgson had never been married, but was engaged as a young man when his fiancée died. It was in connection with her that his interest in spiritism was aroused" (p. 203). In fact he had a vision of her on the day she died.

investigate, and, in most cases, debunk the reports pouring in from all sides" (Burkhardt & Bowers, 1986, p. 381), even though many members hoped that some truth might be hidden somewhere in the mass of reports. However, when it became apparent that the society was becoming more tolerant and less skeptical than originally proposed, spiritualists decreased their initial attacks and the society lost many eminent members, Hall being "the first of the scientific leaders to resign in 1886 or 1887" (D. Ross, 1972, p. 164).

At about this time Hall (1887) published in his newly launched *American Journal of Psychology* an extensive critical review of both Gurney et al.'s (1886) *Phantasms of the Living* and six years of the English Society's *Proceedings*. In the course of describing the myriad tricks that can be used to produce "psychic" phenomena, he pointed out that when conscious deception was not used, another kind of deception, the "tricks of our automatic nature, subtle and manifold beyond all conception" (p. 140), was available. He had already noted one "trick of our automatic nature" when, in psychic experiments with names and letters, "a good muscle reader divines what letter is in mind by unconscious and unavoidable modifications of finger or voice when it is reached" (p. 137).

As I previously mentioned (footnote 7, p. 38), in 1890 the American Society was dissolved, but James remained in the English Society and its American offshoots. In fact he was an active leader who wrote bitingly about those who shunned the subjects of telepathy and spiritism by simply denying their possibility without even examining the evidence, a charge he could not level against Hall, who surely had James in mind when he wrote his introduction to Tanner's book (1910/1994):

> Credence in any of these [psychic] phenomena by cultivated academic minds, or even the admission that there is an open question, presents another difficult problem. Their attitude I believe [is] due partly to a dualistic philosophy that assumes two different world orders, and holds that one [world order] may interfere at certain points with the other, and partly to an inveterate lust for evidence of the independent post-mortem existence of souls. The third factor in their case is found in the utter inadequacy of current psychology in dealing with the unconscious, and a gross underestimation of its range and scope in all our daily lives. Mind, to it, is consciousness and every eruption from the unconscious it regards as of ghostly origin, because it lacks all conception of the intricacy and complexity of the subliminal psychic processes of which introspection gives no glimmer or inkling. (pp. xvii–xviii)

Initially Tanner was inclined to believe in telepathy and even in the possibility of contact with spirits, but by the end of their study she believed in neither and commented in a tone of disillusionment, "Nearly all of the published accounts of the work of the Society for Psychical Research have tended to emphasize the evidence in favour of supposedly supernormal forces, and have largely or wholly ignored the weaknesses in the evidence"

(1910/1994, p. vi). After what she witnessed during her study it was incomprehensible to her that telepathy and spirit communication should ever have been believed, no less that people "should be willing to stake their professional reputations upon the inaccuracies and rubbish that pass for 'scientific' facts" (p. vii). Then, using James's own metaphors, she beseeched James to let the public know about the "marsh of feebleness" as well as the "stream of veridicality." In other words, she faulted James for telling the public why he believed these phenomena were true (veridical) while at the same time neglecting to reveal to the public the feebleness of the evidence.

In his introduction, Hall also provided some interesting autobiographical material. As a boy he had always been fascinated by spiritualists and as a student in Germany had spoken with the astronomer Zöllner and called on Gustav Theodor Fechner, whom psychologists know primarily from his seminal work in psychophysics. Along with Ernst Weber they formed a trio whose late conversion to spritualism had scandalized the academic world. As an adult, Hall became as firm a disbeliever as he had been a believer in his youth. He understood the role of magicians' tricks in séances, and when he was in his early 50s he bought and mastered conjurors' kits and took lessons from professional magicians. When he performed amateur magic shows in his house he was "repeatedly acclaimed as a medium ... by believers," even though in one instance he had explained the trick to an "American member of, and literary contributor to, the English Psychic Research Society" (Tanner, 1910/1994, p. xvii; see also Rosenzweig, 1994). Mrs. Piper, however, did not stoop to knocks on the table, looming apparitions or other such trite physical manifestations, the sources of which magicians can readily unearth; she served only as a medium through which the spirits could speak and write to friends and loved ones.

Tanner and Hall concluded that during her trances Mrs. Piper lapsed into multiple personalities. In his introduction Hall wrote, "In fine, at the very best, I for one can see nothing more in Mrs. Piper than an interesting case of secondary personality with its own unique features.... Even telepathy seems to me a striking case of the subjection of the intellect by the will-to-believe" (Tanner, 1910/1994, p. xxxi). When Hall wrote that "at the very best" he could see nothing more than a case of secondary personality, he apparently was implying that Mrs. Piper was not above a little chicanery. In my view there is no doubt on that score. But she also went into true trances and, as is typical of multiple personality, her different personalities wrote in different handwriting and spoke in different voices.

Hall's amusing sarcasm when writing about the séances were the kinds of refreshing responses we might have expected but never got from James. Hall also showed a compassionate understanding of the psychological dificulties Mrs. Piper must have been experiencing and he offered a penetrating interpretation of the forces working to produce her alternate personalities.

It would be a mistake, nevertheless, to simply ignore what James wrote on this and other topics where Mrs. Piper or other "true" mediums were not involved; much of what he wrote is of obvious merit. But for me at least, something irretrievable is taken from the esteem in which I held this man as a revered and influential psychologist.

We must be careful, likewise, not to take the spurious interpretation of a phenomenon as proof that the phenomenon does not exist. The fact that some individuals describe automatic writing as evidence of telepathy or spiritualism should not invalidate the massive evidence that writing can indeed occur outside of conscious awareness, as it did, in my opinion, with Mrs. Piper. From what we know of involuntary muscle movements there is no reason why automatic writing should not be a natural phenomenon whose study is within the bounds of normal science even though it requires special precautions because of the danger of fraud and deceit.

As noted, William James considered it likely that only a very few mediums are possessed by a paranormal force. To James, when mediums (*most* mediums, and only those who are honest) act as if possessed by the spirit of a departed soul, their trance state is a special form of alternate personality. In showing this kind of understanding he presaged Hall and Tanner, but for whatever reason could not apply it to Mrs. Piper. In its fullest expression, wrote James, the trance state gives rise to changed voice and language. Automatic writing is a lesser or minor evocation by mediums, and within automatic writing the least trance-like expression occurs when the individual "knows what words are coming, but feels impelled to write them as if from without" (1890/1950, Vol. 1, p. 393).

James's interests in the altered states of consciousness revealed by automatic writing clearly influenced two of his students to explore the subject, for James did not consider such altered states to be uncommon even in normal people. The two students were Harvard graduate student Leon Solomons and his close friend Gertrude Stein, an undergraduate at Harvard Annex (shortly thereafter renamed Radcliffe College). Stein had taken a freshman course in psychology given by Hugo Münsterberg, who had recently arrived from Berlin.[17] She was such an excellent student that James acceded to Münsterberg's recommendation that she be permitted to attend James's graduate seminar. The experience was mutually adulatory: Stein was captivated by James's approach and philosophy—which were an inspiration to her for the rest of her life—and James considered her a brilliant student (Mellow, 1974). Under Münsterberg's direction (Stein, 1933) the two students performed a number of experiments on "normal motor automatisms," using themselves as subjects. A pencil was inserted into a planchette upon which one of them would place a hand, but later the pencil was simply handheld.

---

[17]William James was very impressed with Münsterberg's work and managed to lure him to Harvard for the 3-year period of 1892 to 1895 and then permanently in 1897 (Boring, 1950).

Originally, Solomons and Stein had planned to do experiments in fatigue, "and William James added a planchette, he liked a planchette" (Stein, 1937, p. 265). "The fundamental object of these experiments," they wrote, was "to establish an analogy between the acts of the second personality and what is ordinarily called automatism" (Solomons & Stein, 1896, p. 500). They described how, while preoccupied with reading a story, they involuntarily moved a planchette and wrote without conscious control. They also reported automatic reading and automatic speaking. At one point in their experiments they observed "the curious phenomenon of one person unconsciously dictating sentences which the other unconsciously wrote down; both persons meanwhile being absorbed in some thrilling story" (p. 505). Even when they were conscious of the arm movement the movements appeared to them "to be *extra personal*" (p. 494). The subject "gains his knowledge of the movement purely through sensations from the arm. He has no feeling of intention or desire; no foreknowledge of what the movement is to be" (p. 495).

In a subsequent study Stein (1898) tested the automatic writing of a number of students. The subject's arm rested on a board which was suspended from the ceiling, and the subject's hand—extending beyond the board—held a pencil which had been inserted into a planchette. "By lightly resting my hand on the board after starting a movement I could deceive the subject, who sat with closed eyes, as to whether he or I was making the movement" (p. 295). In this way, with the subject distracted, she "taught" all but a couple of them (who produced automatic writing spontaneously) to make rhythmic movements that resulted in the production of various figures, and occasionally words. Once she got the subjects started, Stein would release her own hand from the board. But Stein was less interested in the scientific study of automatic writing than in classifying the subjects into two types, for even then she was more inquisitive about people than curious about science. Solomons was very critical of the prepublication draft of her paper: "The trouble with the article as it stands," he wrote in a letter to her, "is that one has to hunt around too much to find the important points" (Gallup, 1953, p. 15).

There is a sad note to add. When he wrote that letter to his friend Gertrude in 1897, Leon Solomons was in poor health, and he died in 1900 "as the result of an infection contracted in the laboratory" (Gallup, 1953, p. 10).

Three decades later[18] Gertrude Stein (1937) wrote that she was "very much interested [in her experiment] because I gradually found out what ...

---

[18]Taking William James's advice that for psychology you should have a medical degree—which was the path he had taken—Ms. Stein had gone on to matriculate at Johns Hopkins Medical School. Unlike James, however, she did not complete her studies and forsook psychology to become a celebrated expatriate writer and doyen of prominent authors and artists. When James visited Paris she went to his hotel to see him (Stein, 1933), and they occasionally corresponded. His last letter to her was in May 1910, 3 months before he died (Gallup, 1953).

I called the bottom nature of each one of them [the subjects] and I was very much interested in the way they had their nature in them and sitting there while their arm was in the planchette and hardly vaguely talking" (p. 266). Then she made a comment that effectively negated the Solomons and Stein experiment and cast doubt on her own:

> So this was my part of the experiments that were reported in the Psychological Review, Solomons reported what he called his and my automatic writing but I did not think that we either of us had been doing automatic writing, we always knew what we were doing how could we not when every minute in the laboratory we were doing what we were watching others doing, that was our training, but as he wrote the article after all I was an undergraduate and not a professional and as I am always very docile, and all the ideas had been his all that had been mine were the definitions of the characters of the men and women whom I had seen naturally it was as if I had written that I did that automatic writing. (pp. 266–267)

One must decide for oneself whether to believe that Solomons and Stein had truly written without conscious control or were simply consciously pleasing their professor, keeping in mind that Stein's memory of experiments carried out more than 30 years earlier was not always accurate. In either case, pleasing William James would have been a powerful motivator. Perhaps Gertrude Stein later decided that it would be unfortunate if anyone believed that she was not always master of her pen. In saying that she had lied in her brief sojourn into automatic writing—she had earlier denied ever having had any subconscious reactions (Stein, 1933, p. 78)—she made it clear that she was now giving the true explanation "of the article about automatic writing upon which has been based a great deal of theory about my writing" (p. 267)

Obviously she was stung by theories that a part of her writing—with its repetitions, disconnected thought, run-on sentences and indifferent punctuation—actually was automatic writing (e.g., Skinner, 1934). There were good reasons for these speculations; after all, she had written that her automatic writing experiment (presumably meaning her output as a subject) was "the first writing of hers ever to be printed.... [and is] very interesting to read because the method of writing to be afterwards developed in Three Lives and Making of Americans already shows itself" (Stein, 1933, p. 78). It would seem that James Merrill and Gertrude Stein had something interesting in common.

Nineteen years after Solomons and Stein published their paper, June Downey—who, remember, had experimented extensively with mind-reading—joined John Anderson to study automatic writing, also using themselves as subjects (Downey & Anderson, 1915). In their experiments the subject simultaneously read aloud or did arithmetic while writing repetitively (without a planchette) a well-known verse (or, in one study, taking dictation), always screened from seeing their writing arm and hand. After a while they did experience automaticity and periodically lost track of their writing. However, because their reports "showed so much more evidence of conscious control than did the report of Solomons and Stein" (p. 183), they went on to replicate more closely Solomons and Stein's procedures. Nevertheless they found no increase in automatism.

The design of these experiments involved efficiency in a repetitive task while simultaneously attending to a nonrepetitive one, or—in the case of taking dictation—while performing another task. In either case, the task involved splitting attention with the hope that the writing would become automatic or that the writer would become unaware of some aspects of the writing. In the course of the experiment some *novel* content might filter through, for example while making mindless figures or after completing a task, but results of this laboratory demonstration were meager when compared with clinical and other reports of automatic writing in which novel outputs issued abundantly from the pencil.

The experience of perceiving one's own bodily movements as alien is mentioned in automatic writing, as it is in many other phenomena where involuntary muscle movements are involved. In a study to be discussed in Chapter 7, the social psychologist Leon Festinger and his colleagues reported the story of a woman who through automatic writing received warnings of a catastrophic flood (Festinger, Riecken, & Schachter, 1956). She found the experience so inexplicable that she attributed it to possession by an alien being. Thereafter, whenever she met with disappointment she was buoyed by reassuring messages sent by her extraterrestrial masters via automatic writing. Typically, the writing did not emerge full-blown, for in automatic writing the initial output is not always readable and might not consist of words. In time, however, the words flow more easily. Similarly, in facilitated communication it usually takes a short time before facilitators become adept at facilitating words and sentences. They too invariably deny that they are doing the writing (typing, pointing) and even the severest critics of facilitated communication are convinced that this denial is honest.

James (1889) commented that automatic writing is often idiosyncratic and he mentioned "mirror writing, spelling backwards, writing from right to left, and even beginning at the right-hand lower corner of the page and inscribing every word with its last letter first, etc., till the top is reached" (p. 555). In the same paper he remarked that sometimes two people can write automatically with a pencil or with a planchette when neither can do so alone, and he suggested that when each thinks the other is the source of the movement they unknowingly give their hands more freedom.

Morton Prince, following Janet and unlike Freud, spoke of the subconscious or co-conscious (not the unconscious), in which images that were lost, as in amnesias and multiple personalities, were *dissociated* from the waking personality and could be recovered by automatic writing. However, he also believed that automatic writing was often not a subconscious expression but resulted from alternations of mental states (Prince,

1906/1992). On the other hand, such Freudian-oriented workers as Anita Mühl, who wrote frequently about automatic writing, took the position that automatic writing was an effective means of exploring a patient's unconscious. Initially Mühl (1924) uncritically accepted the memories a patient described during automatic writing, and for this she was chastised by Prince (1925):

> Another source of error is the naive acceptance of script [automatic writing] memories as true memories and not hallucinatory memories, as they often are. That is to say the apparent memories are merely expressions of beliefs, not of actual experiences. This is very commonly true of our conscious memories. We often remember as our experiences what really has been told to us, or what we have learned in other ways.... Thus I have frequently induced images of apparently actual past experiences but which were shown to be hallucinatory memories and only expressions of belief. (p. 39)

Prince's warning is by no means outdated in light of the current controversy over false memories.

Later, in her book on automatic writing, Mühl (1930) recognized that some automatic writing was fantasy, but other patients automated very early memories that Mühl verified with their parents. Although she warned that automatic writing must be used with care, she rejected the idea that it is always a sign of pathology, noting that doodlers are unaware of the meaningful writing and drawing they leave on telephone pads or at meetings. She described the variety of talents displayed during automatic writing, such as "writing poetry or stories; composing music; illustrating and designing; while aptitudes for arithmetic, history, and geography may be exhumed where these had remained peacefully interred before" (p. 23). Latent talents such as these, as well as foreign languages that the individuals forgot they had heard, mirror writing with one or both hands, and writing upside down or backward, are phenomena that some people readily attribute to spirits.

Mühl (1930) described a patient who did not simply write automatically while engrossed in reading a book aloud but alternated between writing forward and backward on consecutive lines with the same hand. "The first line would be written from left to right in ordinary writing; then without breaking the connection it would write mirror script from right to left" (p. 82), and she would continue in this manner down the page without lifting her pencil (notice that for Mühl, "it" writes, not "she"). Mühl had to read every other line with a mirror. A sample was reproduced in Mühl's book, where the automatic writing and drawing of many others were also provided.

To induce automatic writing Mühl often suspended the subject's forearm in a sling so it just cleared the paper on the table top. When subjects were engrossed in an interesting book she slipped a pencil into their hand. Her subsequent procedures and alternative methods need not concern us, except to note that the sling could later be eliminated.

Many of Mühl's (1930) examples of automatic writing and drawing were produced by individuals who were in analysis, a number of whom, according to Mühl, harbored hidden secondary or multiple personalities revealed only by their automatic writing. Her longest description (63 pages) was reserved for a friend whose home at the seaside Mühl had visited while writing her book. The friend developed an interest in automatic writing which, with Mühl's assistance, she was able to generate, more as a leisure time activity than anything else. Six months later, however, she asked for Mühl's professional help in working out some distressing fears she had always had. The resulting study, in which automatic writing played a major role, concluded Mühl's book.

In one of her subsequent papers Mühl gave this example of automatic writing:

> While reading aloud one day, she [the patient] covered page after page with relevant conflict material in normal automatic writing. Suddenly she began writing upside down. After she had written several pages this way, she was asked to stop both reading and writing and was then requested to write voluntarily upside down, from dictation, the sentences she had written automatically that way. She was utterly unable to do this, though she really tried hard. The pages written automatically upside down dealt with deeply hidden guilt feelings. (1948/1968, p. 433)

Another patient, after several weeks of automatic writing in a conventional form, suddenly wrote several pages of what appeared to be gibberish, for example, "I dias tuhs pu, tuhs pu Tuhs Pu, uoy era daed, daed" (Mühl, 1948/1968, p. 434). One word cued Mühl to the fact that the patient was writing backward. Translation: "I said shut up, shut up Shut Up, you are dead, dead," addressed to her alternate personality. In contrast to her skill in writing backward automatically, the patient's voluntary attempts to write the same words backward were accomplished very slowly and with many mistakes.

Many other workers have provided illustrations of this kind of facility in automatic writing. What are we to make of it? We might hypothesize that the patients were fooling Mühl, that they really could voluntarily write backward or upside down very easily and were only acting as if they could not ordinarily do so. This is a possible explanation. But there are other, equally plausible (in my mind far more plausible) explanations favored by Mühl and other depth psychologists—including the fact that the individual is very ambivalent about expressing the material—but a fuller discussion of these alternative hypotheses is deferred until Chapter 6.

Informal demonstrations and experiments with automatic writing and drawing have also been carried out in University settings. Milton Erickson (1937) experimented with "college people" (p. 513) at an evening gathering by claiming that something could be written in full consciousness that at the same time would contain another, unconscious meaning. After an argument one of the guests, a woman who had been a subject in one of Erickson's earlier experiments with hypnotism, volunteered to be a subject. Erickson told her to write something clearly and legibly, but also told her that in writing it her unconscious would cause her to write something beyond what could be read by herself or any of the others. What she was asked to write was her guess of the time it had taken one member of the group to move a particular object in the room. There followed a spirited exchange of guesses by the group members, including the subject, who guessed between 2 and 3 minutes, well above the time guessed by any of the others.

Protesting that her unconscious and conscious guesses would be the same, she sat down to write. As she began, "She looked startled and declared emphatically, 'It wasn't either—it was at least two minutes'" and then she wrote, "rather slowly and in ... uncertain juvenile script" (p. 514), the words thirty sec., all the while continuing to protest. A reproduction of her response is given in the paper. Even when finished she protested that what she wrote wasn't so. Without disclosing what she had written, her written estimate was circulated and all agreed she had written thirty sec. The subject said that as she started to write she knew she would write thirty seconds. "I knew it was wrong but my hand just went ahead and wrote it" (p. 515).

Now, this woman was obviously very suggestible and Erickson must have known it. Nonetheless not everyone is going to believe what happened, and some might even suspect a hoax. Certainly we would not want to use this kind of informal "experiment" as support for the existence of automatic writing, even though it does not violate what we know about involuntary muscle movements. But the most interesting part followed. Erickson asked her to answer a series of questions via automatic writing, the essence of which was that the written *thirty sec.* contained an additional meaning. When asked to write what had been omitted she wrote the numeral 8. "Immediately after writing the last reply, the subject picked up the original writing and declared, 'Yes, it does read *38*, only I didn't realize that the *y* was written as an *8*'" (p. 516). And sure enough, in *thirty* the last upswing of the *y*, slightly detached, drifts to the left, making an *8* that is unnoticed until brought to our attention. If it is true that unconsciously she had to spell out thirty (or twenty or fifty) in order to have a final *y* in which to embed a hidden meaning, score a point for clever processes outside our awareness, as there must be when, without conscious direction, we can move a stick, sway a pendulum, agitate a table, spell words, and do mirror writing or write backward.

In two later papers Erickson, joined by Lawrence Kubie, used automatic writing and drawing for both revelatory and therapeutic purposes. The first paper (Erickson & Kubie, 1938) concerned a psychology student who, after attending a clinical demonstration of hypnosis where automatic writing was emphasized, asked if she could acquire the ability to do automatic

writing because she had recently become very uneasy, fearful and depressed. She was given a formal appointment (presumably with the author
who gave the demonstration) and at the initial interview disclosed among
other things that she lived happily with her father and mother, whom she
revered. Her only obvious personal problem was the feeling of a growing,
disturbing estrangement from her close childhood friend, despite the fact
that her friend continued to visit her on weekends. She also disclosed that
she had recently found the subject of symbolism particularly interesting.
Since reading recently about symbolism she noticed that she had been
scribbling meaningless lines and figures when telephoning, in class, or
simply idling (a sample of which is provided in the published paper).

The details of what happened next are too complex to give in full here.[19]
Briefly, the patient, with scarcely any manipulation by the therapist, continued her automatic drawing in the therapist's office. Finally, with assurances
from the therapist—who was, in his view, communicating with processes
outside her awareness—the figures and scribblings were combined into a
coherent whole, a picture that at the time meant nothing to the young
woman. She felt it was important, however, and connected in some way to
a packet of matches from a local hotel which she took from her pocket and
dropped on the therapist's desk.

Some weeks later the patient reported that she had been very cruel to her
friend and they had agreed to separate. She also had a rare fight with her
father. The therapist mentioned her interest in symbolism and picked up
and dropped the packet of matches on the desk. She looked at the drawing,
then grabbed the matches and threw them violently to the floor. She had
suddenly grasped the meaning of the drawing. There followed an outburst
of anger and vilification toward nobody in particular, intermingled with
sympathy for her mother. "'The damned filthy little cheater,'" she said.
"'And she calls herself my friend. She's having an affair with my father.'"
As it turned out this was true, verified to the therapist by her friend. The
friend (former friend, I should say) had lit her cigarette with matches that
came from the hotel, and there were other signs of the misalliance. Intui-
tively the patient had suspected the affair, but it was a denouement she
consciously was unable to accept (after all, consider the devastating consequences). With the help of the therapist, her automatic drawings, made
outside conscious awareness and before she had seen the therapist, were
reassembled by her into a coherent whole whose symbolic meaning she was
finally able to decipher. Automatic drawings were the path to conscious
recognition and acceptance.

The second related publication (Erickson & Kubie, 1939) involved a psychology student who so obsessively feared that various doors (e.g., refrigera-

---

[19]I recognize that a brief digest of clinical cases, here and elsewhere, does little justice to the
material, but it is impossible to expend a great deal of space on the details of every case,
fascinating and revealing though they may be.

tor, laboratory, locker) had been left open that she compulsively checked and rechecked them. She also had an intense hatred of cats, which she described as horrid and repulsive. These facts were unknown to her psychology professor when the student volunteered for some experiments in hypnotism which included hand levitation and catalepsy. "To demonstrate suggestibility a posthypnotic suggestion was given that in the trance her name would be 'Miss Brown'" (p. 472). The next day, by autosuggestion, the student repeatedly induced and then terminated hand levitation and arm catalepsy, repeatedly asking what this behavior meant but ignoring any answers. As her hands levitated to the level of her shoulders there was a short period of time in which she became unresponsive and apparently dissociated, looking terrified. When this was repeated the next day, the professor suggested that she might want to try automatic writing, and she eagerly assented.

She was given an article on Gestalt psychology to read silently. After a short time, while still reading, she started to write in response to the question about why she was interested in hand levitation and catalepsy. As she neared the end of her writing she became very distressed; she couldn't understand why, she said, because there was nothing in what she was reading to distress her. Then just as suddenly her anxiety left her. She was able to adequately summarize what she had read. When she asked if she had written anything she was shown her output, an illegible line of scribbles (reproduced in the article) except for the first section, which she interpreted as the word *trains* but which the authors thought was *trance*. The same conditions were repeated.

Then a second personality (the previously suggested Miss Brown) emerged via automatic writing. (There is, however, a distinct possibility that the therapist created the second personality, a danger that had become a topic of considerable discussion recently.) Erickson and Kubie pointed out that the full name the second personality subsequently took was Jane Brown. They later discovered "that *Jane* signified identification with a favorite childhood literary character, and that Jane was really the important name, the *Brown* having evidently been added to it at the time of the first hypnotic demonstration" (pp. 478–479). This second personality described its role in a crucial event when the subject was 3 years old, but her story probably was not true. In fact, later in their paper the authors, ignoring or forgetting the earlier information, speculated that the alter ego was created *after* the important childhood event.

"A characteristic of Brown's automatic script was its economy. A single letter was written whenever possible in place of a word, or a word for a phrase; abbreviations, condensations, puns, peculiar twists of meaning, all were employed" (pp. 479–480).[20] In the end, according to the authors, the

---

[20] Again we see how surprisingly efficient the processes outside awareness can be. Support for a "smart" unconscious is discussed in Chapter 6.

raising to consciousness of a disturbing experience that occurred when the student was 3 years old finally expunged her compulsion to worry about and repeatedly check that doors were closed.

Philip Harriman (1942b), at Bucknell University, had always been troubled by the skepticism that students in his abnormal psychology class expressed, year after year, about the possibility that two or more minds could exist in one body. To his delight, however, while doing some experiments in automatic writing he discovered by chance a way of producing experimentally some of the features of multiple personality that were suitable for classroom demonstration. "Furthermore, it serves as a basis for pointing out some possible differences between artificially produced multiple personalities and those which may be required in the life history of the individual" (p. 245).

What Harriman did was to put students (individually, of course) who were good hypnotic subjects into a hypnotic trance and then, while they were still in the trance, instruct them to open their eyes. Then they were told that it would seem as though the arm and hand they wrote with were no longer a part of them, but that when a pencil was put in their hand it would write, as though impelled by some force outside their awareness. They were also told that at first they will look around the room indifferently but later they might be interested in watching their hand and arm move. With the subjects still in a trance state, Harriman subsequently induced amnesia for all these instructions.

Subjects continued in a trance state while a board was placed on their lap and they were given a pencil and paper. Their writing was so poor that no one understood it (examples given by Harriman look like indecipherable scribbles). When subjects were awakened and shown the writing, even they were unable to decipher what they wrote.

Harriman described a subject's subsequent experience. "A light trance is now induced, and the subject is told that he fully understands the whole experience.... Upon being awakened now, he is asked to write directly beneath the cryptic automatic writing its exact translation or necessary amplification. Without any hesitancy whatsoever, he complies with this request" (p. 246).

In sum, when awakened the first time the subject could not understand the meaning of his own writing; only after being told, while in a light hypnotic trance, that the entire experience would be understood was he able to decipher what he had written. Note that the automatic writing occurred *following* the command that there would be amnesia for the instruction that the seemingly detached appendage would write as though moved by some outside force. Note also that the writing was understood only when the amnesia was lifted.

To protect the subjects Harriman also told them that although they would be unaware of what they were writing, it should not be about anything embarrassing to them. The dangers of these techniques cannot be overemphasized, and they are best left to the trained therapist and the supervised laboratory. My review only reinforces the opinion of many that the accidental production of automatic writing, as with the Ouija board or during facilitated communication, is loaded with potential peril (see, e.g., Hunt, 1985, who in addition to pointing out the real danger of using the Ouija board was also concerned, unfortunately, about the influence of spirits).

Harriman remarked that with good subjects automatic writing can be readily induced even without hypnosis. "Sometimes this writing is cryptic in nature, and invariably its full meaning is not revealed until after the subject has been given suggestions of the hypnotic or the progressive relaxation type" (p. 246). Elsewhere Harriman (1943) gave 5% as the approximate percentage of subjects who wrote automatically when simply distracted, a figure that I suspect Mühl would have disputed as much too low. Certainly 5% is far too low for conditions in which two people are jointly involved.

Although automatic writing is not necessarily, in fact is not usually, a sign of multiple personality (though too often it is mistakenly thought to be), an association between automatic writing and multiple personality has been reported from at least the 19th century to the present day. George Fraser (1994) commented, "Four of my multiple personality disorders (MPD) patients had childhood traumatic events revealed to them through automatic writing. This all began prior to their clinical diagnosis of MPD and thus, was not an artifact of therapy" (p. 134).

Summing up this small sampling of the extensive literature on automatic writing, I believe that the evidence supports the position that despite its susceptibility to deception, automatic writing is a real phenomenon that can be spontaneously produced by, or otherwise elicited from, many people, perhaps from everyone under suitable conditions. The potential for expressing this form of dissociation has obvious relevance for our understanding of much behavior including, certainly, the behavior of facilitators during facilitated communication. That is not to say that automatic writing is easy to elicit; many workers have depended on hypnotism to induce it or to interpret it. To many, producing automatic writing by hypnotism is not very interesting except as a diagnostic or therapeutic instrument. "As many writers have pointed out, a good [hypnotic] subject will accept various rôles, the nature of which is dependent upon the suggestion. When, however, the rôle is taken without any direct suggestions by the operator the results are more interesting" (Harriman, 1942a, p. 184). For us this observation is particularly pertinent because we are pursuing the consequences of involuntary muscle movements on individuals who are fully awake. Consequently I have avoided focusing on studies that produced automatic writing by hypnotism or posthypnotic suggestion, except for Harriman's classroom demonstration.

Needless to say it is much easier to write automatically when two people are involved, for then the involuntary muscle movements are camouflaged—as on a Ouija board, for example, where one of the partners is unwittingly guiding a planchette to letters or words.

Mühl (1948/1968) defined automatic writing "in its simplest form ... as script which is produced involuntarily by the writer and, in some instances, without his awareness of the process" (p. 426). We can expand this definition to include the involuntary choosing of letters from an alphabet board or a keyboard. "Being a little more modern, one patient stated that while sitting at a computer she found her hands suddenly typing out a message on the computer. One might call this computer age 'automatic typing!'" (Fraser, 1994, p. 134). These variations are no less dependent on involuntary muscle movements than is automatic script writing.

All automatic writing is not the same, and automatic writing during facilitated communication differs from the automatic script writing of a single individual. As noted in Chapter 3, it is likely that in some cases of facilitated communication the involuntary muscle movements of the facilitator cue the partner's movements, much as the muscle movements of the guide unwittingly inform the muscle reader during mind-reading displays (Smith & Belcher, 1994). That is, a slight tightening (or relaxing) of the muscles prompts the partner to press downward. In other cases, however, the facilitators directly move the partner's hand to the desired key.

B. F. Skinner (1957), the founder of modern behaviorism, described automatic verbal behavior as the "inability to respond to one's own verbal behavior or to controlling variables" (p. 388). When he discussed automatic writing he almost always put the word *automatic* within quotation marks, as if holding it at arm's length. He did so because the word suggests the temporary absence of what we now call the writer's primary personality, whereas the real problem, according to Skinner, is the writer's temporary inability to edit or censor his or her own output. Skinner's explanation of why automatic writing occurs could have been written by a Freudian psychologist: "Spontaneous automatic writing frequently suggests an escape from powerful repressing forces" (p. 388). Furthermore, when the writer sees what was written, "The unedited material may be so strange or objectionable as to be unrecognizable" (p. 390).

Genae Hall (1993) applied the Skinnerian approach to facilitator behavior. When distracted, individuals lose stimulus control of their output; they fail to edit what they produce and generate strange or unexpected behavior in the form of automatic writing, in this case via facilitated communication. Hall, as do most other objective observers, agrees that facilitators are exhibiting automatic writing, but she follows Skinner in ascribing such behavior exclusively to relaxed self-editing and in dismissing the need to appeal to unconscious processes. To account for the content of the material—the thematic control, as behaviorists call it—Hall gives a number of likely sources. She even speculates that some cases of sexual abuse allegations may result because the facilitators had been abused, and under the relaxed self-censorship of automatic writing, "verbal behavior concerning prior abuse (punishable under ordinary conditions) might emerge" (p. 95). Gina Green adds that, "When the usual contingencies are not operative, for whatever reason, verbal behavior that usually would not occur 'slips out'" (personal communication, December 8, 1995); that is, as adults in a school setting the facilitators do not openly express such obscenities, but during facilitated communication the usual contingencies are not operative because the facilitators do not believe the words are their own.

It seems to me that automatic writing poses a challenge to some basic tenets of behaviorism, a challenge that was not originally met by Skinner. According to behaviorism, behavior is controlled by a schedule of reinforcement, and the most frequently emitted behavior is generally one that had been most frequently rewarded. Yet in facilitated communication those facilitators who go into minute, obscene detail about sexual abuse do so, if I read Skinner and Hall correctly, because ordinary self-censorship is relaxed when a person is distracted, as in facilitated communication. But why is this *unrewarded* hidden behavior initially expressed when self-censorship is relaxed? Furthermore, in automatic writing people are said by behaviorists to have lost stimulus control. But within the behaviorist system, how can people write meaningfully, and sometimes beautifully, without stimulus control?

Whatever one's orientation (excepting those persuaded that facilitated communication really works) there is no disputing the fact that the output produced by facilitators through their students is simply one more example of automatic writing, from whose voluminous history we can draw upon to inform us about its current alarming manifestation. It should not surprise us that obscene material sometimes issues from facilitated writing; automatic writing frequently consists of material that individuals would never knowingly express, or at least would never express if they were held responsible for it.

SUMMATION

There is a single thread weaving through many apparently diverse phenomena. Animals pick up the slightest movements that people are unaware of making. Automatic script writers, Ouija board users and facilitators do not consciously know what they write and deny that they are directing the writing. Pendulum holders reject the idea that they move the pendulum and dowsers that they move the branch. Table movers believe that they follow, not move, the table. Mind-readers make use of the fact that their guides unwittingly generate muscle movements that can be read by a sensitive and skillful muscle reader. In mind-reading, as in table moving, as on the Ouija board, as in automatic script writing, as in dowsing, pendulum swaying and table moving, people lose conscious control of their muscles and frequently fail to recognize their own movements. For scientists, who seek a unifying principle to explain many different phenomena, these examples are beautiful demonstrations that human beings are influenced by processes outside their awareness and that muscle movements can be driven, unrecognized, by interior (wish-fulfilling, imitative) and exterior suggestion, and—as has been so often said—by dominant ideas. Sometimes the movements lead to an expression of conflicts and memories that are not usually available to primary consciousness.

These follies never end. There is every evidence that we are now entering another cycle, the "New Age" era, which will take its place with the eras of table turning and animal magnetism, to mention just two periods of collective madness. There is renewed enchantment with dowsing rods and pendulums, not for finding water or minerals but for almost anything else imaginable, and believers are dominating the traditional dowsers' conventions. Hope (1996) describes an attorney who asks her pendulum to tell her which video cassette will give her family the greatest enjoyment and benefit, which vitamin pills to choose for her daughter, whether her auto mechanic is lying, and to which partner in a law firm she should send her resumé. "And if I think *she's* weird, I should meet some of the hundreds of other New Yorkers who dowse for everything from stock market buys to whether they should respond to an ad in the 'Personals'" (p. 68). In his description Hope also relates some successes in finding lost objects but we do not know all the circumstances: the cues picked up, the dowser's previous knowledge of the situation, and so on.

The year 2012 marks two centuries after Chevreul carried out his experiments and 179 years since he published his results. To what end?

5

Scientific Studies of Involuntary Muscle Movements

The spread of spiritism, and the covenant of its believers that mystic messages could be received when the faithful touched or held such prosaic objects as tables, pencils, and pendulums, provided a golden opportunity for dynamic psychology. Indeed Ellenberger (1970) was convinced that the epidemic of spiritism in the mid-19th century was "of major importance in the history of dynamic psychiatry, because it indirectly provided psychologists and psychopathologists with new approaches to the mind" (p. 85). From this viewpoint automatic writing, the Ouija board, and the assortment of related instruments that were perceived by so many as manifestations of spirits were in fact manifestations of the unconscious. "A new subject, the medium, became available for experimental psychological investigation, out of which evolved a new model of the human mind" (Ellenberger, 1970, p. 85). At about the time of Sigmund Freud's birth in 1856, mystics and mediums—when they were not outright frauds—were clearing a path to the unconscious.

The mystic messages provided a somewhat different opportunity for physiologists and experimental psychologists, who were less prone to speculate about unseen forces. Clearly, human beings were moving the objects, but just as clearly they had no awareness that they were the source of the movememt. How could that be?

In 1871, again writing as an anonymous reviewer (see footnote 11, p. 63), William Carpenter declared that "the doctrine of 'unconscious muscular action' is not, as the spiritualists allege, a 'hypothesis' invented for the occasion, but is one of the best established principles of physiology" (Spiritualism, 1871, p. 308), and he referred to a memoir published in 1844 by Thomas Laycock in which Laycock "most distinctly showed that involuntary muscular movements take place in respondence not merely to sensations but to ideas" (p. 310). Carpenter then described a lecture he himself had given at the Royal Institution on March 12, 1852, on the "*Ideo-motor* principle of action; which consists in the involuntary response made by the muscles to ideas with which the mind may be possessed when the directing power of the will is in abeyance" (p. 310). *Ideo-motor* was an especially suitable term; it combined the driving force of a dominant *idea* with the resulting involuntary *motor* activity.

In a lecture published in the *Proceedings of the Royal Institution* in 1852, Carpenter explicitly characterized ideo-motor action as a third law of reflex movement. Apparently the earlier practice had been to partition automatic (involuntary) reflex movements into only two kinds: *excito-motor*, such as breathing and swallowing, and *sensori-motor*, such as the startle reaction to a loud sound, or the eye blink response to a sudden light. In order to place certain other phenomena within the known operating principles of the nervous system, however, it was necessary to add a third law of reflex action, *ideo-motor*, in which ideas become the source of involuntary motor movements.

These thoughts must have been largely derived from Laycock, whose 1844 paper (which I have been unable to locate) was titled "Reflex Action of the Brain" (cited in Spiritualism, 1871, p. 310). Carpenter's contribution was to place the site of ideo-motor action in the cerebrum. He excused Laycock for not having done this because, he wrote, Dr. Laycock could not have known of the distinction between the sensory ganglia and the cerebrum:

> The cerebrum is universally admitted to be the portion of the nervous system, which is instrumentally concerned in the formation of ideas, the excitement of the emotions, and the operations of the intellect; and there seems no reason why it should be exempted from the law of "reflex" action which applies to every other part of the nervous system. (Carpenter, 1852, pp. 151–152)

Laycock (1869) was nevertheless concerned that Carpenter was preempting his priority:

> Having first promulgated these views in 1839, 1840, 1844, 1845, and from time to time subsequently … ,[I] was obliged to take serious notice in the first edition of a claim to priority of promulgation of the doctrine of the unconscious cerebral action, set up by Dr. Carpenter in 1855. (p. iii)

To whomever history awards priority, involuntary (unconscious) muscle movements took their place as normal reflexes alongside such reflexes as breathing and eye blinks.

MECHANICAL RECORDING

The basic rationale for a natural explanation of many "mysterious" phenomena had been laid by a number of pioneers including, of course,

Laycock, Carpenter, Chevreul, and Faraday. But science demands measurement. We have already chronicled the fact that Pfungst made permanent records of subjects' involuntary head movements, which he gave as illustrations in his book (Pfungst, 1911/1965). He had adapted for this purpose an instrument that Sommer had used to measure involuntary hand movements. Recall that Pfungst's subjects were asked to think of a number, then Pfungst tapped with his finger (in imitation of Hans tapping with his foot) and was usually able to tap correctly the number the subject had in mind. When the apparatus was attached, a slight movement of the subject's head in any of three directions was transferred by three levers onto smoked paper fastened to the revolving drum of a kymograph (which is all the apparatus description that Pfungst provided, although the Sommer publication is referenced). The resulting records showed a slight involuntary raising of the head when the silent number was reached (with individual differences depending, in part, on the intensity of the subject's concentration). In this way Pfungst demonstrated the kinds of body cues available to a percipient horse. He went on to record the involuntary movements when subjects were asked to think of any of the words up, down, right, left, yes, no, and so on, and performed additional experiments as well.

More than a decade before Pfungst's book appeared, Joseph Jastrow (1892)—an explorer of nonconscious activity and an opponent of irrational thinking—made similar recordings to demonstrate the underlying source of mind-reading. Eight years later he described his experiments more fully. "For a time," he wrote, "the view that mind-reading was muscle-reading rested upon rather indirect evidence.... but the development of experimental research in the domain of psychology has made possible a variety of demonstrations of the truth and adequacy of this explanation" (Jastrow, 1900, p. 309).

To provide a visible record, Jastrow devised what he called the automatograph. The standing subject's arm extended comfortably through a curtain, with fingertips resting on a level glass plate that was secured by a light wooden frame. This framed glass was set on oiled steel or brass balls on a somewhat larger, heavier, stationary glass frame. Because it rested on what were essentially ball bearings, the glass plate, on which the subjects placed the fingertips of one hand, moved with the slightest movement of the subject's hand; yet, according to Jastrow, when subjects closed their eyes and concentrated on an image or thought, they had no sense of hand movement. In order to record the movement, a thin 10-inch rod extended horizontally from the frame of the movable glass plate to a thin vertical rod with a smooth round point, which recorded the subject's hand movement on glazed paper that had been blackened over a flame. This entire arrangement was hidden from the subject by a large screen. Subjects were instructed to think as little as possible about their hand and to make a reasonable effort to keep it from moving.

Jastrow (1900) presented photos of his impressive findings. When subjects were asked to say in order the names of patches of color placed before them from left to right, the hand moved irregularly but consistently from left to right.

> Not infrequently, the movement is performed with complete unconsciousness, and is accompanied by a strong conviction that the apparatus has been stationary.... the hand for a time oscillates about uncertainly, and then moves rather suddenly and quickly in a given direction; then another period of hesitation, again a more or less sharp advance, and so on. (p. 313)

Of course these are precisely the type of movements mind-readers make when searching for hidden objects; Jastrow was providing permanent visual records of the involuntary muscle movements that mind-readers follow. But again, as always, there were marked individual differences, not only in extent of movements but also in timing, just as in mind-reading. Mind-readers always remark that some subjects are easier to read and more reliable than others.

When subjects were asked to count the strokes of a metronome their hand tracings featured back and forth movement. When subjects were given an object to hide, then placed on the automatograph and told to think intensely of the hiding place, an observer could usually tell the direction in which the object was hidden from the direction of the recorded movement, but again with substantial individual differences. Jastrow provided other illustrations, including recordings of head positions made by detaching the recording section of his automatograph, and he pointed out that involuntary head movements are still another clue available to mind-readers.

Tucker (1896–1897) used a slightly modified automatograph to record the involuntary muscle movements of 681 adults and 373 children, athough not all subjects participated in all the experiments. Subjects were unaware of the purpose of the study and were told to pay attention only to what the experimenter instructed them to attend to. When they watched an object drawn along on a string, 88% of the adults and 81% of the children involuntarily moved their hands in the direction of the movement. When an object was moved around the room, the hands of almost all the subjects in this experiment drew circles. Merely thinking of the movements produced results that were just as impressive. In thinking of an object they had hidden, the majority moved their hands in the appropriate direction. Repetition increased the likelihood of a matching involuntary hand response. Tucker's results solidly confirmed Jastrow's.

Because some theories proposed that silent words always accompany thought—that thinking is, in effect, inner speech—there were many attempts, extending from the late 19th century, to use mechanical devices to measure involuntary movements of the tongue or larynx. These were briefly reviewed by Thorson (1925) and Jacobson (1931, 1932), among others. Most of the studies had successfully recorded covert speech. In one of the unsuccessful studies a diagram of the instrument, which K. S. Lashley had modified from Sommer's "movement analyzer," was provided (Thorson, 1925). It consisted of a series of levers that would do justice to Rube Goldberg, starting with a small metal suction cup attached to the tongue and ending with two writing points that recorded tongue movements on smoked paper. To prevent head movements the subject's head was strapped into a headrest. How valid results could have been expected from someone hooked into this apparatus is a mystery, although any physical measurement of involuntary muscle movements raises this problem to a greater or lesser extent.

When the behaviorist John Watson proposed that thinking always requires silent words, a raging debate followed, which, although fascinating, would take us too far afield to consider. The fact that Watson's thesis is unlikely to be universally true (see, e.g., Woodworth & Schlosberg, 1954, p. 807) does not mean that it is not usually true, nor that involuntary muscle movements do not take place in *some* part of the body during thinking, if only in the eyes.

ELECTRICAL RECORDING

The work of Matteucci in 1838 brought the first galvanometric detection of current flow in muscle. (Needham, 1971, p. 311)

According to Rüegg (1986), "During an action potential the membrane potential becomes reversed so that for a brief moment the inside of the muscle cell becomes positively charged with respect to the outside" (p. 3), but almost immediately the negativity is restored. Within milliseconds the muscle fibers contract, then relax. Schneck (1992), giving finer details that are here condensed, described bundles of myofibrils containing nerve and blood vessels, which are wrapped into tightly packed bundles grouped together and covered by a thin membrane called the *sarcolemma* to create a muscle fiber. This sarcolemma is electically polarized by chemical "pumps" in the cell membrane which exchange three sodium ions from the inside of the muscle fiber for two potassium ions from the outside, creating an electric potential "of about 0.10 Volts in the fiber at rest" (p. 14). When a nerve end triggers the muscle, it depolarizes the membrane and causes the muscle to contract.

The essential point is that there is electrochemical action in muscles, just as there is in nerves. This makes it possible to measure large muscle events in humans as, for instance, the electrocardiograph measures contractions of the heart (an organ controlled by the autonomic nervous system). But it also should be possible to amplify and measure even exquisitely fine involuntary muscle movements.

The most prolific and successful of the investigators who took advantage of advances in engineering and design to finally realize this possibility was Edmund Jacobson, for whom it was essential to measure extremely small involuntary muscle activity in order to thoroughly test a technique he had developed called progressive relaxation. In 1925 and 1927 he reported preliminary findings that his subjects could achieve complete muscle re-laxation only when they had no conscious activity. Conversely, muscular activity was necessary for thought. "We find the experience of muscular tenseness is the *sine qua non* of imagery, attention and thought-processes" (Jacobson, 1925, p. 85). These findings were important for the debate on the nature of thinking, but Jacobson initially showed little interest in this debate. His primary focus was on finding, with objective certainty, that complete relaxation could indeed be achieved by his method of progressive relaxation. Consequently Jacobson and his colleagues had to determine whether even miniscule muscle movements accompany conscious thought.

Jacobson (1927) used a "string galvonometer with vacuum tube ampli-fication," which he claimed was "the first application of that instrument … to the question whether action currents are given off by muscular contrac-tions associated with imagery, reflection, attention and other conscious processes" (p. 403). Still, the required measurements of fractions of a microvolt were not easily achieved. In 1928 the chairman of the Department of Physiology at Columbia University introduced Jacobson to two electrical engineers, H. E. Frederick and D. G. Blattner, at Bell Telephone Laboratories who, with others at Bell Labs, collaborated to design and produce an instrument to meet Jacobson's demanding specifications, which they con-tinued to improve and develop (Jacobson, 1930a, 1939, 1940, 1951). Initially, surface electrodes were placed on the skin above the appropriate muscles and photographic records of the voltage changes were impressed on con-tinuously moving bromide paper to provide a continuous visual log. Later the results were registered on a meter, dubbed the neurovoltmeter (and, with further improvements, the integrating neurovoltmeter), eliminating to some extent the need for photography. By inserting very fine needle electrodes directly into specific muscles the contamination of skin effects was avoided, although the procedure could be disturbing for some un-trained subjects. In the end, surface electrodes became the preferred mode of recording, with steps taken to control for such artifacts as the galvanic reflex.

From 1930 through 1931 Jacobson published in the *Journal of Physiology* a numbered series of seven studies measuring subjects' neuromuscular activity while they imagined specific activities (see Jacobson, 1982, for his complete bibliography). For example, when subjects were requested to imagine steadily bending their right arms, electrical potentials were picked up from the biceps region of the arm. The subjects, of course, were unaware that their muscles were moving. Controls included resting potential, the instruction: "Don't bother to imagine the activity," lack of action potentials in other parts of the body, and the instruction to imagine lifting the left arm—which had no electrodes attached—in order to see whether the right arm muscles reacted.

Conditions had to be carefully controlled:

> The subject lies on a couch ... with complete copper shielding on ceiling, walls and floor.... To avert unnecessary movements with unnecessary action potential changes in muscles undergoing measurement requires that the subject receive training in progressive relaxation with daily or frequent practice at home or in the laboratory for months or more (Jacobson, 1982, p. 96).

Subjects could also be taught complete relaxation in other positions if that was called for. Complete relaxation was necessary to have a flat baseline before and after the involuntary muscle movements.

The control tests generally were negative, indicating that positive results in the experimental conditions were not artifacts. Furthermore, curves of action potentials showing slight *voluntary* contractions that accompanied the request to actually bend the arm slightly, were similar in pattern but lower in magnitude to recordings taken during imagined activity involving the same muscle. Another bit of evidence of successful recording of involuntary muscle movements was that subjects who were asked to imagine lifting weights produced higher microvoltage than when they imagined merely bending their arm.

Additionally, Jacobson (1930c) provided conclusive evidence that the action potentials he was picking up were not psychogalvanic (skin) reflex responses, which depend on the autonomic nervous system. Results with many other imagined activities produced varying degrees of success and need not be dwelt on here, although a few of the more interesting findings will be given.

For example, action potentials of eye movements during imagined activity were recorded. In most instances Jacobson (1930b) placed one electrode above the medial portion of the orbital ridge and the other behind the ear (or, in a few experiments, just to the side of the orbital ridge) in order to obtain action potentials from the eye muscles while subjects kept their eyelids closed. First he had the subjects relax, then told them to look slightly in various directions so that the distinctive patterns could be determined. In one study, when subjects were asked to imagine the Eiffel Tower the pattern of involuntary eye movement was practically the same as, although smaller than, the pattern obtained when the subject had been asked to look slightly upward. When asked to imagine reading a newspaper, the eye movement record resembled the pattern previously obtained when the subject had been asked to look to the right. The evidence was clear: Very small but appropriate eye movements occurred during visual imagination, just as muscle movements occurred in the arm that is part of an imagined activity. Furthermore, when subjects were asked to visualize bending an arm and electrodes were attached to both the eye region and the arm, action potentials were always recorded from the arm and many times but not always from the eyes. If there was no muscle contraction in one, there was in the other.

A graduate student of about 40, whose left arm had been amputated above the elbow when he was 8 years old, was tested because he claimed that he could imagine doing anything with his left hand that he could with his right. He later amended this claim by saying that he had to imagine or do the act at the same time with his intact right hand. The results showed that when he imagined bending his left hand, in 13 of 14 trials action potentials were obtained from the partly amputated biceps muscles. When imagining he was lifting a weight with his intact right hand, in most instances activity was also recorded in the remaining left arm muscles, confirming the fact that he did not separate activity in the two arms as readily as did subjects with both arms intact.

Measuring involuntary muscle movements of the speech organs was technically difficult. The apparatus had to be modified, and satisfactory baseline levels were difficult to achieve in the 7 subjects under some conditions. For 1 subject, fine, pointed platinum-iridium wires were inserted about 2 centimeters into the tip of the tongue and under the mucosa in the cheek. Cotton was placed under the tongue to absorb saliva and the mouth was kept closed. Needless to say it was a long time before the subject relaxed enough to give good baseline measures. Other subjects never achieved satisfactory relaxation under these conditions and for them both electrodes were inserted in the interior center of the lip, about 1 centimeter apart.

Tests were successfully made on 5 subjects who achieved satisfactory baselines. When they engaged in mental activity (e.g., thinking of the meaning of the phrase "electrical resistance," or recalling a poem) action potentials were recorded that were easily distinguishable from resting levels. When they imagined counting to three they produced three successive groups of action potentials. Although of lower voltage, the action potentials resembled those of actual speech or faint whispers. Imagining the Eiffel Tower or lifting a weight produced no action potentials in the speech organs. Later Jacobson (1982) described a much less intrusive, "specially designed electrode placed under the tongue, much like the bulb of an oral thermometer," and, in other cases, "EEG electrodes … taped to the upper and lower lip lines" (pp. 103, 107).

Jacobson's initial interest and primary concern were, and remained, relaxation techniques. He was basically atheoretical. Although he was aware that his studies contributed to the debates on thinking and implicit speech, he frequently reminded his readers that he had never advocated the motor theory of consciousness.

Nevertheless he was sensitive to any relevant paper that ignored his work. One study measuring muscular tension annoyed him not only because he was not mentioned but also because the authors ignored the many methodological problems that he had so often raised. "They cite," he commented, "under the caption of 'previous research,' two general reviews … upon muscular tension and its measurement along with a few other references which chiefly bear upon related matters." Then he went on to note that although the two general reviews they cited spoke "in high terms of the pioneering work done [by him], the three current authors give little evidence that they are familiar with the development of the methods of results which I may now give in summary outline" (Jacobson, 1951, p. 112). The rather lame response to this charge was an apology for not crediting Jacobson "with the pioneering work, thinking that it was so well known to all who worked in the field that it did not need mention.... We hope that readers … did not gain the impression that we claim to have invented the instrumentation for the research" (Ryan, Cottrell, & Bitterman, 1951, p. 117).

Jacobson noted that many of his findings "have been confirmed in other laboratories, within the limits of their electronic equipment" (1967, p. 97), and he listed those studies. In the same book he applied his findings to what he described as a new principle of mind and brain, his major point being that "brain and muscle operate simultaneously in one complicated nexus during mental activity" (p. 110). A 1973 edited book to which he contributed the opening chapter was dedicated to him "in recognition of his pioneering research in the psychophysiology of higher mental processes" (McGuigan & Schoonover, 1973).

Whatever the merits of progressive relaxation, which Jacobson advocated as a prescription for sleepless nights, general health and a long life, it certainly seems to have worked for him. He was born in 1888 and his last book was published in 1982. He died in 1983. Jacobson was a brilliant scientist who deserves our deepest respect for resourcefully initiating a significant new research domain, overcoming some daunting problems in pursuing it, and resolutely developing it over his lifetime.

Starting in 1934 Louis William Max published a series of studies closely related to Jacobson's work, although Max was uninterested in relaxation techniques. His motivation for measuring involuntary muscle movements was to test three slightly different variations of the motor theory of consciousness that viewed consciousness as not simply cortical activity but as involving, indeed requiring, motor activity as well. As already noted, an important corollary of the motor theory of consciousness was the idea that thinking must involve implicit speech. This proposal, as Max (1934) pointed out, predated John Watson's (1913) behaviorist views by decades (and, I might add, ruled out the possibility that either toddlers or animals can think). To measure implicit speech Max, like Jacobson, turned to the string galvanometer. He used the novel approach of attaching surface electrodes to the forearms of people who were deaf-mute in order to record their involuntary hand and finger movements, analogous to recording the vocal mechanisms of hearing subjects. In addition to being much less intrusive than electrodes in the mouth, electrodes placed some distance from the hands had the advantage of camouflaging the purpose of the study. However, after some preliminary work it became clear to Max (duplicating Jacobson's experiences) that he would have to transform his equipment in order to amplify and record minute action potentials. When describing his revisions he noted in a footnote the inaccuracies Jacobson must have had in some of his recordings, although he also mentioned the recent revisions that Jacobson made (Max, 1935a).

With his newly improved equipment Max (1937) electrically recorded finger movements by placing surface electrodes near both wrists (over the flexores digitorum), where the deep flexors of the fingers are located. When deaf subjects were asked to solve problems mentally, to imagine scenes and to engage in other mental activity, they more often produced muscle movement (covert) in their fingers than did hearing subjects; and when such movement occurred in the fingers of hearing subjects it was of smaller amplitude. Subsequent studies by Novikova (1961) and McGuigan (1971) with signing deaf subjects who were also learning or had learned oral speech were consistent with these findings. In addition, these subjects produced covert involuntary muscle movements in both the speech apparatus and the muscles used for signing.

Earlier Max (1935b) had recorded action potentials during sleep and while dreaming from the flexores digitorum of people who were deaf-mute. As the subjects relaxed on a bed the action currents began to diminish, and when they fell asleep the currents dropped to a low level or in a minority of cases disappeared altogether. To measure the effects on dreams of external stimulation (which had been discussed by Binet in 1899), disturbances such as gentle taps on the bed (vibrating it slightly), tickling the ear with hair, putting weight on the subject's chest, and so on, were introduced while the subject slept. These intrusions tended to increase the size of the action potentials. Although in some instances putting on a feeble light produced no response or simply awakened the subject, in 12 of 17 instances it too was accompanied by an increase in covert muscle activity and also, most significantly, by dreams.

In fact, Max's most interesting finding was that the periodic presence of more sustained and intense action currents correlated with dreaming, substantiated by the fact that when subjects were awakened during this activity most of them described a dream. One subject, who was deaf, awakened after

> violent electromyographic activity in both arms [as well as] overt arm movements.... had been dreaming of a barbecue party at which he was excitedly arguing [in sign language] with a fellow deaf-mute as to how best to insert the iron spit on which the meat was to be roasted.... [and] he had snatched the spit from the other's hand in the course of it. (Max, 1935, p. 481)

As Max (1937) later noted, sometimes while dreaming a person who was deaf-mute produced finger movements that were sufficiently overt that another person who was deaf-mute could "read" the content of the sleeper's dreams.

Positive action currents indicating finger and arm movement by the deaf subjects occurred in 84% of the instances of dreaming (Max 1935b). In contrast, the dreams of hearing subjects never produced action currents indicating finger and arm movement (but see Stoyva, 1965, for conflicting results).

In 62 instances the deaf-mute subjects were awakened when they were *not* producing action currents and in 53 of these the subjects reported that they were not dreaming. In other words, only in 9 instances were deaf-mute subjects dreaming and not producing muscle movements in the arm or wrist. Wrote Max (1935b): "I do not regard all of these 9 cases as negative, however; in 5 of them the dream content was primarily visual in nature and the seat of activity may have been in their eye muscles" (p. 481). A page later he pointed out:

> [On 33 occcasions when non-impaired (hearing) subjects] were awakened during periods of electrical quiescence, 10 dreams were reported. While the dream results thus far seem to be negative for hearing subjects, additional evidence on this point must be obtained, particularly since some of the dreams were partly visual in nature and no eye records were being taken at the time. (pp. 482–483)

Apparently he never obtained the evidence because of difficulties in making the recordings (Max, 1937), but he was on the right track. Indeed, an association between dreams and retinal activity had long been suspected. George Trumbull Ladd (1892) traced this interest back to 1812, and he himself suggested that when dreams are not due to external stimulation, "both the retina and the visual centres of the brain may prove sources of origin for visual dreams" (p. 30). Furthermore, he was "inclined also to believe that, in somewhat vivid visual dreams, the eyeballs move gently in their sockets, taking various positions induced by the retinal phantasms as they control the dreams" (p. 304). Had Max successfully pursued his own hunch he could have claimed priority for the most important discovery in the history of the scientific study of dreams: Aserinsky and Kleitman's (1953) objective proof that there are "rapid, jerky, and binocularly symmetrical" (p. 273) eye movements —later called rapid eye movement (REM) sleep—associated with dreaming (which, incidentally, provided evidence that nonhuman animals also dream). Nevertheless, Max rightfully took credit for what he did find. "So far as we know," wrote Max (1935b), "this is the first instance of an objective means of detecting dreams" (p. 482).

Involuntary muscle movements are indeed ubiquitous, and they are closely related to the content of thoughts. In addition to evidence that eye movements increase when we think about physical activity—as well as, intriguingly, when we try to suppress or avoid unpleasant thoughts (Antrobus, Antrobus, & Singer, 1964)—Aserinsky and Kleitman's discovery of universal REM sleep demonstrates that involuntary muscle movements play a primary role in still another important aspect of human behavior: eye movements during dreaming. There is even evidence that eye movements during REM sleep follow the direction of the imagined action (Dement & Kleitman, 1957). But the methodological difficulties involved in such research led Allan Rechtschaffen (1973), a leading researcher in this field, to doubt that conclusive empirical evidence could ever be obtained for the hypothesis that eye movements reflect visual scanning of the dream's action. He pointed out that studies with people who were congenitally blind had failed to settle the issue.

The research continued nonetheless, and 2 decades later Herman (1992) argued, on the basis of several studies, "that the thematic narrative of the dream, the sensory-motor aspects of dream content, and the neuromuscular discharges that occur during dreaming (REM sleep only) are isomorphic" (p. 259). It is Herman's position, and he is not alone, that eye movements during REM sleep are the neuromuscular equivalent of the visual activity the dreamers would engage in if they were awake and actually living the dream. This would be consonant with the bulk of evidence that involuntary muscle movements reflect the ideas and activity that the mind (or some facet of the mind) is absorbed in. For example, McGuigan and Tanner (1971) found that when the dream was conversational, covert oral behavior (measured by chin and lip electrodes) was greater during REM sleep than during nonREM sleep, but that this was not true for visual dreams.

Many other laboratories have recorded covert muscle activity using a variety of ingenious methods, and the field continues to be active. As a preface to his own experiments, Shaw (1940) provided a useful listing of "the more important literature [from 1889 to 1939] dealing with the relation between the mental processes and muscular activity" (p. 8). Studies using mechanical and electrical recording systems predominated, but Shaw's brief review also described some ingenious observational and photographic methods for monitoring eye movements of awake subjects during visual imaging.

In his own study Shaw tested two male graduate students and a 45-year-old man trained as a mechanic. During testing the subject sat in a chair with his right arm screened from sight, was given a weight (unseen), and was asked to lift it using a single up-and-down wrist motion. When the lift was completed and as soon as the oscilloscope indicated return to a baseline level of relaxation, the subject was asked to *imagine* lifting the weight. For the two graduate students the weights ranged from 100 to 500 grams, "within the range of weights that can be lifted by a wrist motion without undue strain" (Shaw, 1940, p. 18). A surface electrode recorded from the outer surface of the upper right forearm. After each imagined lift the subject was asked to rate the quality of his imaging (vague, fair, clear, vivid) and to classify its modality (which, it turned out, was almost always kinesthetic). For the third subject the weight was always the same but the interval between actual and imagined lifting varied. He too reported modality and vividness.

As expected, when the amplitude of the action potentials during *actual* lifting by the two graduate students was plotted on a graph it described a steep, linear slope; that is, the muscle activity when lifting a 500-gram weight was much greater than when lifting a 400-gram weight, which in turn was greater than when lifting a 300-gram weight, and so on. But the result of interest was the muscle activity of the *imagined* lifts. Although not as steep, they too described a linear slope; that is, the increased involuntary muscle movements were directly related to the imagined weight of the object. And for all three subjects, the higher the rated vividness of the image the greater the amount of involuntary muscle activity. In sum, covert muscle activity was greater when subjects imagined lifting a heavier than a lighter weight and greater also when the kinesthetic image of lifting a weight was more vivid.

Although the sample is too small to be conclusive, these results have suggestive implications for the phenomena we have been examining. The relationship of vividness and extent of covert muscle movements suggests a basis for individual differences, and the adjustment of the covert muscle movement to the type of imagined activity (e.g., lifting heavier vs. lighter weights) can account for the wide range of phenomena in which the extent of involuntary muscle movements is adjusted for the requirements of the activity (e.g., slowly setting in motion a small weight held by a string vs. the sudden downward twist of a dowsing stick).

Curiously, none (or at least none that I have read) of the researchers and theorists in this domain—broadly labeled psychophysiology—traced the path that led from Chevreul through Pfungst to their own work. Of course many were caught up in the debate over the motor theory of thinking, but even Jacobson, who eschewed that debate, never mentioned that path. Their books and papers never refer to "involuntary muscle movements" or "ideo-motor action" despite the fact that the assumption underlying much of their research (as well as the motor theory of thinking itself) echoes Laycock, Carpenter, Chevreul and Pfungst in maintaining that thoughts are invariably accompanied by involuntary muscle activity directly related to those thoughts.

Recall that in Chapter 4 we reviewed Mühl's work on automatic writing and drawing. In her book (Mühl, 1930) she gave an interesting suggestion for how a righthanded writer could simultaneously mirror-write with the left hand during automatic writing. Because "movements of symmetrically placed parts of the body tend to produce symmetrical movements" (p. 29), during normal writing there are natural, minute *covert* involuntary muscle movements of the opposite arm, registered in the opposite hemisphere of the brain. The *overt* expression of these covert involuntary muscle movements, repressed during normal writing, are expressed as mirror writing during automatic writing, when normal inhibitions are not operating. Of course for people who are naturally lefthanded but were forced to write with their right hand this reaction would be even more pronounced.

Anyone wishing to follow more recent developments should start with the work of the behaviorist F. Joseph McGuigan (e.g., 1978), who published a textbook in which his own work and that of Jacobson figure prominently (McGuigan, 1994). His major thesis is much the same as Jacobson's: that we think not only with our brain but with our entire body, that in fact thought is impossible without the "selective interaction of complex circuits within the brain and between the brain and body" (p. 77). By now some readers must have raised for themselves the question of what occurs when the muscles are blocked from communication with the brain, either by a naturally occuring injury or by the administration of drugs. McGuigan (1978) cites and replies to a number of such experiments which, by their nature, challenge the motor theory of thinking and the Jacobson–McGuigan position.

A century after Chevreul's convincing although indirect demonstrations that our muscles are involuntarily activated by our thoughts, empirical demonstrations have provided direct physical evidence. Many of the measurements have been of small, covert involuntary muscle activity, but there is ample evidence that small involuntary muscle movements can rapidly develop into larger ones. But this occurs only under certain conditions. When we lie in bed at night and think of running, our legs do not churn, athough they harbor covert muscle activity. Other factors, such as wish fulfillment and the powerful force of suggestion, must operate in order to produce not simply involuntary covert muscle activity but involuntary *overt* muscle activity as well. Most people, standing relaxed with eyes closed and repeatedly given the suggestion that they are falling forward, sway forward to various extents or even fall forward (Eysenck & Furneaux, 1945; Hull, 1933; Weitzenhoffer, 1989), an example, presumably, of neuromotor enhancement following repeated suggestion. In general, those who sway the farthest are the most readily hypnotized.

To say that the brain is a complex organ is a sizable understatement. Indeed, how mind and consciousness emerged remains a mystery. From our explorations thus far it is clear that involuntary muscle movements manifest themselves in a variety of ways. In numerous experiments, asking subjects to think of an activity was enough to set the muscles required for that activity into action. Jastrow's studies with his automatograph, for example, were intended to demonstrate that thought produces small muscle movements that can be read by mind-readers, who, remember, instruct their subjects to think about where the object is hidden. No instructions were given to the questioners of Clever Hans or to those who held Chevreul's pendulum, but clearly they were thinking about the outcome, thereby setting small involuntary muscle movements into action. In automatic writing attention is usually directed away from the writing hand, and the hand seems to perform on its own. On the Ouija board when two people produce larger and more continuous movements that are guided by one of them, the involuntary muscle movements of one person's hand are camouflaged by the hand of the partner, as they are also in facilitated communication. A related situation occurs in table moving and table rapping, where many hands are on the table, with the added catalyst that numbing of the fingers impedes feedback. In all these phenomena wishful thinking abounds.

Involuntary movements of the entire body (involuntary body movements) require additional explanation. Ordinarily the body moves involuntarily when attention is riveted on an idea or thought, a routine occurrence that everyone must have experienced. However, people who obey a posthypnotic suggestion that they move to some location will fabricate for themselves and others some reason for going there (Hull, 1933; Myers, 1886b), because they must account for the fact that their bodies took them there involuntarily. Somnambulism (sleepwalking) is another example of involuntary body movements under unusual circumstances. These are dramatic instances when control of the body is involuntary as far as the primary personality is concerned; less dramatic instances occur routinely.

6

Additional Psychological Mechanisms Relevant for Understanding Facilitator Behavior

---

Earlier we explored the way that involuntary muscle movement combined with suggestion, wishful thinking and fixed ideas to blind Herr von Osten to the role he played in cueing Clever Hans. Substantial evidence has been compiled to suggest that the same mechanisms blinded table movers, pendulum holders, dowsers, facilitators and many others to their own roles in producing phenomena they erroneously ascribed to other forces. But many questions remain unanswered. Why do we humans have the power to produce movements without recognizing that we initiate those movements? What possible reason could there be for its evolution as a favored trait?

Moreover, we have not yet tried to explain the single most startling and frightening aspect of facilitated communication: the frequency of false sexual abuse charges. To explore the full range of possibilities—for no doubt there are many different reasons—we must delve into areas in which, unlike involuntary muscle movements, there is much disagreement among psychologists.

SURFACE AND DEPTH PSYCHOLOGY

Scientists … employ all ways of "knowing" available to them in generating their theories, hypotheses, and explanations. They differ, to the extent they differ, from nonscientists in putting whatever it is they have come to "know" to rigorous and objective tests. (Vogt & Hyman, 1979, p. 232)

In his outstanding book *The Hans Legacy* Dodge Fernald (1983) discussed two contributions and approaches to psychology, one represented by Pfungst's study of Clever Hans—a horse very sensitive to people—and the other by Freud's study of Little Hans—a boy very sensitive to horses. Both studies were dependent on careful observation, the *sine qua non* of any good scientist. To understand the horse's response to his master, Pfungst analyzed the surface interaction between von Osten and his horse. He had to ferret out the overt cues evoking the specific responses that earned the horse his edible rewards.

On the other hand, to understand Little Hans's sudden phobic reaction toward horses, no amount of study of this kind of interaction would have sufficed. Freud had to somehow get into Little Hans's head and try to understand what was producing his strange, unrealistic behavior. Freud's armchair deductions and developing theory were no less important (and certainly more influential) to psychology than was Pfungst's manipulation of variables. At the same time, the psychodynamic approach has the far greater danger of being influenced by the desires of the theorist or experimenter, for it lacks the careful control of variables that surface psychology enjoys.

For a complete understanding of facilitated communication I believe that the approaches of both surface and depth psychology are required, for here we have both Clever Hans and Little Hans in a single package. By surface psychology I refer to a psychology that deals only with observable behavior. By depth (dynamic) psychology I mean a psychology that, in addition, deals with and speculates about what goes on in the mind, by definition unobservable. For depth psychologists overt behavior and conscious thought are only the tip of the iceberg.

Surface psychologists object to the concepts of depth psychology. They point out that the premise of an unconscious system or unconscious processes such as dissociation assumes the existence of variables that cannot be observed or manipulated and are therefore unworthy of scientific interest. We are not doing good science, they say, unless we study only observable, manipulable variables. Depth psychologists respond that deducing the existence of a system or a variable is actually in the best scientific tradition. Electrons and atoms were inferred before they were observed. Black holes are by definition invisible, but astrophysicists deduced their existence—on the basis of Einstein's general theory of relativity—from the behavior of surrounding matter.

Where controls are possible they are of course eminently desirable. But in these examples from the physical sciences controls were, for the moment, neither possible nor indispensable. Theories are propagated based on the best available data. They go beyond the data and are tested by how well they explain what is known and how well they predict what is at present unknown. In subsequent years they will be confirmed or rejected, often by ingenious experiments. In the social sciences Noam Chomsky's (1965) proposal that humans are born with a template for learning language was derived not from direct experiments but from deductions about the nature of language. Subsequent empirical evidence has not only supported his conclusions and changed the course of language research but also influenced the thinking of psychologists in many other fields. Yet Chomsky's language template is unobservable.

The study of facilitated communication provides an excellent example of these disparate approaches. The two reasonable hypotheses to account for the startling results of facilitated communication are that the responses come from the students or from the facilitators. Rigorous, controlled "surface" study has proven that in almost all instances the facilitator is the source of the responses, and researchers generally agree that facilitors are unaware of controlling their students' responses. Yet the conclusion that facilitators are not lying can only be *inferred* from our knowledge of involuntary muscle movements, from the enthusiasm of those who continue to believe that their students are making all the responses, and from the shocked and distraught behavior of those facilitators who—after long periods of turmoil and anguish—finally accept the objective evidence.

Depth psychologists make the same kinds of inferences about such phenomena as somnambulism, posthypnotic suggestion and automatic writing. Once we accept the fact that people experiencing these and related phenomena are telling the truth, we must search for mechanisms that can account for their behavior. That does not mean there are no cases of fraud; it means only that the phenomena are usually real and therefore must reflect some aspects of the human mind. Additional hypotheses must then be proposed, one of which is that there is in the human organism a mental system or mental processes existing outside of conscious awareness that can affect conscious thought and behavior. Another is that the mind is capable of multiple consciousnesses and that extreme dissociations can manifest themselves as a result of mental stress, disease, brain damage, or suggestion.

The subtle responses of the facilitators and the ample rewards their responses evoke—all made easier by the ubiquity of involuntary muscle movements—fall into the domain of surface psychology and reveal its power. As for the accusations of sexual abuse, one might propose that the rewards for accusations of abuse are great enough to produce such behavior; but in many instances the charges of abuse contain such specific, lurid, obscene detail that I can only conclude that much more is going on here.

Needless to say, assumptions concerning the dynamics of certain kinds of facilitator behavior are here advanced as hypotheses only. Before speculating on what might be occurring to produce false accusations of sexual abuse we must take a careful look at a few of the mental mechanisms that have been proposed by depth psychologists, mechanisms that may help to explain some of the more extreme charges of sexual abuse.

THE UNCONSCIOUS

> There seems to be a presence-chamber in my mind where full consciousness
> holds court, and where two or three ideas are at the same time in audience,
> and an antechamber full of more or less allied ideas, which is situated just
> beyond the full ken of consciousness.... The thronging of the antechamber is,
> I am convinced, altogether beyond my control; if the ideas do not appear, I
> cannot create them, nor compel them to come.... The consequence of all this
> is that the mind frequently does good work without the slightest exertion.
> (Galton, 1883, pp. 203–204)

> That those sudden enlightenments which can be called inspirations cannot
> be produced by chance alone is already evident by what we have said: there
> can be no doubt of the necessary intervention of some previous mental
> process unknown to the inventor, in other terms, of an unconscious one.
> Indeed, after having seen, as we shall at many places in the following, the
> unconscious at work, any doubt as to its existence can hardly arise.
> (Hadamard, 1954, p. 21)

These two assertions were not made by psychologists. The mathematician
Jacques Hadamard (who quoted Galton's statement in his book) summed
up his thoughts on intuitive mathematical discoveries, instances of which
he goes on to recount in fascinating detail. Francis Galton—anthropologist,
hereditarian, statistician—described what many would now call the preconscious, in which reside ideas and words ready to come to consciousness.
A remarkable aspect of these underground ideas is that they are not random
but, without the person's conscious effort, are related in some way to
conscious thought. Unlike many unconscious processes, preconscious
thoughts very likely will, like most memories, reach consciousness. However referred to: preconscious, nonconscious, subconscious, or unconscious, there are mental activities (as well as overt behaviors) over which
we have no conscious control.

These quotations describe only one aspect of unconscious processes, the
creative aspect as manifested in discoveries and artistic endeavors. Other
aspects, more germane to our inquiry, are the province of dynamic psychology. It is primarily, though not exclusively, these other aspects that we will
explore.

I define unconscious processes as active thinking and behavior of which
we are not aware and cannot at will make ourselves aware. These processes
affect our conscious thoughts and behavior so that we often consciously
think and behave for reasons we do not understand. That this idea predates
Freud is by now a truism.

> There have probably been individuals in every culture who knew that factors
> of which we are not directly aware influence thought and behavior. As I have
> suggested, this recognition must have been widespread, for example in China
> where a more balanced and unified view of mind than that of Cartesian

Europe was prevalent in some periods. And certainly in ancient Greece, in Rome, and through the centuries of the Middle Ages many thinkers, some of great influence, avoided the self-centered mistake of treating the awareness of the individual as primary in the realm either of value or of philosophical thought. (Whyte, 1960, pp. 59–60)

Whyte nevertheless concentrated on the two centuries preceding Freud, whom he saw as "the most influential thinker in a succession of thinkers, all recognizing aspects of the truth" (p. viii). Our inquiry will proceed not from Freudian insights but from current academic thought, clothed in quite a different cloth than the Freudian one. This is not in any way to denigrate Freud's achievements, which hardly need my defense.

Pfungst (1911/1965) wrote in a footnote that although his subjects could not describe their own involuntary muscle movements, he himself could with practice describe in detail even the slightest of his own. Consequently he doubted that the movements were, as he put it, "quite unconscious" (p. 203). Rather, he reasoned that the movements went unrecognized because his subjects were concentrating on an idea. Any attempt to divide their attention between their thoughts and their movements decreased the force of the movements, making them even more difficult to discover. In a word, the movements were unattended to, not unconscious. However, Pfungst chose to avoid both these terms ("unattended to" or "unconscious") in the text so as "not to be guilty of premature judgment" (p. 203). He apparently forgot that he had previously used the term *unconscious* (if the translation is accurate) when he wrote, "And yet she, too, soon fell into line in the matter of executing unconsciously the characteristic head movement" (p. 115).

In any case, Pfungst was typically prudent in not prejudging the issue, and his cautiousness gives us some idea of the apprehension harbored by his era's scientists about the use of the term *unconscious*, a vigilance that persists today. Pfungst was not denying the possibility of unconscious processes; he was implying only that if his own involuntary movements had been unconscious he would not have been able to describe them. But that does not necessarily follow. As noted in Chapter 4, in automatic writing there are descriptions of observing one's own movements as if they were someone else's; there is no feeling of intention or conscious knowledge of what is to be written. By Pfungst's definition, Chevreul's (1833) movements were unconscious, for Chevreul was surprised that the pendulum he held over mercury was swaying when he had no feeling of moving it. Indeed, Chevreul was "quite amazed" (p. 250) when the oscillations diminished and then stopped entirely after a glass pane was placed between the pendulum and the mercury. Of course Chevreul was observing the effect of his muscle movements on the pendulum, not the actual muscle movements, but since both he and Pfungst described their own movements as "involuntary" we must assume that neither of them was intentionally activating his muscles. Even for Pfungst there was no conscious intention to move.

A refusal to understand that adjustments and adaptations occurring during eons of evolution are harbored in our genes—and consequently in our central nervous systems—and affect our behavior in various ways, is only one of the many arrogances that have deluded many people into believing that all thinking and behavior are on the surface and suitably under control. But it seems to me that the evidence is overwhelming that human beings frequently learn without conscious awareness, perform acts that they are unaware of, and behave for reasons other than the ones they consciously believe (see, e.g., Nisbett & Wilson, 1977). In the mind-reading section of Chapter 4 I noted that the terms *smart unconscious* and *dumb unconscious*, used in a recent symposium (Loftus & Klinger, 1992), were presaged by June Downey in 1908. As she noted, it is hardly much of a step to concede that there are well-learned habits that we no longer need to attend to—a "dumb" unconscious as we might now call it. But to claim that unconscious processes are more than that, that there is in fact a "smart" unconscious where processes occur that are organized and creative, was a paradigmatic leap (e.g., Bowers, Farvolden, & Mermigis, 1995). Is this smart unconscious a complex, organized, encapsulated, permanent *system, the* unconscious, or is it several less organized *processes* that only occasionally coalesce into organized systems? Morton Prince, whose 1906 book on a case of multiple personality is considered a classic, was firm in declaring that—except in such extreme dissociations as double personality—there is no "subconscious mind," although he conceded that there could be temporarily organized systems.

> There are subconscious processes any of which may take on autonomous activity and determine "automatic" and other kinds of behavior (including conscious mental processes of the personal consciousness); and among these activities may be automatic writing and hallucinations. Theoretically, therefore, such script [automatic writing] may be written by any number of different, and more or less independent, systems of integrated dispositions, *i.e.*, subconscious processes. (Prince, 1925, p. 37)

Unfortunately, from just about the time Prince wrote those words until quite recently the scientific study of unconscious processes was not in the mainstream of academic, experimental psychology in the United States. That is not to say that there were no experiments at all; there was a very large number of empirical tests of Freudian psychoanalytic concepts (reviewed, e.g., by Sears, 1947, and later by Fisher & Greenberg, 1977). Nevertheless the unconscious was long considered fringe territory for many reasons, some of which are discussed by Kihlstrom (1995). Happily, the long sleep is over. Renewed, vibrant interest in the subject along with the publication of many ingenious experiments permitted Kihlstrom (1995) to say with confidence,

> We now have good evidence, from a wide variety of research paradigms, that our experience, thought, and action is influenced by mental structures and processes of which we are not aware. The unconscious is not, as William James feared it would be, merely a 'tumbling-ground for whimsies'; rather, it is an empirical fact of mind, and can be studied by the conventional techniques of psychological science. (p. 138)

The James quote is from his masterwork volumes *The Principles of Psychology* (1890/1950, p. 163), in a section where he systematically attempted to shatter the validity of the current concepts of an unconscious. James preferred an unconscious that mediated the psychic phenomena of the spiritualists, and it was this kind of thinking that frightened away academic psychology (Fuller, 1986).

The central fact upon which all else hinges is that we can process only a limited amount of information, be it outside stimuli or interior thoughts, in a given period of time (Miller, 1956). Obviously our remote ancestors were similarly limited. Not only are conscious mental operations limited, but attention is also limited. These are major bottlenecks. One way in which these bottlenecks are eased is the spontaneous assignment of well-learned activities to another system, one that does not use precious space in consciousness. Another is to supplement learning by gathering information outside of conscious attention. For Arthur Reber (1992) this is a fundamental process in evolution because an organism that can extract information without attending to it and that can "use that information to guide its actions is going to have a decided advantage over organisms with similar overall design but lacking such a facility" (p. 33).

The existence of unconscious processes need not be perceived as unnatural, supernatural or mysterious. The real mystery is that a capability that evolved as an adaptation in response to one particular set of circumstances can be recruited to serve the organism in a number of other ways, a not uncommon source of many different kinds of adaptations (Gould & Vrba, 1982; Rozin, 1976; Sherry & Schacter, 1987). One original, indeed fundamental, adaptation was the ability to automatically carry out motor functions. No organism could survive without this capability and surely the reactions of rudimentary organisms were automatic and without consciousness. During evolutionary development consciousness was a relative newcomer, emerging from the base of implicit, unconscious processes (Reber, 1992). Likewise, since perception predated thinking it is likely that thinking evolved from perception. There are in fact innumerable thought processes that mirror perception (Shepard, 1981; Shepard & Podgorny, 1978).

One can give countless illustrations of the value of unattended motor reactions in situations that would have confronted our hominid ancestors, but a frequently used example that has nothing to do with survival might be more meaningful for many readers. When people learn to drive they must give all their attention to driving. Once they have learned and are comfortable driving they can talk with a friend or think about a problem. Meanwhile, the unattended movements that must be made to control the car are never exactly the same as in previous instances, so there must be some intelligence guiding them. For this reason the dissociated secondary system can never really be "dumb."

When driving we can always turn our attention to (and control) the motor activity if we wish to or need to. But many of the phenomena we have examined occur when we cannot consciously control them no matter how much attention we give them. We cannot even acknowledge that we are the source of the movement. The processes designed to ease the burden on a limited information-processing system have taken on a certain amount of independence and can turn into a Frankenstein monster.

The idea that certain habits need not be attended to is not a new concept; Hilgard (1992) cited William James as having proposed it in 1890 in his *Principles*. However, James (1890/1950) was referring only to habits that are established by practice, thereby setting the conscious "brain and mind ... comparatively free" (pp. 114–116). Unlike Downey (1908), James would not have subscribed to the idea that processes outside awareness (*extra-marginal* is a term he sometimes used) could perform cognitive operations—be "creative," as it were, or "smart," unless supernormal forces were operating. For James, subliminal consciousness operated at two levels: Its lower regions were revealed in certain pathological cases, but the upper regions were of most interest to him. According to Fuller (1986), James believed these upper regions could "be studied in such phenomena as telepathy, clairvoyance, religious experience, and the mediumistic trance state" (p. 87). This would be enough to frighten away any hard-nosed empirical scientist, and with good reason. But we need not be forever paralyzed by James's misreading; it is possible to explore "subliminal consciousness" in a sensible and productive way.

As noted above, a trait that developed during evolution can be recruited for other purposes. The ability to carry out motor activity outside conscious awareness, while remaining an indispensable trait, can be recruited for learning without attention as well as for solving problems without wasting precious space in consciousness.

There have been a substantial number of recent studies of unconscious processes and many commentaries about its "rediscovery" and its role in current empirical psychology (e.g., Bowers, 1987; Greenwald, 1992; Kihlstrom, 1995). Writers have likened or contrasted the cognitive unconscious of experimentally oriented psychologists to the dynamic unconscious of those more clinically oriented (e.g., Eagle, 1987; Epstein, 1994; Shevrin & Dickman, 1980). As Whyte (1960) astutely observed, "The discovery of the unconscious is the recognition of a Goethean order, as much as of a Freudian disorder, in the depths of the mind" (p. 71). Talented, experimentally oriented psychologists are making a concerted and knowledgeable effort to understand unconscious processes because they believe them to be fundamental.

Implicit Learning and Problem Solving

The current terms under which many studies of unconscious processes are carried out are implicit learning and implicit memory, which in a short time have accumulated a sizable literature. Reber (1992) defined implicit learning as "a fundamental cognitive/perceptual process whereby tacit knowledge about a complex environment is acquired" (p. 33). The key word here is *tacit*. Unlike explicit learning, where people intentionally acquire knowledge, implicit learning is the acquisition of knowledge without conscious intent. The evidence for these processes is very impressive (Reber, 1993). Objections have been raised, of course; claims and evidence for learning without awareness will not be accepted by experimental psychologists without passing the most exacting tests (Shanks & St. John, 1994), even more exacting, it seems, than those applied to other studies (Berry, 1994).

Albert Einstein (1970) had no doubt that unconscious processes contribute to thinking:

> What, precisely, is thinking? When, at the reception of sense-impressions, memory-pictures emerge, this is not yet "thinking." And when such pictures form series each member of which calls forth another, this too is not yet "thinking." When, however, a certain picture turns up in many such series, then—precisely through such return—it becomes an ordering element for such series, in that it connects series which in themselves are unconnected. Such an element becomes an instrument, a concept. I think that the transition from free association or "dreaming" to thinking is characterized by the more or less dominating rôle which the "concept" plays in it.... For me it is not dubious that our thinking goes on for the most part without use of signs (words) and beyond that to a considerable degree unconsciously. (pp. 7, 9)

In introducing this section on unconscious processes it was noted that many intuitive problem solutions and insights which develop just outside of awareness, in the preconscious, will reach consciousness, but nevertheless we usually arrive at solutions never knowing how we got there, or with some mistaken belief to account for our journey there. We unknowingly make associations among many things and find patterns and redundancies without ever realizing we have done so.

Many studies have documented this fact (see Spitz, 1993, for a brief review). An impressive recent series of studies have been those of Pawel Lewicki and his colleagues (Lewicki, Hill, & Czyzewska, 1992). In one study, college students were asked to locate a target (e.g., the number 6) that was presented in one of four quadrants of a matrix. On every seventh trial (the critical trials) throughout the experiment (i.e., on trials 21, 28, etc.) the target number was embedded with many other numbers and of course took longer to find. Trials continued over 12 days (32,256 exposures). Unknown to the subjects a complex sequential placement of the target number on the trials when it was presented alone was a cue (heuristic) to where it would appear when it was embedded among many other numbers on the critical trials. If the subjects knew the pattern they could find the target more quickly on the critical trials than if they had no cue to its placement.

When the experimenters suddenly changed the hidden pattern the subjects' performance dropped, so obviously they had used the pattern to help them locate the target. But—and here's the point—they did not know they were using it. After the experiment the subjects were surprised to learn there was a hidden pattern, and none of them could figure out what it was. In other experiments subjects knew what the experiments were about but still could not figure out the patterns. They tried to explain why they suddenly had performed more poorly (e.g., the experimenters must have subliminally flashed a threatening stimulus). Even when the college students were given unlimited time and promised a $100 reward they could not consciously discover the hidden pattern. Faculty members were equally ineffective.

On the basis of these and other experiments Lewicki et al. (1992) concluded that when it comes to efficiently processing complex information, not only are unconscious processes smart, they are even smarter than conscious processes:

> Our nonconscious information-processing system appears to be incomparably more able to process formally complex knowledge structures, faster, and 'smarter' overall than our ability to think and identify meanings of stimuli in a consciously controlled manner.... Most of the 'real work,' both in the acquisition of cognitive procedures and skills and in the execution of cognitive operations, such as encoding and interpretation of stimuli, is being done at the level to which our consciousness has no access. (p. 801)

Many others are contributing to the growing storehouse of empirically derived knowledge that documents the role of unconscious processes in thinking (see Bowers, Farvolden, & Mermigis, 1995, for a recent review of the literature on intuition, insight and creativity).

If implicit learning and unconscious problem solution occur automatically then it follows that they will be, under certain circumstances, largely age- and IQ-independent, and this too has been documented. These findings suggest a solution to the conundrum of how some people of very low general intelligence can become calendar calculators of prodigious skills, able to give the name of the day that falls on any date many years in the past and future. When extraordinary amounts of time are spent studying calendars the rules and regularities that govern the calendar are automatically (unconsciously) extracted from it (Hermelin & O'Connor, 1986; Spitz, 1995). They are, in other words, implicitly discovered and used.

But whether unconscious processes are studied by cognitive psychologists or explored within the framework of dynamic psychology is irrelevant for our purposes. The fact that unconscious processes are experimentally verified simply strengthens our case when we draw on these processes in order to understand the phenomena under discussion, including facilitated communication.

Dreams

Dreams are an obvious illustration of an organized narrative generated without conscious control. Here is Dr. Henry Jekyll describing the growing disaster of his fateful experiment:

> At that time [when he, Dr. Jekyll, had first taken the drug] my virtue slumbered; my evil, kept awake by ambition, was alert and swift to seize the occasion; and the thing that was projected was Edward Hyde. Hence, although I had now two characters as well as two appearances, one [Mr. Hyde] was wholly evil, and the other was still the old Henry Jekyll, that incongruous compound of whose reformation and improvement I had already learned to despair. The movement was thus wholly toward the worse. (Stevenson, 1886/1898, p. 356)

Here is an interesting case of alternate personality with the evil second personality gradually taking over, but alas, not an actual case study; just a wonderfully perceptive figment of an active imagination. On the other hand the author's description of his dreams' contribution to the writing of his story is not fiction and to that extent is of even greater value for understanding the mind. Here is Stevenson (1897) struggling to germinate an idea:

> For two days I went about racking my brains for a plot of any sort; and on the second night I dreamed the scene at the window, and a scene afterwards split in two, in which Hyde, pursued for some crime, took the powder and underwent the change in the presence of his pursuers. All the rest was made awake, and consciously, although I think I can trace in much of it the manner of my Brownies. (p. 250)

To describe the unconscious, Stevenson (1897) used the analogy of "little people [Brownies] who manage man's internal theatre" (p. 238), and in time he learned to make use of the productions of his little people, "to write and sell his tales" (p. 238). He wrote in the third person about his own experiences, as if he were writing about someone else.

> When he lay down to prepare himself for sleep, he [Stevenson] no longer sought amusement but printable and profitable tales; and after he had dozed off in his box-seat, his little people continued their evolutions with the same mercantile designs. (p. 239)

Of course the stories still had to be, as he described it, "trimmed and pared and set upon all fours" (p. 238), but he depended on the Little People (suddenly capitalized) for his ideas. Who are these Little People, he asks, who have more talent than he, and who "can tell him a story piece by piece, like a serial, and keep him all the while in ignorance of where they aim"? (p. 247).

> And for the Little People, what shall I say they are but just my Brownies, God bless them! who do one-half my work for me while I am fast asleep, and in all human likelihood, do the rest for me as well, when I am wide awake and fondly suppose I do it for myself. That part which is done while I am sleeping is the Brownies' part beyond contention; but that which is done when I am up and about is by no means necessarily mine, since all goes to show the Brownies have a hand in it even then. (pp. 247–248)

Stevenson expressed regret that he—the conscious he—might be no storyteller at all, that all his works were the product of an unseen collaborator, although he did claim some credit for his role in editing the Brownies' productions and taking care of the mundane necessities that go into publishing a polished and finished work. Then unexpectedly he rebelled, in indecisive desperation. It was he, Robert Louis Stevenson, who should nevertheless receive the credit and the praise, not the elusive Brownies!

> All the rest [of Jekyll and Hyde] was made awake, and consciously, although I think I can trace in much of it the manner of my Brownies. The meaning of the tale is therefore mine.... Mine too is the setting, mine the characters. All that was given me was the matter of three scenes, and the central idea of the voluntary change becoming involuntary. (pp. 250–251)

It was not easy for Stevenson to give credit to nonconscious processes. Nor is it easy for most of us, who like to feel in complete control.

Consider also the remarkable fact that while sleeping we incorporate outside stimuli into our dreams, or perhaps outside stimuli induce dreaming. Most people have had this experience. I recall a dream about elephants I had one morning just before awakening, in which I heard their trumpeting very clearly. When I awoke I again heard an elephant trumpet, and although I live in a small town we are not accustomed to having elephants wandering about. The mystery evaporated when I learned that a traveling circus, elephant and all, was setting up its tent in a nearby lot.

Binet (1899) recorded an experiment by M. Maury on this very subject. Maury asked someone to variously stimulate him while he slept and shortly thereafter to awaken him:

> His lips and the end of his nose are tickled with a feather; he dreams that he is undergoing a horrible torture, that a mask of wax is being pulled off, the skin of his lips, nose and face is torn. A pair of tongs is rubbed with steel scissors a short distance from his ear; he dreams he hears the sound of bells;

He is made to breathe eau de cologne; he dreams he is in a perfumer's shop, and the idea of perfume arouses that of the Orient; he is at Jean Farina's shop in Cairo. (p. 130)

Several other illustrations are given, and I'm sure most readers can supply their own. This is very nice evidence that our minds can organize unexpected exterior stimuli into an interior narrative without our conscious effort and without conscious awareness.

The concept of secondary processes that lessen the information load must also encompass, by its nature, the concept of dissociation—that is, the concept that those processes are separated in varying degrees from primary consciousness. Separation can be such that developments in this secondary system influence primary thought and behavior, including muscle movements. We have seen an example of very minor dissociation in the inability of the questioners of Clever Hans to consciously control the head nods that cued Hans to respond. Somnambulism, amnesia, possession, and multiple personality—altered states of consciousness—are examples of a major loss of control. In such instances what was formerly a secondary automatic process operating in parallel with primary consciousness becomes the primary consciousness; that is to say, the secondary process does not simply influence primary thinking, it becomes primary thinking.

As an evolutionary heritage, primary consciousness can release control of some or all of its mental and physical capabilities to a secondary process for varying periods of time, depending on the situation and the person's innate propensity to dissociate. I believe that this is what occurs in many of the phenomena we have looked at, including facilitated communication.

As we shall see, this interpretation of altered states of consciousness (ASC, of which so much has been written) as well as this general proposal for how the human mind operates, is not the sort of thinking that every psychologist is comfortable with; in fact the concept of an altered state of consciousness itself is by no means universally accepted (e.g., Kirsch & Lynn, 1995).

Even more controverial is the proposal that in some instances secondary systems are activated to protect a person from mental trauma grave enough to cause serious mental disorder. At such times, goes this line of reasoning, the secondary process takes control to protect the individual.

MULTIPLE PERSONALITIES
AND OTHER DISSOCIATIONS

Gloucester. Better I were distract:
  So should my thoughts be sever'd from my griefs,
  And woes by wrong imaginations lose
  The knowledge of themselves. (Shakespeare, *The Tragedy of King Lear*, Act V, Scene VI)

The principle of dissociation of the mind is very important. Only by thoroughly grasping it can one understand multiple personality and other phenomena of abnormal psychology. (Prince , 1906/1992, p. 75)

The idea of MPD [Multiple Personality Disorder] strikes many people as too outlandish and metaphysically bizarre to believe—a "paranormal" phenomenon to discard along with ESP, close encounters of the third kind, and witches on broomsticks. I suspect that some of these people have made a simple arithmetical mistake: they have failed to notice that two or three or seventeen selves per body is really no more metaphysically extravagant than one self per body. (Dennett, 1991, p. 419)

The unity of consciousness is illusory. (Hilgard, 1992, p. 16)

I have been reiterating that involuntary muscle movements are a natural human attribute that is manifested in a variety of ways, many of which are often misunderstood. Involuntary muscle movements are also intimately interrelated with another natural human attribute to which we have given rather perfunctory attention: the capacity to dissociate. According to Erdelyi (1994), "Dissociationism designates theoretical commitment to the notion that integrated systems such as the self are made up of subsystems that may become—or may normally be—relatively disconnected in terms of information exchange or mutual control" (p. 3). Extreme dissociation is often found in pathology, but dissociation is usually not pathological.

Any form of involuntary muscle movement or involuntary body movement involves some degree of dissociation, from the most banal activity such as doodling to multiple personality, an extraordinary human curiosity in which one or more "hidden" personas are said to alternate as the primary persona. An essential feature of dissociation disorders, according to Kihlstrom (1994), "is a disruption of the monitoring and controlling functions of consciousness … not attributable to insult, injury or disease affecting the brain tissue, or to psychotropic drugs" (p. 384).

As previously noted, instances of dissociation, such as automatic writing, are not by themselves indicators of a multiple personality disorder.[21] In a sense we are all multiple personalities. For one thing, different people see us differently. "Properly speaking, *a man has as many social selves as there are individuals who recognize him* and carry an image of him in their mind" (James, 1890/1950, Vol. 1, p. 294). But more importantly, we behave differently toward different people. We are one personality with our children, a different personality with our parents, different with our spouses, different with our colleagues, different with our friends. We are not pathological multiple personalities, however, because the different personalities are

---

[21]The label of Multiple Personality Disorder (MPD) has been changed to Dissociative Identity Disorder and placed under the general category of Dissociative Disorders in the latest diagnostic manual of the American Psychiatric Association (1994), but I will continue to use the former designation.

usually not warring or isolated from each other, and are amenable to conscious awareness. The point at which multiple personality is considered pathological is an interesting question; in some conceptions of mind unitary consciousness is the illusion, not multiple selves. Although automatic writing is not by itself an indicator, it is frequently by means of automatic writing that an alternate persona announces itself and communicates.

Some workers have taken a second look at the few recorded cases of dual personality from the late 18th and early 19th centuries and attribute many of them to organic damage, lengthy amnesia, somnambulisms, and bipolar affective disorder (manic depression; Carlson, 1981; Merskey, 1992). Many question the validity of the dynamics said to underlie multiple personality, and the recent upsurge in the number of cases suggests to them that therapists are being duped or unwittingly create the phenomenon. Few question that multiple personality exists, but there is strong disagreement about whether the symptoms are driven by interior dynamics or by exterior social forces, and consequently there is a major dichotomy in the way it is perceived (Spanos, 1994).

There is also some disagreement, though far less, about the existence and ubiquity of dissociation. However, the view taken here is that the capacity for dissociation is an essential aspect of the human mind, and that the mental mechanism of dissociation, accompanied by involuntary muscle movements, is crucial to an understanding of many phenomena we are interested in, from swinging pendulums to facilitated communication. Because the source of some communications during facilitated communication (in particular exaggerated sexual abuse allegations) is still wrapped in mystery, the debate over multiple personality, in which communications also circumvent the primary personality, is of interest to us. Whether one sees multiple personality as socially constructed (driven by exterior forces) or dynamically constructed (internally activated) is not as important in the present context as the fact of its existence, for in either case it is enabled and sustained by the human capacity to dissociate. By the same token, it matters little whether a case is described as an instance of possession or of multiple personality.

A Brief Look at the Early History of Multiple Personality

Challenges to the illusory idea that individuals are mentally unitary have existed since Plato and St. Augustine, but in terms of later conceptions of multiple personality the year 1816 stands out despite scattered reports of earlier cases. It was in 1816 that a most influential case of "double consciousness" was published in the United States, followed in Europe 14 years later by a book on the case and 44 years later by a magazine article in *Harper's* (Bliss, 1980; Carlson, 1981, 1984; Ellenberger, 1970). It was the case of Mary Reynolds of Titusville, Pennsylvania, whose condition had developed in

1811. As with many cases described in earlier times, her experiences were unlike those currently being published. She was reported to have had a severe seizure at the age of 25 after which she lost consciousness. When she regained consciousness she was blind and deaf, but recovered these senses about 6 weeks later. Subsequently she went into another coma and after about 19 hours awoke with a blank mind, in need of complete reeducation. One morning 5 weeks later, she awoke as her original self, but a few weeks later, after a heavy sleep, she awoke as her second self again. These amnesic fluctuations continued to occur periodically and at no time did she remember the alternate state. As her second self she was wittier, cheerier, and more mischievous and imaginative than she was in her original state, even writing poetry. From the age of 44 she remained permanently in her second state.

A case in Bavaria was published in 1828 after which a few additional cases were reported. In 1840 a detailed monograph describing the case of an 11-year-old Swiss girl, "Estelle," was published in France.[22] This case takes on special significance because many years later it influenced the work of Pierre Janet, whose concepts of dissociation in turn strongly influenced (temporarily) many psychologists in the United States, including Morton Prince, his contemporary and friend. Janet visited the United States a number of times and gave a course of lectures at Harvard in 1906. In fact the French—in particular Charcot, Janet, Ribot and Binet—dominated the field of abnormal psychology until Freud's concepts prevailed (Barresi, 1994; Ellenberger, 1970; Fahy, 1988; Taylor & Martin, 1944).

Before that happened, however, Alfred Binet (1896) summarized the French claim, or at least one Frenchman's claim, to France's preeminence. After pointing out that in France there was no school of psychology, he noted that

> With relatively few exceptions, the psychologists of my country have left the investigations of psychophysics to the Germans, and the study of comparative psychology to the English. They have devoted themselves almost exclusively to the study of pathological psychology, that is to say psychology affected by disease. (pp. 8–9)

Obviously influenced by Janet, Binet preferred the term subconscious to unconscious (which he nevertheless continued to use) and thought of the processes occurring in amnesias and multiple personalities as the product of a second consciousness. Binet even suggested that the automatic writing of healthy subjects is a product of secondary personalities and has its origin in dissociation, although the unconscious personality is not as developed as it is in hysterics. Divided attention produces a division of consciousness, and a secondary consciousness is a secondary personality. In Binet's view,

---

[22]Merskey (1992) argued that these and other early cases were not multiple personalities at all, and he suggested alternative diagnoses. Furthermore, the book on Estelle "provides no evidence for a second 'personality'" (p. 330).

then, automatic writing is not simply a function of the effect of ideas on involuntary muscle movements, but is dependent also on the division of consciousness (Binet, 1891/1896).

Despite Binet's somewhat disdainful remarks about the failure of foreign psychologists to study pathological psychology, he himself soon went off in many other directions—much too many, really. In the end his fame rested, as everyone knows, not on his work on double consciousness or automatic writing or the subconscious but on developing, with Théodore Simon, the first functional and reliable children's intelligence scale. Janet, on the other hand, continued his studies in abnormal psychology. Ellenberger (1970) described a sample of Janet's early work (in the late 1880s) on psychological automatism:

> By means of automatic writing, Janet found both the cause and the meaning of the terror fits. When she was seven, two men hiding behind a curtain had made a practical joke of frightening her. A second personality within Lucie, Adrienne, was reliving this initial episode when she had her fits of terror. Janet described how he made use of the rapport in order to relieve the patient of her symptoms, and how the second personality eventually disappeared. Lucie had a relapse eight months later, which, however, receded rapidly with the help of a therapy combining hypnosis and automatic writing. (p. 358)

In experiments with another patient, Léonie,

> He showed that, under hypnosis, two very different sets of psychological manifestations can be elicited: on one side are the "roles" played by the subject in order to please the hypnotist, on the other side is the unknown personality, which can manifest itself spontaneously, particularly as a return to childhood. (Ellenberger, 1970, pp. 358–359)

When hypnotized, Léonie referred to her childhood self as Nichette but "behind the hypnotic personality, a third hidden one may exist.... a product of an old hypnotic personality that magnetizers had elicited in Léonie in the past" (Ellenberger, 1970, p. 359).

But was this third personality elicited or created? The charge that therapists *create* multiple personalities (iatrogenic induction, as it is called) is a serious one. It is clear that alternate personalities can be created by therapists, particularly under hypnosis. Some critics have claimed that they are *always* externally created, either by therapists or by other social influences. In one description of multiple personality Janet (quoted in Myers, 1886a) described how he had induced automatic writing by posthypnotic suggestion. Then, by means of the automatic writing, the patient (the same one described above as Lucie) responded to Janet's altered, more commanding voice, while she continued to talk with other persons:

> "Do you hear me?" asked Professor Janet. Answer (by writing), "No." "But in order to answer one must hear?" "Certainly." "Then how do you manage?" "I don't know." "There must be somebody who hears me?" "Yes." "Who is it?" "Not Louise [the patient]." "Oh, someone else? Shall we call her Blanche?" "Yes, Blanche." (Myers, 1886a, p. 240)

This exchange was also quoted in Binet's book (1891/1896, p. 147) where, however, not only did the patient's name differ (Lucie rather than Louise) but there was no mention of the name Blanche. Myers wrote that the name Blanche had to be changed because it had a bad association for the patient (which one could not know from the Binet version) and then quoted this later exchange after the patient had rejected the name Blanche: "'What name will you have?' 'No name.' 'You must—it will be more convenient.' 'Well then, Adrienne'" (Myers, 1886a, p. 240).

On this Myers (1886a) sardonically commented, "Never, perhaps, has a personality had less spontaneity about it" (p. 240). Binet (1891/1896) was even more direct: "It is plain that M. Janet, by christening this unconscious person, and, more still, by declaring that someone must exist in order to answer him, aided materially in the formation of the person; he himself created her by suggestion" (p. 147). But Binet added that the secondary personality could be created only because in this patient it took very little to gather and crystallize the scattered disaggregated (dissociated) elements existing apart from normal consciousness. He also noted that in many instances this process occurs spontaneously.

For Janet it was important to give names to hypnotic subpersonalities: "Once baptized, the unconscious personality is more clear and definite; it shows its psychological traits more clearly" (quoted by Ellenberger, 1970, p. 139). Theoretically, when a name is given to an unorganized group of memories and impulses that are unacceptable to the primary consciousness they take on a life of their own, created by the mind's capacity for self-organization. Of another case Janet wrote: "It seemed as though this newly-evoked personality consisted of the synthesis of all the psychological phenomena of which the primary personality was unconscious" (quoted by Myers, 1886a, p. 250).

For Janet, a major mechanism in neurosis is the detachment of certain ideas from consciousness, a process he called *désagrégation*, or disaggregation, which was loosely translated as dissociation. This concept was never adopted by Freud. As Erdelyi (1994) points out, Freud's approach to what Janet called *désagrégation* was to implicate active defense—the concept that threats to the integrity of the unitary system are repressed. Janet's was rather a deficit approach, positing that the individual is unable to preserve a unitary system. However, his companion concept—that dissociation occurs only in people who have a genetic weakness in the ability to hold psychic functions together, and that it is dissociation that causes subconscious activity and symptom formation—faded before the onslaught of Freud's contention, and much evidence, that unconscious processes are universal (Ellenberger, 1970; Nemiah, 1984; Perry & Laurence, 1984). In sum, whereas Janet emphasized more passive elements, such as dissociation, Freud emphasized dynamic elements, such as repression.

Morton Prince was generally sympathetic to Janet's approach, not only in his theoretical stance but also in his desire to unite clinical with academic psychology. Prince founded and was the first editor of the *Journal of Abnormal Psychology*, the first volume of which covered the years 1906–1907. At about that time his *The Dissociation of a Personality* was published—the first book-length description of a case of multiple personality. Much later, in 1927, he founded the Harvard Psychological Clinic.

The Dissociation of a Personality (Prince, 1906/1992) aroused great public interest and was extremely influential, at least for a while (Marx, 1970). Perhaps of minor significance, but relevant for us, was Prince's (1906/1992) departure from his previous position that alternate personalities revealed during hypnosis (as opposed to those that developed spontaneously) were artificially created by the therapist's suggestion, "sort of unconscious and unspoken mutual understandings between the experimenter and the subject, by which the subject accepted certain ideas unwittingly suggested by the experimenter" (p. 26). Prince was following in the footsteps of his mentor, for Janet was so aware of the influence of therapists on their patients that he insisted on seeing only patients who had not previously seen a therapist. Janet had noted "with a certain wry humor that a clinician could recognize by whom a patient had been treated by the way this patient behaved" (Perry & Laurence, 1984, p. 27). But with the publication of his book Prince's previous opinion was jettisoned. His patient's principal alter was depicted as a true alternate personality despite its first appearance during hypnosis.

In his book Prince described the case of Christine L. Beauchamp (pronounced Beecham), the name given to herself by one of her alternate personalities.[23] In addition to her presenting self the patient initially was said to have one altered state and two altered personalities. The presenting personality was the refined, saintly, overly conscientious and reticent Miss Christine Beauchamp, whom Prince labelled B I. Then there was Miss Beauchamp as she was when hypnotized, labelled B II, who was not a separate personality but only a hypnotic state described by Prince as "herself intensified but without the artificial reserve" (p. 25).[24]

---

[23]See Rosenzweig (1987) for some fascinating speculation about the significance of this pseudonym, taken from a novel by George Meredith titled *Beauchamp's Career*. Rosenzweig, a student of Prince's from 1928 to 1929, discovered after a long investigative journey that Miss Beauchamp's real name was Clara Ellen Fowler. In tracing her early life he suggested a number of possible precipitating factors.

[24]Later, B II (the hypnotized state of B I) spun off a different personality—the New B II, as Prince originally called it—and so the original B II, which occasionally reappeared, had to be renamed B Ia. "B I when hypnotized went into two different states: B Ia, and B II" (p. 307). And so it went, through many complications, additions, changes, combinations, contradictions and speculations. Unmentioned here are the names of new permutations such as B Ib, B IIa, B IIb, B IVa, B V, B Vb, B VI and so on, many of them associated with transitory stress and therefore ephemeral, and most (but not all) gathered together in a graph of 16 such symbols on p. 465 of Prince's book. For the sake of my sanity as well as the readers', I make no attempt to detail or follow it all.

During the hypnotized state a new character surfaced that "at first appeared to be [only] a second hypnotic state, but later proved a veritable personality, with an individuality that was fascinating to watch" (p. 25). She came in with a stutter that soon abated and only occasionally recurred. This was the devilish, mischievous, rebellious, saucy, influential alternate (indeed co-conscious) personality, B III, whom Prince named Chris but who subsequently called herself Sally. By *co-conscious* Prince meant that she existed simultaneously with primary consciousness. It was his experience with B III (Sally) that persuaded Prince to abandon the idea that true alternates could not be revealed by hypnosis, and one need only read his book to understand why he was persuaded. Later Sally insisted that she had existed as a personality co-conscious with Miss Beauchamp since childhood but had only achieved fully independent existence (ability to control consciousness) during therapy.

Finally there was the selfish, formal, quick-tempered B IV, who was in some respects more normal and certainly healthier (physically and mentally) than B I and who arrived without hypnosis about a year after Sally's appearance. Sally called B IV the "Idiot" because B IV knew nothing directly of Miss Beauchamp's recent and current life or what Miss Beauchamp (B I) and Sally (B III) thought and did (although she soon found ways to gather partial information).

But other states and personas soon arrived. In the tradition of Janet, Prince believed that multiple personality was not the result of material being repressed but rather of the disintegration of the primary personality. In this case not only had a primary personality disintegrated but the disintegrated parts had also disintegrated, and those disintegrated parts had further disintegrated. "There is no limit to the modes and degrees in which personality may be disintegrated, or to the combinations in which psychical (or cortical) elements may be arranged and rearranged" (pp. 444–445). Two processes were operating: First, certain memories and perceptions were lost to the normal personal consciousness by dissociation (the disintegration), and second, there was a rearrangement or new synthesis of the memories, moods, and so on. When the new synthesis was very limited, Prince thought of it as a *state* that sensitive subjects could readily be thrown into, not a true alternate personality that occurs only when the network is sizable. "When the new synthesis is complex and embraces a wide field of consciousness, we have what to all intents and purposes is a complete personality" (pp. 474–475). Near the end of the book Prince argued that these disintegrated selves could in turn be influenced by subconscious processes: "B I and B IV were disintegrated selves, with B III an abnormal subconsciousness (Sally)" (p. 505). In other words, B III was *their* subconscious.

Throughout, Prince sought a way to find the original primary personality (the Real Miss Beauchamp, as he called it) or recreate it by unifying the disintegrated parts, for it was obvious that the Miss Beauchamp who had come to him for help was herself an alternate personality. "Close observa-tion of B IV soon awakened the suspicion that it was she who was the true Miss Beauchamp, who, for some unexplained reason, had disappeared some time in the past" (p. 186). For a time Prince worked on this assumption and also found what he believed to be the precipitating shock that had submerged B IV and replaced her with B I 5 years before Miss Beauchamp (as B I) had come to him for help. Gradually and spontaneously, but also with Prince's encouragement and (for a time) the assistance of Sally, B IV took over more and more of the consciousness previously taken by B I, and even took on Sally in a resolute but losing battle.

Then Prince dropped a little bombshell: He decided that neither B IV nor B I alone was the Real Miss Beauchamp, and that the division between B I and B IV was not as complete as he had previously believed. The two were now thought to be disintegrated parts of the real self. Two years into therapy he tried, through B II, to integrate them. This was initially unsuccessful because the fusion, although giving the patient some peace and mental stability, never lasted very long. A final reconstruction had to be postponed for 2 years because of the strong opposition and clever disrupting and scheming tactics of B III and B IV, to say nothing of the conflicts between all the alternates. None of the personalities wanted to die: "Each wanted to be the one that should live, and each was unwilling to be snuffed out for someone else" (p. 455).

Later, a cataclysmic confrontation between B III and B IV took place over a 2-week period, with B III inflicting great damage on B IV. Prince inter-vened and was able to shut down B III for the moment, then aimed to once again, and finally, unite B IV with B I via B II. To do so he had to control B IV and change her into B II, not an easy job. In fact Miss Beauchamp as B IV engaged in a 2-hour physical struggle with Prince until gradually her will weakened and Prince brought up B II. Prince had broken through, but the ordeal was not yet over. Sally was still present and B IV conspired with her to share the power. After many difficulties a healthy personality repre-senting a combination of B I and B IV was obtained, one who remembered all that had occurred except for the times that Sally was in control. Prince was satisfied that he had put together the Real Miss Beauchamp. She was not at first permanent, but once he had solved the problem of how to bring her at will and how to keep her, the case could be closed.

And what of Sally? With great difficulty Prince brought her up, for she could no longer easily appear. Nor was she now the saucy one; she was very meek, feeling "squeezed out," and she confessed that it was indeed the Real Miss Beauchamp who had been present. Under coercion she further re-vealed that "B II was the Real Miss Beauchamp with her eyes closed" (p. 519)—that is, under conditions in which Prince declined to permit her, under hypnosis, to open her eyes. Hypnotizing Miss Beauchamp, Prince brought up B II but this time induced her to open her eyes, and there again was the Real Miss Beauchamp. Prince had for some time theorized that she was the Real Miss Beauchamp but had discarded this theory without having known that Sally had blocked the disclosure. "When the real Miss Beauchamp was finally permanently obtained, Sally 'went back to where she came from,' without power to produce sensory or motor automatisms or other dissociation phenomena" (p. 512).

After much work and many setbacks during 7 years of treatment, Prince closed the case in 1905. He noted that his patient suffered slight lapses following physical illness and other strains and required occasional therapeutic support. "The problem still remains, How far and for how long can she be protected?" (p. 524). And Sally had not evaporated. "When, however, as a result of some mental catastrophe, she [Sally] appeared again as an alternating personality, her language implied a persistent existence as a subconscious like that of her early youth" (p. 524).

In the course of this case a novel automatism had occurred: B IV (the Idiot) took over and managed to have B III (Sally) respond to B IV's spoken questions by means of automatic writing (of which Prince provided a sample). Obviously this woman was very disturbed (Rosenzweig, 1987).

> As a child [she] frequently had visions of the Madonna and Christ, and used to believe that she had actually seen them.... She constantly used to have the sense of the presence of some one (Christ, or the Madonna, or a Saint) near her, and on the occasion of the visions it seemed simply that this person had become visible. (Prince, 1906/1992, p. 548)

During therapy she again had a vision of Christ and at one point was determined to join the Catholic Church and enter a convent.

There were other things that, unfortunately, Prince would not print. For example, Sally (B III) agreed to write an autobiography in which much was revealed: "As a dissociated consciousness she claimed to see and hear much that did not enter the consciousness of the primary self. A good deal of this, of course, is too private to put into print" (p. 368). This statement, made by Prince despite the fact that Christine Beauchamp was a pseudonym, seriously compromises the value to clinicians and theorists of this extensive report, and decisively separates Prince from the Freudians. At one point Sally wrote that Christine's mother "never wanted C. [Christine] near her after we grew older. She didn't even want to see her, but was always saying, 'keep out of my sight.' And I know why, because of something that happened when C. had been taking medicine and was sound asleep—If I had been asleep too I shouldn't have known it....." (p. 387). The ellipsis indicates that Prince omitted material about what Sally saw when Christine was supposed to be asleep, the importance of which we can only speculate about. In addition, Prince was apparently oblivious to the obvious transference and counter-transference that was occurring in this case (McCurdy, 1941), which further separated him from the Freudian school.

Nothing of a sexual nature was ever mentioned by Prince. He did however print Sally's description, in her autobiography, of Christine as a 13-year-old stealing into a room one evening to take her crying 4-day-old sister—"nasty squally little thing," Sally called her—into her arms to soothe her so she wouldn't awaken their mother. The infant did grow quiet, and she held it in her arms till morning without noticing that the infant had died. In fact, wrote Sally, Christine "had entirely forgotten the child in going over and over for the ten thousandth time her sins" (Prince, 1906/1992, p. 387). A few days later her beloved mother, whom she idolized but by whom she was rejected and disparaged, died. Christine believed her mother's illness "had all come about because of her; that she had fallen short of God's requirements" (p. 387).

According to Rosenzweig (1987), 5½ years earlier *another* sibling had died, a 4-day-old brother (whose twin sister survived), whom Prince probably knew nothing about. For a number of reasons this earlier death was even more traumatic than the later one, and the linkage of the two events probably had a profound effect on the patient. Rosenzweig also speculated that Christine was severely abused by her widowed father, causing her to run away from home at age 16, never to return. In any case it is surprising that Prince did not discuss the ramifications of the infant sister's death described in Sally's autobiography.

The Miss Beauchamp who presented herself was extraordinarily suggestible and Prince related that without hypnosis he had induced anaesthesia in one of her forefingers and even blindness for a particular object. He reasoned that the mechanism involved was dissociation, because when he subsequently hypnotized Miss Beauchamp, B II was able to describe the sensations in detail. Prince's explanation:

> The sensory impressions from the forefinger were no longer synthesized with (and therefore had become split off from), the personal consciousness, that great group of perceptions and memories which at any given moment makes up the ego or personality. These tactile sensations, then, existed in a dissociated state, and to this extent there was a doubling of consciousness. (Prince, 1996/1992, pp. 73–74)

Being also a dissociated state, B II was able to recall the event.

About a year after treatment had begun, Prince requested assistance from Richard Hodgson, who could be accessible to Miss Beauchamp when Prince was unavailable. We know Richard Hodgson as a friend of William James and the organizer sent from England to put the American Society for Psychical Research on a sound financial footing. For 18 years Hodgson was, remember, the manager of James's favorite medium, Mrs. Piper. Although B IV referred to him as Dr. Hodgson, the flippant Sally (B III) referred to him in a familiar and rather belittling fashion as "Dicky." In his masterly though often quite speculative analysis of the Beauchamp case, Rosenzweig (1987) reprinted a letter from James to Prince complimenting Prince on the publication of his book, and Rosenzweig later raised the possibility that it was James who recommended Hodgson as Prince's assistant. Presumably Hodgson did not consider Miss Beauchamp subject to paranormal influence, as he did Mrs. Piper. After Hodgson's sudden death he was often Mrs. Piper's medium control—a controlling spirit who summons those whom sitters wish to contact—and it was Hodgson who communicated through Mrs. Piper with G. Stanley Hall from the great beyond.

John Barresi (1994) believed that a crucial event in Prince's confrontation with psychoanalysis was another case of multiple personality that came under Prince's care, the case of Nellie Parsons Bean, also known as B. C. A. after the abbreviations representing her three personalities. As with Miss Beauchamp, Prince ultimately determined that the presenting personality (A) was a dissociated personality. Another, different alternating personality called B was discovered during hypnosis. After prolonged treatment her presumably normal state (C), absent for almost 2 years, was hypnotically attained and after some early instability was, with great difficulty, finally stabilized and remained as the primary personality. Prince reasoned that two systems, A and B, into which her normal state had been split during a 2-year period, had now been reunited.

As the reintegrated personality (C), Mrs. Bean was able to remember herself as alternating personalities A and B, so Prince asked her to write an account describing herself as she had been in A and B. In the first of two publications (B. C. A., 1908) she described the times when she behaved in ways that were out of character, and for which at that time she had been amnesic. Her personality alternated completely, sometimes for short periods and sometimes for weeks at a time:

> How can I describe or give any idea of what it is to wake suddenly, as it were, and not know the day of the week, the time of the day, or why one is in any given position? I would come to myself as A, perhaps on the street, with no idea where I had been or where I was going.... Often it happened that I [as A] came to myself at some social gathering ... to find I had taken wine (a thing I, as A, felt bound not to do), and what was to me most shocking and horrifying, smoking a cigarette; never in my life had I done such a thing and my humiliation was deep and keen. (p. 249)

B was not only an alternate personality, but at times co-conscious:

> I remember, in the *alternating* state of B, telling you that I could when *co-conscious* control A by *willing*.... I will give one instance.... As A I felt it my duty to go often to the cemetery to which, as B, I objected. In fact, B said she would not go there nor allow A to do so. A writes in the diary as follows: "Another queer thing happened to-day.... I had gone only a little way [to the cemetery] when I began to feel that I could not go on.... It was as if some physical force was restraining me, or like walking against a heavy wind. I kept on, however, and finally reached the entrance, but further I found it impossible to go.... I set my will and said to myself I *will* go, I *can* go and I will,

but I could not do it. I began to feel very tired—exhausted—and turned back.
As soon as I turned away I had no trouble in walking but I was very tired. (B.
C. A., 1908, pp. 255–256)

As B she wrote letters to Prince and notes to A by automatic writing, and
B was given as the author of the second publication (By a personality,
1908–1909). One would think she could not write the autobiography if she
had been fused with A for the final integration of C, but the explanation
given was that B had been writing this autobiography for some time and
continued to write it while C was still unstable. In his prefatory note to B's
autobiography (By a personality, 1908–1909) Prince wrote:

> Later this completely integrated and stable personality [C] was obtained. The
> writer [of the autobiography], B, claims to have the same co-conscious life
> with this apparently normal stable personality [C], only she has not the power
> to influence her, and therefore cannot "come" voluntarily. She can, however,
> perform automatic writing (as many normal persons can), and thus give
> evidence of a co-conscious existence. Through hypnosis, too, the alternating
> state B can be obtained. Afterward the normal C becomes integrated again
> and retains memories of this state as explained in this account. (p. 313)

At one point in the autobiography B made a statement that required the
following footnote: "Being in hypnosis now I remember this, but when I
wake up as an alternating personality I lose this part of my *co-conscious*
memory" (p. 321). This indicates that B wrote parts of her autobiography
when the patient was hypnotized.

Considering the confusing explanations and twisted logic, one can sym-
pathize with skeptical readers who did not agree that the dissociations of
thought and action—first occurring when she was a young adult—produced hidden "personalities" (full-fledged homunculi). For multiple personality in general, some writers believe that only if it began in childhood
can we call a multiple personality genuine. Others are convinced that
multiple personality is *never* genuine. They contend that the behavior is not
spontaneously created by inner dynamics and that true alternate personas
do not exist, although the individual imagines that they do and acts as if
they do.

Few would accuse Mrs. Bean of purposely lying or knowingly acting.
She had experienced a childhood trauma, the stress of a dying husband,
and events that were shocking to her restricted character. Evidently she was
a prudish, dedicated, suggestible person who dealt with stresses and unacceptable drives in a histrionic and dissociative manner. Her suggestibility
is evident in an incident that B related. Prince invited Mrs. Bean to observe
a patient who showed the interesting symptom of being unable to put her
feet flat on the floor. When Mrs. Bean returned home she developed the
same symptoms and called Dr. Prince for help. "She was in great distress
of mind, as she thought her condition was caused by her extreme suggesti-

bility, and that she must be very ill to be so easily affected" (By a personality, 1908–1909, p. 332).

Mrs. Bean later collaborated with Prince in his investigations, particularly in the analysis of her dreams. The precarious nature of this kind of relationship reveals itself when Prince discreetly but unscientifically omitted intimate aspects of the dreams. This refusal to deal frankly with sexual material is apparently part of what Barresi was alluding to when he wrote that this case was a significant event in Prince's confrontation with psychoanalysis. Barresi (1994) and Rosenzweig (1987) have interesting comments to make about the undercurrent of unanalyzed reciprocal feelings between Prince and his two famous patients.

One thing struck me about several of these early cases of multiple personality: The presenting individuals were repeatedly described as very proper, courteous, prudish, restricted and usually depressed whereas their principal alternates were outgoing, outspoken, lively, and sometimes reckless and troublesome. (For an example of an early case demonstrating these features, see Goddard, 1926.) Much can be, and has been, made of this, not only in terms of the release of urges and thoughts that the patients were consciously unwilling to express or even admit to themselves, but also in terms of the position of women in the family and in society. Rosenzweig (1987) emphasized this latter point in his discussion of Miss Beauchamp. Where available, their histories were invariably traumatic; many patients were the victims of unfortunate experiences and monstrous insensitivity. Their escape into daydreaming can readily be understood.

Current Controversies

Not long after the publication of Prince's two cases, the concept of dissociation all but disappeared and reported cases of multiple personality became quite rare. They were unimportant to the Freudians who dominated clinical and abnormal psychology, as well as to the behaviorists, who later dominated experimental psychology. However, as the influences of Freudian theory and behaviorism declined, the concept of dissociation re-emerged, in large part as a result of Ernest Hilgard's work.

The explanation for the genesis of multiple personality given by many depth psychologists is (in brief and much simplified) that alternate personalities (alters) are created when a child can cope with an extreme trauma such as physical or sexual abuse, including incest, only by dissociating it (the Janetians) or repressing it (the Freudians). One might say that multiple personality disorder is a form of post-traumatic stress disorder. The dissociated (repressed) aspect develops into an alternate persona or personas capable of expressing some of the feelings the person is unable to express.

In the view of those who stress dissociation as a primary mechanism, individual differences in dissociative susceptibility permit some children, but not others, to escape the trauma through dissociation. The nature and predictability of the abuse suffered by the child also determine whether the trauma is dissociated. I will make no attempt to cover, even cursorily, the enormous literature linking dissociation, repression and multiple personality disorder; but these concepts have been seriously challenged, and it is necessary to present opposing viewpoints in some detail.

For one thing, questions are raised about the extraordinary increase in the United States of patients diagnosed as having multiple personality disorder. An examination of the number of articles on multiple personality in a selected sample of popular magazines, newspapers and professional journals from 1899 to 1988 reported the trend over the years. From 1909 to 1913 publications in both outlets increased slightly, but the number stayed low, with some sporadic increases, until 1973 and 1974. From then on, the clinical articles increased steeply, with some fluctuations, until the end of the study period, and no doubt they continue to rise. Although the popular articles also increased early in the span from 1973 to 1988, they peaked in 1979 then dropped sharply in 1980 and never again reached their 1979 peak (Fleming, Shilony, Sanchez, Hiam, & Rodehaver, 1995).

The authors of the survey believed that a relationship between the number of publications of popular compared with clinical articles might indicate that many people developed the syndrome because they had heard or read about it. In fact they did find a significant correlation of .43 when they compared the number of publications for every year between 1899 and 1988. When the articles were grouped into 5-year periods the correlation rose to .59. In other words, an increase or decrease in the number of articles in the popular magazines was accompanied to a modest degree by a parallel increase or decrease in the professional journals. Although the authors warned that correlations prove neither the presence nor the direction of causality, they nevertheless raised the possibility that popular culture influences clinical conceptions of psychological constructs.

Neither popular books nor television programs were included in the survey, nor was there any measure of the separate impact of individual publications, movies or television programs, although there were some popular events during that period.[25] In 1976 television audiences saw *Sybil*, a made-for-TV movie from the book by Schreiber (1973) about a patient with multiple personality. Five years after *Sybil*, a popular biography on the same topic, *The Minds of Billy Milligan* (Keyes, 1981), was published. Returning to the results of the survey, we find that the Sybil book and movie coincided with the initial rise in the number of articles in popular maga-

---

[25]The literature on multiple personality is immense. In 1983 Boor and Coons published a bibliography of 350 references, restricted primarily to English references. Two years later Damgaard, Van Benschoten, and Fagan (1985) added 90 more references, two of which were French publications. One can imagine what the number is now, when there are societies and journals dedicated to dissociation and multiple personality.

zines, and both they and the Milligan biography coincided with the initial period of sharp escalation of articles in clinical journals. On the other hand, almost 20 years earlier, in 1957, *The Three Faces of Eve*—a notable film about a case of multiple personality—had been released. If multiple personality were a social construction a rise in number of articles should have occurred at that time, but there was no dramatic increase.

Another puzzle raised by skeptics is the fact that the increase in cases of multiple personality in North America is not matched elsewhere, which is supportive evidence for those who posit a strong cultural component. The British psychologist Aldridge-Morris (1989), among others, has raised serious questions about the diagnosis. Yet in his book *Multiple Personality: An Exercise in Deception* he did not say that the disorder does not exist, only that it is grossly overdiagnosed. He also pointed out that it is rare outside the United States. From a survey he made in Great Britain he quoted this response by a consultant psychiatrist: "In the UK, we react to any suggestion by patients or relatives that there are two or more personalities by immediately saying that there are two or more aspects to one personality and asserting that the individual must take responsibility for both of these aspects. It works" (p. 15). At least one Canadian publication also expressed skepticism: "We think it is very unlikely that a sustained diagnosis of an alternate personality ever occurs without social or medical encouragement. Where occasional cases of dissociation do arise in which another identity is assumed, they do not appear to last long if they lack subsequent fostering" (Freeland, Manchanda, Chiu, Sharma, & Merskey, 1993).

Although multiple personality is much more frequently diagnosed in North America than in other parts of the world, even taking into account the size of its population, it does occur in other countries; some of the earliest reported case were from France and Italy, although the diagnoses of those cases have been questioned (see footnote 22, p. 132). A literature search revealed that since 1840 multiple personality disorder has been reported in 1 territory and 13 countries other than the United States and Canada. Following this search, questionnaires were mailed to 132 individuals in 27 countries outside of North America, resulting in reports of from 1 to as many as 20 new cases from 10 of the countries (Coons, Bowman, Kluft, & Milstein, 1991). The reported number of alternates per patient ranged from 2 to 20 with a median of 5, only slightly higher, according to the authors, than the median of 4 found in North American surveys. Six of the countries had not previously been reported in the literature, making a total of 1 territory and 19 countries outside the United States and Canada in which multiple personality disorder has been reported.

But this study was flawed because the list of people to whom the questionnaire was mailed was compiled from reprint requests sent to the authors before this study was undertaken. We can therefore assume that those receiving the questionnaire already had a particular interest in the subject of multiple personality and therefore also had an incentive to create (unwittingly, of course) multiples in their practice. Nevertheless, though biased and extremely restricted, this survey confirmed the fact that multiple personality disorder, however induced, is not limited to any one country. Still, considering how much more pervasive the diagnosis is in North America, if multiple personality is not completely culture-bound (or country-bound) it is at the very least culture-sensitive. The social climate cannot be ignored.

Why look for multiple personality disorders in other cultures in order to prove that it is "real?" Such a strategy is counterproductive when dissociations are expressed differently in different cultures. According to Kluft (1994),

> Over 90% of studied cultures have dissociative syndromes in which another entity takes over control of the body and behaves in a different manner. Some of these conditions appear to be related to unique social stressors within those societies, some to the life experiences of the victims. These syndromes are often described as *possession*. (p. 17)

A colleague who grew up in rural Jamaica told Kluft that all the girls who developed the "multiple souls" syndrome, common in Jamaica, were incest victims. How much stock can be put in that anecdote remains to be seen.

Thigpen and Cleckley (1984), whose treatment of a patient with multiple personality disorder had inspired the 1957 movie *The Three Faces of Eve*, also warned of false diagnoses. In the 25 years following the publication of their book, hundreds of patients, many sent by therapists, came to them for treatment of multiple personality. Yet in the 30 years that the two had practiced and had seen thousands of patients, only one other case, aside from Eve, appeared to be a genuine multiple personality:

> Before assuming ... that the patient's "personalities" or "ego fragments" are long-standing, autonomous entities that are fully dissociated from the original personality—and therefore serve separate motives, impulses, and feelings—we have found it useful to consider whether there might not be instead a pseudo- or quasi-dissociation that functions to help the patient gain attention, or maintain an acceptable self-image, or accrue financial gain, or even escape responsibility for actions. (p. 65)

They made the important point that there are degrees of dissociation and that great care must be taken to reserve the disorder "for those very few persons who are truly fragmented in the most extreme manner" (p. 66). In the case of Eve they worked for almost a year to rule out psychosis, partial dissociation, feigning, and secondary gains before feeling confident in their diagnosis. Not many therapists are that cautious.

Thigpen and Cleckley used the pseudonym Eve White for their patient and Eve Black for her first alternate. Merskey (1992), while agreeing that Thigpen initially witnessed a dissociative episode, revealed that the actual name of the patient was Christine "Chris" Sizemore and that she called her alternate personality Chris Costner, her maiden name, which readers of Thigpen and Cleckley's work could not have known. The fact that she used her maiden name for the alter was an important detail, as it suggested the possibility that the first alter was not so much another personality as "an affirmation of a previous (real) single state which the patient regretted leaving" (Merskey, 1992, p. 335). Thereafter, however, 22 different personalities emerged.

Thigpen and Cleckley (1984) also remarked that some patients sample different therapists until they find one who will give them the diagnosis they seek, then compete with each other to have the most personalities. Even more disturbing is Thigpen and Cleckley's report that there are therapists who compete over the number of multiple personality patients they have seen. Why, many people ask, do some therapists see so many multiple personality patients while others see so few, or none at all? Of course the former believe that other therapists are misdiagnosing many patients and are too insensitive to, or unfamiliar with, such cases to pick up the presence of alters.

We are reminded of the "states" that Prince spoke of, easily produced by sensitive patients but not true alternate personalities. And recall that both Janet and Prince had warned about therapist influence, although that did not necessarily immunize them then, nor does it protect any therapist now, from unwittingly influencing their patients (any more than knowledgeable observers were protected from cuing Clever Hans with involuntary muscle movements, or than facilitators recognize they are doing the typing simply because someone raises that possibility). With patients seeking therapists who will diagnose them as multiples and with therapists seeking to increase their caseload of multiples it is not surprising that the diagnosis of multiple personality is sharply and steadily increasing in the United States.

Films such as *The Three Faces of Eve* are a powerful evocative force, particularly for unstable or very suggestible people, and they can trigger unexpressed emotional problems. After *The Exorcist* was released there was a sudden spurt of activity in the offices of psychiatrists. Bozzuto (1975) described four patients who had difficulty sleeping and developed other very disturbing symptoms. Three of them feared an approach by the Devil, and the fourth was preoccupied with "the Devil aspect" and evil forces.

Many critics have raised objections to the explanation for multiple personality disorder given by depth psychologists, despite the fact that the literature is flooded with reports that individuals with multiple personality disorder had been abused as children. Most of these critics do not deny that sexual abuse, physical abuse and neglect of children has been occurring in epidemic profusion, perpetrated by children's biological parents and parent surrogates as well as by others. Even Spanos (1994), a major critic of the depth psychology view of multiple personality, acknowledged that "many people who become MPD patients were abused during childhood" (p. 158).

The question is: How often do children forget or repress these appalling events, and how often, if ever, does the forgotten or repressed material metamorphose into an alternate persona? Critics point out that it does not necessarily follow that memory for these events has been lost, and they raise the possibility that in many other instances memories of abuse have been implanted by therapists who expected that abuse caused their patients' multiple personality—which itself was implanted.

Among the most heinous examples of therapists creating multiple personality disorders were those perpetrated by a group of therapists in Chicago and elsewhere, disclosed to the public in a *Frontline* television broadcast, "The Search for Satan" (Bikel & Dretzin, 1995). Patients were talked into believing they had been members of an international satanic sect and had engaged in the sect's loathsome activities, including ritual abuse of their own children and cannibalism of infants roasted on a skewer. Placed into the therapists' private clinics, brainwashing techniques—such as isolation from friends and relatives, administration of massive amounts of drugs, constant interrogations and even restraints—were applied. The patients were told that their ancestors had been members of the sect and that the torch was being passed as the patients initiated their own children into the cult. The children were induced to describe the terrible acts that occurred and that they themselves performed, and were given stars for particularly colorful revelations. Patients were told that as a result of their experiences in the satanic cult they and their children had developed multiple personality disorder. Children as young as 4 years of age were placed into the clinics for as long as 3 years. Nurses and teachers who witnessed these events were appalled, but when they protested they were accused of being satanists themselves, and warned that the doctors were the experts. Indeed, the doctors *were* the experts: They spoke at meetings, wrote books and articles, and received awards for their achievements in uncovering the sources of multiple personality disorder.

There is no evidence that satanic cults of this nature exist. The therapists have bought into a paranoid system of beliefs in an ancient international satanic cult that implanted cryptic messages, including Greek letters that stood for various types of programming the patients had presumably undergone. It doesn't seem to bother the therapists that this ancient international conspiracy, causing thousands of deaths and presumably implicating thousands of people, has somehow eluded the police for centuries. How much of this the therapists actually believe is impossible to determine, but they made millions of dollars from the patients' insurance companies, apparently choosing patients with the kinds of insurance that would pay well. In my view they do believe it, or at least many of them believe it. Ironically, it is the therapists who are part of a cult: a fully developed, paranoid belief system reinforced by their own arrogant, mutual, exclusionary folly. They destroyed families and created emotional disturbance in previously normal, healthy children. The State of Illinois finally closed one of the clinics, and therapists are now being sued by their former patients. Yet belief in satanic cults continues, spurred on by unscrupulous elements of the media and irresponsible members of the clergy (Spanos, 1994, among many others, has reviewed the literature on satanic and other spurious creations).

A Side Trip Into the False Memory Syndrome

The Chicago episode is a particularly graphic example of the false memory syndrome (FMS). The syndrome most frequently occurs when patients are convinced, usually (and sometimes unwittingly) by their therapists and often during hypnosis, that the source of their problems is sexual abuse by a parent or parents, which the patients had repressed, and that the only way they can get well is to remember these repressed events. Many times the patients are induced to believe that because they were abused as children they must have multiple personalities, so of course many alternate personalities emerge. Eventually, subject to both the subtle and blatant suggestions of their therapists, they produce false memories of abuse, confront their parents with these "facts," and in time isolate themselves from all contact with their families, resulting in untold and unnecessary sorrow and distress. (This is not to say that true memories of abuse cannot be forgotten, a not uncommon event as we shall see.)

In one case it was a parent who was induced into believing he had repressed memories as an abuser. In this case a father was induced into believing he had repressed memories of events described by his two adult daughters: that he had been a member of a baby-murdering satanic cult and, programmed by this cult, had raped his daughters when they were young children (Ofshe, 1992). The allegations had begun when one of the daughters attended a church-sponsored retreat during which women were encouraged to reveal abuse. Her sister joined in the accusations and blamed her recent misconduct in school on the fact that she had been raped when she was 4 years old. After 5 months of extended questioning and harangues this rigidly conventional, suggestible, very religious man (who had converted to fundamentalism more than 10 years before these events), never doubting the power of Satan, was manipulated by investigators, two psychologists and a Pastor into believing the allegations and producing pseudomemories of the crime. In Ofshe's view, once the questioning had produced a dissociative state, the suggested pseudomemories were incorporated. He was convicted and imprisoned. After he had entered a guilty plea and his interrogators stopped seeing him, however, his belief in his own guilt eroded. His case, which demonstrates the monstrous creations that the human mind is subject to when pressured by constant harangues and repeated suggestions, is being appealed.

But this case is atypical: The emotionally disturbed daughters were, I think, consciously manipulative and the *parent* produced the false memories. Typically it is the *children* who are manipulated into producing false memories of parental childhood abuse.

There are similarities between the false memory syndrome and facilitated communication. The same wish-fulfilling mechanisms that drive believers in facilitated communication find fertile ground in the expectancy fulfillment of therapists who believe in the ubiquity of repressed memories of abuse and therefore induce "memories," usually unwittingly. Occasionally a person not in therapy produces false memories of abuse, in which case a therapist can hardly be held responsible. However, we have already noted how books and the media can strongly influence suggestible people, so it is not surprising that dramatic instances of recovered memories have become fashionable. Unfortunately such revelations are often presented in the press or in professional journals without cautionary warnings about their validity (Loftus, 1993). In addition, people in our cultural climate are expected to blame others for their problems, making it easier for some patients to accept suggestions that their problems are a result of repressed childhood abuse (Yapko, 1994).

I know of no support group for disillusioned therapists similar to the one for disillusioned facilitators. There is, though, a support group for patients who have recanted accusations they made against their parents on the basis of what they thought were recovered memories. "Two such recanters have formed an association for others like them and published a newsletter called *The Retractor*" (Yapko, 1994). A major organization, the FMS Foundation, supports primarily the parents of these children. Its newsletter disseminates information about the baleful effects of false memories of abuse, presents the outcome of numerous law suits against the therapists and reports litigation in process. The foundation does not minimize the frequency of, or damage caused by, actual sexual or physical abuse of children, nor does it question memories that are only suspected or partial, as long as the memories are continuous throughout childhood and adolescence. The point of contention is the accuracy of recall by adults who had never before entertained such thoughts.

In 1993 the American Psychological Association appointed a Working Group on Investigation of Memories of Childhood Abuse. The Interim Report concluded that most people who were sexually abused remember all or part of what happened to them, but the report also pointed out that it is possible for long-forgotten memories of actual abuse to later be remembered.

In this regard, in one objective study 129 young women were interviewed 17 years after an abuse for which they had been brought to a hospital emergency department for treatment and collection of forensic evidence. At the time of the abuse their ages ranged from 10 months to 12 years. A significant minority (38%) had forgotten that particular abuse although many recalled other abuses. If they were 6 years old or younger at the time of the abuse they were more likely to recall the specified abuse than if they were older. Twelve percent reported no sexual abuse of any kind despite hospital records to the contrary (L. M. Williams, 1994a, 1994b). In Williams's (1994b) opinion, research such as hers provides support for trauma theory, "which suggests that forgetting abuse reflects the use of psychological mechanism such as cognitive avoidance, dissociation or repression as coping strategies for the psychological distress associated with previous traumatic events" (p. 1182). However, questions have been raised about the ability to discriminate between different kinds of repression as well as the tendency to overuse the concept, and it has been proposed that in some instances mechanisms such as "normal forgetting, deliberate avoidance, attentional overfocusing, and infantile amnesia" (Ceci & Loftus, 1994, p. 352) can be invoked more parsimoniously than can repression.

There is no doubt that forgotten memories of *true* events can be recovered in many cases—all sorts of forgotten memories, not just of sexual abuse but also of long-forgotten abilities. As one venerable example, in 1902 Freeborn reported the case of a 70-year-old woman who while in a delirium caused by broncho-pneumonia spoke in Hindustani and kept repeating a Hindustani poem. Before and after her illness she could not speak Hindustani, nor could she recall having spoken it when she was a child or during her recent delirium. Later it was discovered that Hindustani was a language she had spoken until some time in her 3rd year, when she had returned to England from India and her Indian servant had left her.

The recovery of *pseudo* events can seem just as vivid as the recovery of real events, despite the fact that objective evidence indicates they never could have occurred. This is particularly true if the false memory image is repeatedly induced. Likewise, both true and false memories can be indistinct. Memories, particularly recovered memories long lost, are very often unreliable. Finally, as Williams (1994b) points out, in many instances child abuse occurs in private and because perpetrators deny their roles the offense is almost impossible to document. It is important, nevertheless, to try to differentiate between true and falsely created recovered memories, or at the very least to be extremely cautious.

It is difficult to summarize the conflicting views that have created two warring camps, both of which can find cases that support their beliefs. The evidence indicates that although in most instances sexual and other abuses are not forgotten (although the abused people may wish that they were), in a number of cases they are indeed forgotten, and in some instances they are forgotten and later recovered. But the evidence also indicates that *false* memories of abuse are common when the "memories" are "recovered" during therapy with therapists dedicated to the theory that repressed memories of abuse are the cause of most disorders. This is reminiscent of the false hopes created during facilitated communication among facilitators imbued with the proposition that, with their help, all autistic and retarded children can communicate at a high level. The most serious question, amounting to an indictment, concerns the grave consequences resulting from the creation of false memories of abuse, just as grave consequences result from facilitators' creation of false perceptions of communication.

Back to Multiple Personalities

Belief in multiple personality is tempered by questions of origin as well as by criticism of the lax conditions of diagnosis. The alternates in Prince's case of B. C. A. would not qualify as authentic on the basis of Thigpen and Cleckley's (1984) requirement of good evidence that fully developed alternate personalities, with a life of their own, must exist before therapy, prior to hypnosis, and usually from a very young age. Nor would all but one of the alternate personalities in his Beauchamp case qualify. The problem is that evidence for the birthdate of an alter must come from the patient and consequently is of questionable reliability. Circumstantial evidence from friends and family can help but is unlikely to be obtained by busy therapists who, like lawyers, could use the services of investigators. Many times the evidence clearly indicates the presence of alters or periods of dissociation prior to therapy. In such cases the therapist cannot be accused of creating the multiple personality, although the influence of information the patient derived elsewhere or the influence of a previous therapist could have contributed to the disorder.

Nor can the therapist be implicated when the presenting personality *is* an alter, a situation more typical of cases reported in the past than at present. In fact, charges of therapist creation of multiples apply almost exclusively to the recent upsurge of cases of multiple personality disorder in North America; the older cases (and perhaps a very few of the recent ones) seem to be of a completely different order.

In 1973 Hilgard introduced his neodissociation theory, so called "because it derives from the classical theory of Janet ... but adds a new dimension" (p. 397). The idea of dissociation remained a central concept but the hypothesized mental structures producing the dissociation and functioning during the dissociation were greatly changed. This new dimension was required because Hilgard discovered in the early 1970s that some hypnotized individuals were not completely oblivious to what they were doing, that a part of them observed what was going on. In a word, the dissociation was not complete.

In 1994 Hilgard recounted (as he had in his 1977 book) the events that led to the detection of this observing component, which had taken place during a class demonstration with a subject who happened to be blind and whom Hilgard described as "of known hypnotic talent" (p. 34). (In a manner typical of these kinds of studies, Hilgard preferred to work with subjects in the top 1% to 2% of hypnotic susceptibility.) After the student was hypnotized he was told that at the count of three he would become deaf. The suggestion appeared to work, for he showed no reaction to a sudden loud sound next to his ear or to the taunts of other students. "One student in the class raised the question whether some part of the subject might not know what was going on, for, after all, there was nothing wrong with his ears" (p. 34). Hilgard followed this up and, lo and behold, elicited a sign from the subject (a raising of his index finger) that some part of him heard Hilgard's voice. The still-hypnotized student then requested that Hilgard restore his hearing so he could know why he felt his finger rise. Hilgard restored his hearing, and the student, still hypnotized, explained that when everything got quiet he became bored and busied himself with a statistical problem, when suddenly he had felt his finger lift. Then Hilgard made contact with the other part, which was able to describe the noises and the request to lift his finger. Finally, leaving this other (dissociated) part and restoring the student to his usual hypnotic self, Hilgard told the student that upon being aroused from his hypnotic state he would remember everything that happened, and he did.

The serendipitous seeds of a new hypothesis were sown. Hilgard labeled the other part a "hidden observer," and verified its presence in a number of subsequent experiments. However, it is not a pervasive phenomenon: In cited studies it was found in only 25% to 40% of highly hypnotizable subjects. Considering that the number of highly hypnotizable individuals is limited, Hilgard estimated that the hidden observer effect can be found in less than 5% of the general student population. He emphasized that the metaphor of the hidden observer was not to be confused with a well developed second personality; it was not multiple personality (although a process very much like it occurred often in Prince's case of Miss Beauchamp). "The 'hidden observer' was intended merely as a convenient label for the information source capable of a high level of cognitive functioning [that was] not consciously experienced by the hypnotized person" (Hilgard, 1994, p. 36). Nevertheless the existence of a separate part that, among other things, reported pain via key presses (à la automatic writing) when the primary hypnotized person reported very little pain, was for Hilgard "evidence of a split in consciousness between the overt (conscious) level and the covert (subconscious) level, and hence evidence of dissociative processes" (p. 37). (Note that the lifting of the finger and the key presses were involuntary muscle movements as far as the primary part of the hypnotized subject was concerned.)

To explain these and other experimental findings Hilgard (1991) turned to cognitive psychology's hierarchical model in which an executive control monitors and directs various subordinate systems (lower level cognitive control systems), themselves hierarchically arranged, "each of which has some degree of unity, persistence, and autonomy of function" (pp. 94–95). These subsystems usually work under the guidance of the executive control to produce normal functioning. When, for whatever reason, constraints are put on the executive control or the executive control is bypassed or hidden behind an "amnesic barrier," a subordinate system takes over control of behavior and consequently behavior is dissociated in varying degrees from the intents and plans that go along with executive control. These occurrences are usually benign, even necessary, like the executive's relaxation of control over well-learned activities such as driving, but the same essential process occurs in automatic writing, sleep, hypnotism and multiple personality; that is, subordinate systems operate independently from (are dissociated from) executive control and, although usually interactive, may become isolated from each other as well.

In hypnosis the primary hypnotic component and the hidden observer can then be seen as two subordinate systems isolated from conscious awareness and also isolated in varying degrees from each other. We do not yet know how significant the hidden-observer effect will be for increasing our understanding of multiple personality disorders, or if it will increase our understanding at all. According to Horevitz (1994), Hilgard cautioned that his investigations were "much too limited in scope to use when drawing conclusions about MPD" (p. 446). Kenneth Bowers's theory of dissociated control is similar to Hilgard's neodissociationist theory in incorporating cognitive psychology's hierarchical model, but he has introduced some important variations as well (Bowers, 1992; Kirsch & Lynn, 1995; Woody & Bowers, 1994).

Toward the end of his career Donald Hebb, the distinguished neuropsychologist, became unusually intrigued by Hilgard's work. Hebb (1978) believed that his own cell-assembly theory provided a physiological substratum for the hidden observer phenomenon, "the two consciousnesses being considered as two groups of assemblies temporarily cohering in separate systems" (p. 547). For Hebb, cognitive theories were incomplete if they could not account for the kinds of phenomena that Hilgard described.

Classical and modern dissociation theories have been challenged by several alternative theories, the most fully developed of which is the social-psychological (sociocognitive, cognitive-behavioral) concept identified with Theodore Sarbin, Theodore Barber, William Coe, and represented in a large corpus of published papers by the late Nicholas P. Spanos and his colleagues. As they see it, hypnosis and multiple personality are products of externally driven role playing that takes place outside of awareness, rather than altered states imposed from within. "Multiple identities are rule-governed social constructions, which are created, legitimated, maintained, and altered through social interaction" (Spanos & Burgess, 1994, p. 137). Among his final published papers Spanos (1994) provided a comprehensive description of the sociocognitive interpretation of multiple personality.[26]

---

[26]For a neodissociative critique of Spanos's research as it has been applied to an understanding of hypnosis, along with divergent results supporting the neodissociative model, see Bowers and Davidson (1991).

The role-playing perspective is particularly provocative when one considers that, as already noted, altered states of consciousness are expressed differently in different cultures. Suryani and Jensen (1993) compared trance states in Bali with multiple personality in the United States. In Bali, trance and the ritual possession that occurs during a trance (trance-possession) are commonplace; they are part of normal life and are usually a positive experience because the person is said to be possessed by good spirits. Occasionally, however, possession by evil spirits produces unhappy consequences. Unlike most Westerners, the Balinese have no concern about being controlled; their lives "have in the main been controlled by their families, their ancestors, and the supernatural" (p. 173). Other differences were found. Balinese trance-possession usually occurs in a social, religious setting where the person is typically possessed by God, a god, or a spirit, although in some instances possession is by an internally driven power. "The most salient characteristic of trance-possession in the Balinese is the meaning it has for the culture" (p. 172). In Bali, personal identity is likely to be fused with a broader cultural, natural and spiritual world and the possession is driven by positive cultural approval. In the United States, on the other hand, the unitary personality is prized and an alternate persona or personas, perceived as the result of negative internal stress, is a much more private affair. Of course spiritism and other supernatural phenomena play a role in Western religions, but for most people they are not so pervasive a part of everyday existence as they are in Bali.

But there are also many similarities in the way that altered states of consciousness are expressed in the two cultures. "In the Balinese, most trancers experience the core 'symptoms' of dissociative disorders in the West" (Suryani & Jensen, p. 172). Suryani and Jensen list 36 similarities between multiple personality disorder and trance-possession in Bali.[27] "The psychobiological mechanism and the phenomenology of MPD and possession both in the West and in Bali are similar if not the same; MPD alters are viewed as psychological entities equivalent to Balinese possessions.... [In both] some other entity or part of the self that to them has a real existence takes over" (pp. 219–220).

Instances of possession in the United States take many forms, including mediums who act as channels for spirits of the dead, people who are

---

[27]After pointing out the ubiquitous nature of dissociation, they mention that other possible universals include psychic or parapsychological processes such as "clairvoyance, ESP, the ability to divine, predict, or know aspects of a person's life and problems without having heard of them" (Suryani & Jensen, 1993, p. 174). A generous interpretation of this uncritical proposal of paranormal explanations (dispensed in a scholarly book published by Oxford University Press) is that it reflects the senior author's upbringing in a society where the supernatural and parapsychological are indigenous. Eight pages earlier they had written: "Suryani feels that by using her psychic abilities it is possible to determine if her patients have black magic; it is not necessary for her to use any specific ritual or diagnostic techniques, as most traditional healers do" (p. 166).

possessed by a satanic presence that must be exorcised, and ritual expressions in isolated sects such as the Shakers. These and other forms of possession, however, are not a normal constituent of the larger culture as they are in Bali. On the other hand, multiple personality disorder does not exist in Bali, at least in the form that we know it. Suryani and Jensen suggest that this is because child abuse and neglect are so rare. In the end, they propose a new theory of multiple personality disorder, in which it is redefined as "self-hypnosis or trance with a possession process" (p. 232). By this definition, possession becomes an integral part of the major dissociations that occur in both cultures.

A Proposed Rapprochement

If we can generalize a principle from the dissociative expressions of two very different cultures, Bali and the United States—a reasonable extrapolation in view of the fact that the possession experiences of a great many non-Western cultures are similar in many ways to those of the Balinese (Kirmayer, 1994; Krippner, 1994)—the larger meaning to be drawn from cultural comparisons is that similarities represent the underlying, universal nature of dissociation and altered states of consciousness. Differences in how these dissociations are expressed stem from the influence of culture and/or the personality structures of the members of the disparate ethnic groups: unitary personality structures in Westerners compared with fragmented personality structures (in which supernatural elements are an important part) in cultures like the Balinese (see also Lewis-Fernández, 1994).

This general viewpoint provides a rapprochement between the neodissociation and sociocognitive perspectives. Even Spanos agreed that patients are not for the most part consciously fabricating their alternate personalities. Evidence for role playing does "not mean that multiple personality patients simply fabricate their retrospective reports out of whole cloth, or that they are necessarily dishonest or insincere when they provide such reports" (Spanos, Weekes, Menary, & Bertrand, 1986, p. 310). Even more relevant was his acknowledgment, when discussing the origins of hypnosis, that many processes take place outside of awareness.

> It is now generally accepted by investigators in cognitive and social psychology that a great deal of information processing occurs outside of awareness; that people are unable to specify the most important variables that determine their behavior; and that the causal attributions people do develop to explain behavior are often inaccurate and reflect cultural convention rather than accurate information. (Spanos & Chaves, 1991, p. 70)

Spanos and Chaves did not dispute the insistence of neodissociation theorists that processes about which people are unaware (that is, unconscious) are important; they claimed only that "notions of unconscious processing and misattribution are not inconsistent with the [sociocognitive] concept of goal-directed action" (p. 70; see also Kirsch & Lynn, 1995). They proposed that combining concepts of information processing outside awareness with such concepts as misattribution, self-deception and other mechanisms used by sociocognitivists might "allow for some rapprochement between neodissociation and sociocognitive theorists" (p. 71). But without a role for dissociation, which sociocognitivists spurn, how can there be a rapprochement with neo*dissociationists*? By insisting on a crucial role for dissociation my suggested rapprochement is quite different than theirs.

But we need not enter more deeply into the voluminous literature of this simmering controversy. For present purposes it is important simply to note the general agreement by both sides that people experiencing these phenomena are not faking and that unconscious processes exist. As for dissociation, I think that once you concede that involuntary processes exist you must also concede that dissociation exists. They are both natural processes and everything that can be said about unconscious processes applies to the concept of dissociation; in fact, dissociation is one kind of unconscious process. The two are inseparable, a result—as I have proposed—of the adaptation during evolution of an innate, subconscious capacity that supplements our limited capacity to consciously process information and to physically perform routine operations.

If, as sociocognitivists insist, multiple personality and related phenomena are *externally* driven, they nevertheless have a convenient *internal* mechanism—the capacity for dissociation—to attach to. The phenomena reviewed in Chapter 4, along with facilitated communication, are excellent examples of events produced by people who for the most part are not frauds. They illustrate too the operation of unconscious and dissociated (in sum, secondary) processes. A strong critic of the diagnosis of multiple personality disorder—who says, "It is likely that MPD never occurs as a spontaneous persistent natural event in adults (Merskey, 1992, p. 337)—nevertheless had this to say about dissociation: "In 89 cases of classic dissociative or conversion disorder ... I encountered no MPD.... One patient dissociated and talked to herself in a detached fashion. In that instance the genesis of MPD was carefully avoided" (p. 328). In other words, dissociations occur; what you do with them and what you call them are personal matters.

All humans habitually dissociate or they could not function. Exceptional dissociations also occur, although there are large individual differences in susceptibility to these more surprising manifestations. The behavior of facilitators during facilitated communication is an excellent example of minor, nonpathological dissociation. It is a form of dissociation that touches, however wispily, the deeper dissociation of multiple personality disorder. The large variability in facilitators illustrates the role played by individual differences. Not everyone can be a facilitator, for not everyone succeeds in producing coherent communication from a partner. "Social construction" is fundamental in facilitated communication as it often is in multiple personality: Facilitators are expected to produce communication in their retarded and autistic partners and suggestible facilitators will comply, using whatever mental mechanisms they have at their disposal.

Secondary processes, by whatever name, exist. They are self-organizing processes that can influence, accompany, or even displace currently primary conscious processes and, most important in the present context, can manifest themselves via such involuntary muscle movements as automatic writing and automatic speech. I have called them *smart* because they act in an organized fashion for discernible ends. It is no great inferential leap to suggest that during facilitated communication the facilitator is writing automatically (a form of dissociation) and that consequently, in selected instances, emotionally charged, personally meaningful unconscious content can manifest itself in what is written. There is no need for an alternate personality; in facilitated communication the second persona can be played by the client.

Sadly, the founder and disseminators of facilitated communication created a fertile breeding ground for automatic writing in which a ventriloquist communicates through a live mannequin who cannot speak out in denial. If we were asked to design conditions in which individuals could unwittingly release inner material of which they were unaware or which they would not have released under ordinary circumstances, we could do no better than invent facilitated communication, an environment that produces automatic writing that is "hidden" because the real writers cannot (in their mind and in the mind of many others) be held responsible for it.

WHY ARE THERE ACCUSATIONS OF SEXUAL ABUSE?

As pointed out in Chapter 1, anyone familiar with the laws of probability understands that some of the sexual abuse charges occurring during facilitated communication will be corroborated because of the outrageous fact that there are many instances of mentally disabled individuals being sexually abused. But in most instances the specific accusations are false.

On February 12, 1994 *The New York Times* published an article about a 14-year-old girl who was severely retarded and autistic. She had facilitated in lewd language that her father had repeatedly sexually abused her and that her mother had ignored the abuse.[28] She later claimed to have been

---

[28]On April 29, 1994, this family appeared on the television program 20/20, in a segment titled "Where Do the Words Come From?" The young girl with autism had two facilitators whose later reactions to facilitated communication were very different. One continued her adherance and became intensely emotionally involved with the daughter, whereas the other, Janyce Boynton, courageously renounced it and helped form a support group for former facilitators (see Chapter 7).

abused by a grandfather, who had actually died before she ever saw him, and by an uncle living across the country. When another facilitator was brought in the girl typed a new set of allegations, which maintained that she had been molested hundreds of times. She was taken from her parents, but after 10 months the family court ruled that the evidence derived from facilitated communication was invalid and she was returned to her family. The lawyer for the parents argued that the sexual allegations were the fantasies of the woman who occasionally cared for the daughter and facilitated with her, a woman who was a college graduate and worked as an aide—as did the mother—at the special school the daughter attended. According to the mother, the woman had "once confided that she had been sexually abused as a child" (Berger, 1994, p. 27). The parents felt they should have been suspicious of the intensity of her attentiveness: The woman frequently visited their daughter when the girl moved to a new facility and even wrote poems about her deep love for her:

I am happy to watch you grow
Feeling torn between rejoicing
In your new-found power to express
And my fear
That I might find you don't love me after all
You just tolerated me
Because you had no choice. (Quoted by Berger, 1994, p. 27)

Although professional and public groups should require greater discernment from certain mental health workers and educators, as well as a more questioning and skeptical attitude toward the recurrent selling of new panaceas, it is unfair to label as emotionally disturbed all facilitators who, through their partners, have falsely accused others of sexual abuse. During training facilitators are told to expect their students to raise charges of sexual abuse, and many facilitators may be unconsciously fulfilling that prophecy. Gina Green (1995) noted that suggestions of sexual abuse permeate our culture, and some facilitators may be eager to rescue disabled people from mistreatment. Finally, simple, direct motives of revenge, power and attention must drive some facilitators, who literally have in their hands a potent instrument for controlling others, for exacting revenge on parents and colleagues, for drawing attention to themselves, and for social power they never before experienced.

But that does not mean that most of those who raise charges of sexual abuse in lurid detail do not have an emotional problem. Considering the possibility that a stronger than ordinary tendency to dissociate can result from abuse in childhood (a possibility challenged by Spanos, 1994), any facilitators who had been abused as children are presented with a situation ready made for creating what might be called a "pseudo-alter" in the guise of the person being facilitated. In this way these faciitators can release conflicting and troubling feelings that resulted from their own abuse and at the same time finally gain revenge on their (substitute) abuser.

The sociocognitive perspective, closely related to behaviorism but not burdened by Skinnerian precepts of response–reward contingencies, emphasizes the impact of external, cultural forces. Neodissociationism, on the other hand, stresses internal processes. The position taken here is that dissociation is an innate attribute of the human animal and that both external experiences and internal dynamics determine the form that a dissociation will take, whether it be a trance state in Bali, a multiple personality, or a bizarre sexual message written automatically during facilitated communication. Facilitators buy into the social world of facilitated communication, with all its social pressures, and while facilitating they exhibit automatic writing, a form of dissociation. Grievous consequences can result when social pressures produce the opportunity for the dissociated expression of private conflicts that are disguised by unconscious processes.

7

Confirming False Beliefs

Though we especially prize reason, it is just one adaptive form mental processes can take.

—Johnston (1988, p. 89)

When Sanford (1914b) was reviewing the books and articles on clever horses he made an observation that must have occurred to many readers: that an understanding of evolution precludes the possibility of authentic human behavior in horses.

> But this [the evolution of animal intelligence] is a very different matter from saying that the minds of horses, which are now fitted to a horse body and a horse life and have back of them untold ages of horse development can by a few months' teaching be transformed into tolerable likeness to the mind of man which is associated with a human body, has been moulded [sic] to a human environment and has had a human evolutionary history. (pp. 29–30)

The phenomenon that requires explanation is not the intelligence of horses; rather, it is the astonishing fact that intelligent people believed that horses could be taught to perform complex mathematics and elaborate spelling. If Sanford could return to us today he would no doubt marvel at our scientific and technological advances but despair at our continuing follies. We would ask him what qualities the human mind had incorporated over its long evolutionary journey that imbued it with logic enough to reach the moon at the same time that it is vulnerable enough to believe in utter nonsense. Perhaps he would agree with Robyn Dawes (1976) that we are confusing "cumulative technological advances" with the limited power of a single mind. "The fact that a lot of us with the aid of the printing press, telephone, and verbal communication can create an H bomb does not mean that any of us singly can think very straight" (p. 10). And Sanford might join others in suggesting that the adaptive strategy of searching for causes—so useful during evolutionary development—backfires when the need to believe in a favorite explanation overrides everything else.[29] So powerful is this need to find causes, joined by the need to be right, that it tenaciously resists disconfirmation. The popularity of facilitated communication adds weight to this hypothesis and provides further evidence for the presence of a mechanism, the self-fulfilling prophecy, that serves to reinforce faulty assumptions.

THE SELF-FULFILLING PROPHECY

In his Introduction to the 1965 edition of Pfungst's (1911/1965) book, Robert Rosenthal mentioned Merton's (1948) concept of the self-fulfilling prophecy as relevant for understanding that Clever Hans "performed accurately only for those who unconsciously believed he could" (p. xvii). Travis Thompson's (1994) scathing review of Biklen's *Communication Unbound* (to which Biklen, 1995, responded) also alluded to the self-fulfilling prophecy. In introducing the term, sociologist Robert K. Merton had suggested that many of the finest minds in human history have variously described a principle of human behavior that W. I. Thomas had summed up succinctly: "If men define situations as real, they are real in their consequences" (quoted in Merton, 1948, p. 193). For example, when the public defines a situation by making prophecies or predictions about it, these become part of the situation and consequently affect its outcome; "a rumor of insolvency, once believed by enough depositors, would result in the insolvency of the bank.... The self-fulfilling prophecy is, in the beginning, a *false* definition of the situation evoking a new behavior which makes the originally false conception come *true*.... [and] the prophet will cite the actual course of events as proof that he was right from the very beginning" (pp. 194–195).

Merton applied this concept primarily to ethnic and racial conflicts but one can see why it has been mentioned in relation to Clever Hans and facilitated communication. Questioners who falsely believe that horses can spell—as well as facilitators who falsely believe that their charges have remarkable hidden capacities—see their beliefs come true by unconsciously making the muscle movements required to produce the desired outcome. The circle of self-fulfilling prophecies can be broken by abandoning the basic assumptions, but—as we have seen—these are not easily surrendered. "In the social realm, no more than in the psychological realm, do false ideas

---

[29]The study of attributing causes is a major area of research in social psychology, under the general term, logically enough, of "attribution theory" (see, e.g., Försterling, 1988; Kelley & Michela, 1980). Most relevant for us are studies of irrational attributions of causality (e.g., Gilovich, 1991; L. Ross, 1977).

quietly vanish when confronted with the truth" (Merton, 1948, p. 197). To break the circle requires, according to Merton, "deliberate institutional controls" (p. 210).[30]

The concept of the self-fulfilling prophecy generated a voluminous body of research, much of it under the term "expectancy confirmation effects" (Darley & Fazio, 1980; Hilton, Darley, & Fleming, 1989), which was used interchangeably with "interpersonal expectancy effects" and "interpersonal (or interorganism) self-fulfilling prophecy" (Rosenthal & Rubin, 1978, p. 377). In one incongruous episode, however, an experimenter—a principal player in this movement—and his co-author were unwittingly led astray by *their* expectancies in a study of the influence of *teachers'* expectancies. In the study (Rosenthal & Jacobson, 1968), experimenters gave teachers the names of students who were expected to spurt academically and intellectually (although in fact the students were picked at random). Unfortunately, the teachers' expectancies could hardly have influenced the students since most of the teachers forgot which students were expected to be "spurters" (Snow, 1969; see also Thorndike, 1968). Undaunted, the researchers claimed that students' IQs were raised merely by raising teachers' expectations.

Whereas early studies demonstrated that experimenters unwittingly influence their human and animal subjects, later studies examined interpersonal effects outside the experimental situation; that is, how one person's expectancies affect another person. I suggest an extension: facilitated communication as an example of a self-fulfilling prophecy that is *intra*personal. The facilitators' prophecies are fulfilled when they unwittingly affect their own actions through the medium of passive agents (their partners).

COGNITIVE DISSONANCE

The self-fulfilling prophecy is a means of confirming a false belief, but what happens when the disconfirming evidence is overwhelming, as it is in facilitated communication and was with Clever Hans? Why do proponents persist in their beliefs? We can draw some clues from studies of a still more obvious disconfirmation: when an individual or a group predicts that a catastrophic event will occur on a certain date and the date passes without incident. A fascinating field study of the reaction to disconfirmation in just this kind of situation was carried out by the social psychologist Leon Festinger and his colleagues (Festinger, Riecken, & Schacter, 1956).

It began when a local paper carried the announcement by a woman (called Mrs. Keech in the book) claiming that by means of automatic writing

---

[30]Such controls would imply that professional organizations and institutions must announce, as official policy, that facilitated communication is an experimental method only and should not be used as an approved educational clinical procedure. Many organizations have already done this, but unfortunately some government agencies have ignored warnings about, and even supported, facilitated communication.

she had received a message from superior beings on a planet called Clarion. These beings had been visiting the earth and determined that a great flood would occur 3 months hence, on December 21. Festinger, Riecken, and Schacter, along with hired observers, joined Mrs. Keech and other believers, two of whom—a physician and his wife—had been convinced believers in Mrs. Keech's powers for many months before her flood prediction.

During the previous 15 years Mrs. Keech had joined several marginal groups and had become interested in occult phenomena and flying saucers. She had initially experienced automatic writing when, upon awakening one morning, she felt a tingling and numbness in her arm. Without knowing why, she picked up a pencil and pad and her hand began to write. The handwriting, although familiar, wasn't hers; someone was using her hand. She immediately learned that it was her deceased father writing a letter through her to her mother. Although her mother admonished her daughter about such nonsense, Mrs. Keech persisted, enduring many frustrations—the early messages contained incoherent passages and indecipherable words and neologisms—before discovering that other spirits were trying to reach her. As her facility in automatic writing improved she received messages from powerful beings who asked her to share with others the knowledge and information they were imparting. It was in this setting that she received the warning of the flood. A number of people joined her, making major commitments by leaving jobs and spending money to travel to her.

On December 17 Mrs. Keech received a phone call informing her that she would be picked up in her backyard by a flying saucer at 4:00 that afternoon. When no saucer appeared, the group said little about the failure, but then Mrs. Keech received a message informing her that when the group is picked up she needn't return to earth again, which made her weep with joy. Later that day, group members began to offer various explanations for the disconfirmation, settling finally on the rationalization that the incident had served as an alert, a drill for the real thing. Still, they lost one member, their most recent convert.

That night, at about midnight, Mrs. Keech received yet another message that a flying saucer was on the way to pick them up. Out they went to the backyard, but again they were disappointed and again they explained away the disconfirmation as a drill. As always, Mrs. Keech later received reassuring messages through automatic writing from the Guardians on the planet Clarion, and a visit by five young men the following evening was interpreted by the group as contact by spacemen in disguise. Two more members left the group, never to return; three others wavered but stayed.

Parenthetically, it should be noted that one of the believers, who could not always be with the group, held a doctorate in "one of the rigorous natural sciences" (Festinger et al., 1956, p. 90), another instance of an accomplished person believing in nonsense (see Chapter 4). Biklen (1993) often cites the supporting letters of a Nobel Prize winner in physics who, with his wife, had independently discovered how to facilitate their autistic son's pointing and typing:

> The tape [of the son's performance] showed his typing, usually with seemingly little attention on his part to the keyboard. "He does it often without looking at the keyboard" … [his mother] noted. "Don't ask me how he does it but he does." She assumed that he might be able to do it as a result of his seemingly exceptional peripheral vision. (pp. 95–96)

The emotional need to believe in their son's performance is a strong catalyst, but intelligence and scientific training do not prevent people from having irrational beliefs.

Final messages of instruction were received on December 20 and the group sat expectantly in the living room waiting to be evacuated by the Guardians at midnight, well before the predicted time of the cataclysmic flood, scheduled for 7:00 a.m. Shortly after midnight, as they awaited the cars that were to take them to the saucers, another message was received, this time *spoken* by the voice of the Creator through a group member who periodically had served as an alternative channel for messages. The message assured them that plans were intact but there was a slight delay. The delay lengthened and the group became distraught. At about 4:30 a.m. Mrs. Keech read a message that the group, "sitting all night long, had spread so much light that God had saved the world from destruction" (Festinger et al., 1956, p. 169). An additional message told the group to release this "Christmas Message" to the newspapers. This was too much for one participant who departed, permanently.

What happened then, and subsequently, is at the heart of the study. For the first time, Mrs. Keech called a newspaper. The group followed up by calling other newspapers and the major wire services. The voice of the Creator announced that the formerly secret tape recordings (made through an earthly agent, of course) should be made public, and that the Creator would make special new tapes. Whereas before the disconfirmation the group did not actively proselytize, they now became very active in spreading the word. During the rest of the day, "the group sought frantically to convince the world of their beliefs" (Festinger et al., 1956, p. 174), and the media gave them ample opportunity. Mrs. Keech, meanwhile, grasped at anything that would counteract the disappointment, and was even convinced that a phone call she received the evening of December 21 was from a spaceman. She continued to receive messages. Any natural disaster, even those that had occurred before the predicted date, was somehow incorporated into their belief system.

Although the group was disorganized and looked everywhere for guidance—seeing disguised spacemen at every opportunity— even the failure of subsequent prophecies did not discourage the most dedicated believers. On the other hand, those who were not deeply committed were able to discard their beliefs instead of increasing their proselytizing. When the prophecy failed, the faith of those who were not with the main group began to weaken; even if they had been deeply committed they did not proselytize.

In sum, when the prophecy failed, the core group of dedicated believers did not concede that perhaps they were wrong, that perhaps they were not receiving messages from the Guardians, that it was all a mistake. On the contrary, they not only continued to believe but became newly active in trying to convince others to become believers.

For Festinger, (1957) these events supported and extended his theory of cognitive dissonance, which states that "dissonance, being psychologically uncomfortable, will motivate the person to try to reduce the dissonance and achieve consonance" (p. 3). At the same time, the person will actively avoid any situations and information that are likely to increase the dissonance. Festinger et al. (1956) had posited five conditions, paraphrased below, which lead to increased fervor after disconfirmation.

The first two are associated with the believer's resistance to change:

1. The belief is held with deep conviction and influences the believer's behavior.
2. In general, the more important and irrevocable the actions taken for the belief, the greater the believer's commitment.

The next two exert pressure on the believer to disbelieve:

3. The commitment must be amenable to unequivocal disconfirmation.
4. The undeniable disconfirmatory evidence must be recognized by the believer.

When the first two conditions are pitted against the second two, people face a dilemma that must be resolved. They are, in Festinger's words, experiencing dissonance, which is very stressful and must be reduced. They can either maintain their belief, in which case they must ignore or rationalize the disconfirming evidence, or they can discard their belief, in which case they must admit they were wrong and had wasted energy, time, and resources.

One way to resolve the dissonance is to find new evidence that their beliefs are in fact correct, and one important piece of new evidence is that others have the same beliefs. Consequently it is necessary not only to maintain group support but also to convert others. The fifth condition specifies those circumstances under which believers, when facing disconfirmation, are expected to either discard their beliefs or maintain them with increased fervor:

5. With group support a believer is likely to maintain belief and also to proselytize, whereas an isolated believer is likely to succumb to the disconfirming evidence.

Five years later Hardyck and Braden (1962) added further qualifications based on their experiences with a religious cult that for many years had lived separately from society. The group had recently received a message that it had 6 months to prepare for a nuclear disaster. When the prophecy failed, the group had a rationalization: "They had discovered by looking back over all their messages that it had never been stated that the attack was imminent; they had simply misinterpreted God's purposes" (p. 139). However, unlike the group studied by Festinger et al. (1956), this group did not seek publicity and did not proselytize, even though their fervor, if anything, increased. Hardyck and Braden suggested that they did not proselytize because they were a more closely knit, unquestioning group that had been in existence for a much longer time than the group studied by Festinger et al. They gave each other sufficient support to preclude the need for support from outside the group. Also, they did not experience as much ridicule as did Mrs. Leech's group. Ridicule adds dissonance that can be reduced by persuading those who mock them that the group was right after all. Another condition, then, must be added:

6. For proselytizing to occur, the group must "provide only minimal social support for its members and ... receive ridicule from the outside world" (Hardyck & Braden, 1962, p. 141).

EXPLAINING AWAY THE EVIDENCE

What does dissonance theory predict about the behavior of supporters and proponents of facilitated communication? For one thing, we cannot expect them to curtail their excessive claims, nor should we expect facilitated communication to fade away in the near future despite warning statements from organizations such as the American Academy of Child and Adolescent Psychiatry, the American Academy of Pediatrics, the American Association on Mental Retardation, the American Psychological Association, and the American Speech-Language-Hearing Association. Conditions 1 and 2 of the theory of cognitive dissonance are robustly fulfilled by believers in facilitated communication, and heavily outweigh conditions 3 and 4. Although facilitated communication has been unequivocally disconfirmed, advocates have found numerous rationalizations for the disconfirmations, just as Herr Krall and others did with Clever Hans. Summing up nearly 3 decades of work on dissonance theory, Aronson (1980) remarked that it was now understood that "when an individual is personally involved in a situation wherein he might consider himself to be stupid or immoral, he engages in self-justifying behavior which involves some form of self-persuasion" (p. 21).

In response to the drum beat of negative reports on the validity of facilitated communication, Biklen and Duchan (1994) simply moved the playing field and rewrote the rules. Whereas the "normative" approach views mental retardation as a departure from typical behavor, Biklen and Duchan subscribe to the "competence" view, in which people with mental retardation are considered basically competent. Any discrepancy in their performance compared with other people is perceived as a departure from their natural competence. The replacement of the normative position by the competence position is accompanied by differences in philosophies of science. Whereas the normative approach accepts the traditional "positivist" viewpoint that retardation exists "as an objective fact that is measurable through objective means" (p. 176), the competence approach "views reality as being different depending on one's point of view."

Research within the competence position is "experiential" and

> does not lend itself to quantitative methods.... A competence view lends itself more to a philosophical perspective that sees truth as a matter of interpretation. The aim of the researcher is to take bias as given and to examine how particular interpretations are socially constructed through different frameworks. (Biklen & Duchan, p. 177)

Consequently the debate, as they see it, is not just about who authors the communications and other such mundane matters; rather, it has more to do with the different views of mental retardation and science.

Within the competence-experiential approach, the fact that facilitators may author the messages that are said to come from the students is not a particular matter of concern. "The aim is to understand the facilitated exchange as a highly complex activity in which different messages are negotiated in different ways, with varying degrees of contribution from each of the partners" (p. 178). It's all relative, you see, and "acceptance, confirmation, or validation of the theories will reflect the theorizers' approach to disability and to research" (p. 181).

In commenting on this strange view of science, Whitehurst and Crone (1994) surmise that consumers of facilitated communication are not expending huge amounts of time and effort because of their commitment to this particular belief system and "would certainly be surprised to learn that the world has no objective truths" (p. 194). Perhaps they would. But on the other hand, many parents of facilitated children are content to use any rationale for maintaining a utopian illusion, as indeed are many professionals. Jacobson, Mulick, and Schwartz (1995) have discussed the curious redefinitions of science that allow social theorists, human service advocates and other professionals and paraprofessionals to accept uncritically whatever they wish to be true.

One thing is certain: Additional reports of failure to replicate will simply fall on deaf ears. As far as the leaders of the facilitated communication movement in the United States are concerned, all the negative studies are irrelevent because they spring from an entirely different tradition. Biklen and his cohorts will continue to avoid or rationalize disconfirming evidence, secure within the cocoon of their belief system where mainstream science cannot reach them.

The group support among leaders of facilitated communication, at centers such as the Biklen's Facilitated Communication Institute at Syracuse University, provides powerful reinforcement that acts to resist disconfirmation. When facilitators return to their schools, however, many are more isolated and consequently more vulnerable to disconfirmation. A poignant example of a facilitator's disillusion was given on April 29, 1994, in a segment of the television program *20/20* titled "Where Do the Words Come From?" (which I referred to in footnote 28, p. 157). A speech therapist was facilitating a student with autism who typed graphic descriptions of being sexually abused by her father and brother. The child was taken away from her parents until objective tests indicated that all communication was coming from the facilitator. At first recalcitrant, the facilitator, after a lengthy struggle, eventually accepted the objective findings that she was the source of the communication, and she was devastated. She began to understand that her training had really been indoctrination carried out in a cult-like atmosphere. She apologized to the parents and convinced her school to discontinue facilitated communication. Her subsequent description is especially instructive:

> My belief in FC did not fade quickly. In fact it took over a year for me to fully accept my role in what happened. I received complete copies of those "negative" studies. These articles so closely matched my experiences with FC that I could no longer ignore the fact that the communication was coming from those of us facilitating and not the clients.... The emotional impact of my experiences with FC has been long-term and far-reaching. I soon discovered that FC promoters do not support facilitators who question FC. They have characterized me as a "bad" and "poorly trained" facilitator. Community members assumed that I had something against the family and wanted to know why I was still teaching. The "experts" speculated about my sexual and emotional well being. (Boynton, 1994, p. 4)

Although in this case disconfirmation was convincing, it is unlikely that empirical results alone would have been enough. It was Ms. Boynton's courage and integrity that, after intense soul searching, resolved the dissonance by relinquishing the false belief. This has occurred often enough, and the struggle is devastating enough, to induce many disillusioned facilitators to form a support group,[31] an instance in which loss of support from one group is alleviated by the substitution of another. But such groups are countered by the existence of antithetical support groups formed by facilitators who bolster each other in their loyalty to facilitated communication.

---

[31]Concerned facilitators may contact Janyce L. Boynton, P.O. Box 1343, Ellsworth, ME 04605 or Marian Pitsas, O. D. Heck Developmental Center, Balltown and Consaul Roads, Schenectady, NY 12304. Ms. Pitsas appeared on PBS's *Frontline* television show of October 19, 1993, "Prisoners of Silence," which was also very critical of facilitated communication.

To take the first step into dissonance, facilitators must experience discon-firmation. Unfortunately, they rarely have the opportunity to witness an objective demonstration that might raise doubts about the source of the communication. If doubts are raised, a trip to Syracuse or some other center, or a conference with other facilitators, can dispel them. It takes courage for facilitators to accept the extraordinary fact that they produced words without knowing they were doing it, that they were conversing with themselves, and that they must relinquish the illusion that the autistic or profoundly retarded child was reaching out to them from a hidden world of normal competence. When parents are facilitating, the emotional invest-ment and the wish to believe can be overwhelming.

Based on a number of psychological experiments over the past few decades, the position of some philosophers that human beings are rational creatures, reasoning with competence in everyday affairs, has suffered major damage (reviews of this literature can be found in Gilovich, 1991, and Sutherland, 1992). Inarguably some people some of the time are capable of excellent reasoning, or we could not have planted a flag on the moon, but I think everyone would agree that there is a lot of irrationality out there (in others, of course, not in you and me). A revealing experiment illustrates the remarkable resistance of belief systems (Benassi, Singer, & Reynolds, 1980). Subjects were 189 students enrolled in six introductory psychology classes at the California State University, Long Branch. The experimenters ar-ranged for an amateur magician—bearded, impressively dressed in a pur-ple choir robe and sandals, and adorned with a medallion hanging from his neck—to perform three tricks: blindfold reading, teleportation of ashes, and mental bending of a metal rod. Subjects were partitioned into three groups, each of which watched under three conditions. In the psychic condition the performer was introduced as a psychic, in the weak-magic condition he was introduced as a magician, and in the strong-magic condition the weak-magic instructions were augmented to emphasize that the performer was doing magic tricks. Despite this, 65% of those in the weak-magic condition and 58% of those in the strong magic condition believed the performer was psychic, compared with 77% in the psychic condition. In other words, despite being informed that the performer was a magician doing tricks, more than 60% of these college students refused to believe it. The numbers are even more startling when the undecided subjects are eliminated. This raised to over 70 the percentage of students who, despite being told the performer was a magician, believed he was a psychic. In a subsequent paper Singer and Benassi (1981) commented on their findings:

If the need to maintain an irrational belief outweighs any cost associated with maintaining it, the fact that the belief is not rational or not scientifically supportable does not usually enter the equation. If cognitive dissonance does occur in maintaining an occult belief in spite of scientific debunking, any number of rationalizations ... will serve to reduce the cognitive tension. (pp. 53–54)

An apt description indeed of the behavior of the proponents of facilitated communication and of the believers of the many other phenomena that owe their existence to involuntary muscle movements, suggestion, and a will to believe that is so powerful that it leads people to follow clearly irrational tenets and to exhibit behavior that is often described, as was von Osten's, as self-deceptive.

SELF-DECEPTION

Our fundamental tactic of self-protection, self-control, and self-definition is not spinning webs or building dams, but telling stories, and more particularly concocting and controlling the story we tell others—and ourselves—about who we are. (Dennett, 1991, p. 418)

Human beings are cause seeking, story making, storytelling animals. To explain why we possess these traits requires an examination of their adaptive value during the course of evolution, a shadowy area where different candidates vie for favor and one person's reasonable hypothesis is often as credible as another's. One might propose, for example, that cause seeking is a method of gaining information that allows the members of the species to both avoid danger and gain benefits. Hunters who discovered that it was the wind at their backs that alerted their prey (carried their scent) would increase their success. Turning information into a narrative makes sense of it and is a means of preserving it. Transmitting information by telling stories would likewise be a favored trait for a social animal. For that matter, the present utility of a trait might have nothing to do with its evolutionary origin, as discussed in Chapter 6.

Cause seeking is applied to every event, large or small. The variety of explanations that are generated in order to attribute causes is astonishing, as if it is simply unbearable for anything to remain unexplained without a known cause. This trait has spurred humans to numerous discoveries that have advanced civilization but also to erroneous attributions, exemplified in the myths endemic to every culture as well as in the chimerical solutions to intractable problems. For our ancestors, the sun was driven across the sky by a chariot. For judges in Salem, Massachusetts, strange behavior was valid evidence of witchcraft. The archeological findings of advanced thought and technology by an ancient people must reflect the presence of aliens. A sickness is caused by a voodoo curse. It is God's will.

Sarbin (1981) believed that storytelling, including silent storytelling with the self as principal figure, is central to human conduct. As he saw it, the plot of any narrative has a central theme, and a story is embellished by fictions and by strategically ignored material in order to maintain its theme and make it coherent and orderly, to satisfy the human need to see things as sequential and connected. Stories create order out of chaos at the same time that they are satisfying to the narrator.

Herr von Osten's interior narrative had a story line attributing human qualities to animals, qualities that were for the first time freed by his patient teaching techniques. Unknowingly, involuntary muscle movements served to satisfy and maintain this story line. Involuntary muscle movements created a situation that satisfied von Osten's fondest wish and deepest intellectual convictions. To admit the power of involuntary muscle movements and their role in Hans's performance would be to destroy his deeply held and deeply satisfying narrative, which he could not do. To the outside observer, he was deceiving himself. Yet, strangely, von Osten was aware that gross body movements could control Hans and even demonstrated it.

> He undertook to show us what we already knew—that, when he remained standing perfectly erect, he could elicit no sort of response from Hans. Furthermore, that whenever he continued to bend forward, Hans would always respond incorrectly and with very high numbers.... Mr. von Osten, however, believed this to be a caprice of the horse and at first declared that he would yet be able to eliminate it, but later became resigned to it as an irremediable evil. (Pfungst, 1911/1965, p. 230)

Pfungst was quick to point out that von Osten was nevertheless unaware of the more minute signals, and Pfungst saw no way that von Osten could have discovered them. Indeed, Pfungst did not become aware of *his* own movements until he finally observed their analogue in von Osten. "In fine, everything would indicate that we have here not an intention to deceive the public, but a case of pure self-deception" (Pfungst, 1911/1965, pp. 235–236), which Pfungst attributed to von Osten's pedantic obsession with a single idea combined with his extraordinarily uncritical attitude. Von Osten always met objections by attributing to Hans "certain remarkable qualities, such as extraordinary keenness of hearing and a wonderful power of memory, or again, certain defects, such as moodiness and stubborness" (p. 237). As one example, when the horse repeatedly gave 5 as his response to 2 x 2, von Osten would shrug it off as animal stubbornness. Other difficulties, such as failures when the correct response was the number 1, he simply ignored.

According to Stumpf, when Hans failed the test in which he wore blinders, von Osten was genuinely surprised and was so enraged with the horse that Stumpf and his associates

> finally believed that his views in the matter would be changed beyond doubt. "The gentlemen must admit," he [von Osten] said at the time, "that after seeing the objective success of my efforts at instruction, I was warranted in my belief in the horse's power of independent thought." Nevertheless, upon the following day he was as ardent an exponent of the belief in the horse's intelligence as he ever had been. (Stumpf's Introduction in Pfungst, 1911/1965, pp. 13–14)

From this description it is apparent that immediately after the blinders test von Osten admitted failure, only to return as a firm believer the very next day. As I noted in Chapter 1, he rationalized the experimental results by blaming the experimenters for training the horse to respond to signals (Sanford, 1914b). As he saw it, this placed on him the additional burden of erasing the damage they had done. In this way he deflected a catastrophic blow by changing its meaning, a universal ploy whenever incontrovertible evidence is obtained that would destroy the essence of a personal narrative. Von Osten briefly acknowledged failure but apparently only until the consequences of such a concession overwhelmed him, at which time he found a way out.

But is this self-deception, self-persuasion, or simply wishful thinking? Or are they all the same? Von Osten could not have deceived himself, in the classical definition of the term, unless he *continued* to believe, somewhere in his mind, that the professors were right, that his horse was not intelligent, at the same time that he declared the opposite position. We can never know whether he harbored these contrasting views, just as we cannot know whether the leaders of the facilitated communication movement have an intuition or unconscious acceptance of the validity of the extensive experimental evidence demonstrating that the facilitators are doing the typing. To maintain their belief system they, like von Osten, cannot accept the power of involuntary muscle movement and its role in the facilitators' behavior. The same can be said of dowsers, automatic writers, and believers in the Ouija board. In fact, people can recognize the truth and simultaneously accept the fable simply because the fable is so much more gratifying, like a drug. This must be the case with some of the parents who want to believe that their children are finally speaking to them through facilitated communication.

Proclaiming that von Osten was deceiving himself is a colorful description, but the term self-deception is inherently paradoxical, which apparently makes it a fascinating subject to philosophers (e.g., McLaughlin & Rorty, 1988). That people recognize or sense the truth at the same time that they refuse to acknowledge it is difficult to explain when the mind is seen as a single entity controlled by a monolithic conscious awareness. But if like Charcot, Janet, Binet, and Prince we think it possible that the mind is capable of splitting, of having more than one consciousness—or, as Freud and his followers and many others might say, of having more than one system—then the dilemma disappears. Fingarette (1974), who emphasized the role of defense in self-deception, suggested that the ego (the primary self) defends itself from overwhelming anxiety by forming a rudimentary "nuclear dynamic complex" (p. 93) which the central rational system detaches from itself, thereby defending the ego from the threatening material (like putting into orbit radioactive waste). The longer this complex remains split off, the more disparate it becomes and the more likely it is to remain detached. Although Fingarette goes no farther, this description parallels the dynamic interpretation of dissociation. Indeed, what else is behavior we usually describe as self-deceptive but a (usually) mild form of dissociation?

Davidson (1982) believed that overlapping mental compartments—semi-autonomous structures, as he put it—are necessary to explain certain kinds of irrationality. Another philosopher, Amélie Oksenberg Rorty (1988), considered two major perspectives: on the one hand a single consciousness as a unified rational overseer of all mental operations, and on the other hand "a loosely organized system of relatively autonomous subsystems." From this second perspective, which "seems hospitable to the possibility of self-deception" (p. 12), it is not difficult to explain how an individual "can be aware and not aware of herself as holding contradictory views" so long as "psychological and intellectual activities are performed by loosely conjoined subsystems" and when there is "failure of integration among systems that are standardly coordinated" (p. 21).

Of course self-deception is not always deleterious; it can serve a protective function. Without it everyone might be in a perpetual state of melancholia or in a state of constantly vacillating beliefs. But there are times when self-deception can lead to tragic consequences, as we have seen.

We have barely brushed the surface of the sizable domain of self-deception, seemingly of more interest to philosophers than to psychologists. To go farther would be beyond the scope of this book. In my view, however, even a searching examination of the concept would not add to our understanding of the behavior we have met in our explorations; dissonance theory and concepts from dynamic psychology, such as rationalization, are sufficient to provide some underlying theoretical understanding. Simply put, when humans are locked into a belief system that is rewarding and satisfying to them (for any number of reasons), and to which they have extensively committed themselves, they do not readily accept any assault on the core of their beliefs. They will protect this core by any means at their disposal unless it is more beneficial to release the beliefs than preserve them, or unless they can muster the strength to bear the mental pain that such a renunciation entails. Most important, when a belief system and personal ego are intimately linked, any threat to the belief system is a threat to the ego. Then humans act as though they have two minds: a rational mind dealing with commonplace functions and an irrational mind involved with the belief system.

In merely touching on explorations into self-deception we encounter important attributes—some of which I have discussed in detail—that many philosophers and psychologists find indispensable to explain it: the narrative imperative, the storytelling embellishments and deletions, and dissociative and unconscious processes. These are useful constructs—in my view indispensable—and certainly worth careful consideration by anyone attempting to understand the curious behavior that so often arises in response to a misunderstanding, or lack of understanding, of involuntary muscle movements.

8

Summing Up

We have traveled a considerable distance across time, across space, and across a variety of human (and animal) attributes. From a clever scientist dangling a pendulum in Paris to a clever horse spelling words in a courtyard in Berlin. From a mind-reader in London to a seer writing automatically in Boston. From a poet writing poems on a homemade Ouija board in Stonington, Connecticut, to a dowser obeying a forked stick in the woods of Biddeford, Maine. From a dedicated scientist recording minute muscle movements in a laboratory at the University of Chicago to autistic children who—hands guided by others—write sophisticated messages in a classroom in a suburb of Melbourne, Australia. Side trips have been made: to watch another clever horse, one so very clever that she received messages telepathically; to observe master logicians listening to spirits from dead souls; to travel into the world of dreams and witness hidden lives and multiple personas. Through it all a single phenomenon kept recurring—not in every bit of unusual behavior, certainly, yet so pervasively that it became our key concept: involuntary muscle movements.

Awareness of the control of muscle movement via feedback is necessary in mastering new motor skills, but this awareness is no longer necessary once the skills are mastered. In fact it would be catastrophic if there were continuous consciousness of the control of and feedback from every muscle movement, because the mind would have no room for the vast amount of information to which it must attend. The natural state of living organisms is to be unaware of the control of their own muscle movements.

That does not mean that awareness cannot be reinstated at any time. If we wish, we can attend to our leg movements while walking, and we are certainly aware of muscle movements when we have muscular pain. However, there are a number of circumstances in which individuals are unable to recapture the state of awareness; that is, circumstances in which they cannot (or will not) induce consciousness of control and feedback. The

174

concept of dissociation has been invoked as a companion to involuntary muscle movements.

The evidence is compelling that involuntary movements can serve as an outlet for interactions that we are unaware of, not only for mundane thoughts but also for thoughts that would otherwise be withheld. Driven by a person's will to believe, involuntary muscle movements can be exceedingly dangerous, serving as instruments of a mind we are struggling to understand.

Facilitated communication—the latest example of a particular kind of human folly that has recurred through the ages—cannot be encompassed by a single explanation; involuntary muscle movements are only part of the complex key to understanding. That is why I have moved beyond involuntary muscle movements into such diverse areas as social and interpersonal theory, dissociation, and the role of unconscious processes in human activity. The behavior exhibited by defenders of facilitated communication and by the facilitators themselves should remind us of the complexity of the mind and of the seemingly inexplicable behavior the mind can produce, but it is well to remember that facilitated communication is just one in a long inventory of basically similar phenomena.

As with those related phenomena, facilitated communication is not easily expunged; indeed, it continues to spread like a virus run rampant. The antidote is knowledge, and for involuntary muscle movements and dissociated experiences we have a rich stock of evidence and a storehouse full of knowledge. Because proponents of facilitated communication do not know or choose to ignore this enlightening history, facilitated communication now takes its place alongside the witch trials, magic cures, animal magnetism, and other such phenomena in the long struggle of our species to emerge from the grip of irrationality.

References

Aldridge-Morris, R. (1989). *Multiple personality: An exercise in deception.* Hillsdale, NJ: Lawrence Erlbaum Associates.

American Psychiatric Association. (1994). *Diagnostic and statistical manual of mental disorders* (4th ed.). Washington, DC: Author.

Antrobus, J. S., Antrobus, J. S., & Singer, J. L. (1964). Eye movements during daydreaming, visual imagery, and thought suppression. *Journal of Abnormal and Social Psychology, 69,* 244–252.

Aronson, E. (1980). Persuasion via self-justification: Large commitments for small rewards. In L. Festinger (Ed.), *Retrospections on social psychology* (pp. 3–21). New York: Oxford University Press.

Aserinsky, E., & Kleitman, N. (1953). Regularly occurring periods of ocular motility and concomitant phenomena during sleep. *Science, 118,* 273–274.

B. C. A. (1908). My life as a dissociated personality. *Journal of Abnormal Psychology, 3,* 240–260.

Baladarian, N. J. (1991). Sexual abuse of people with developmental disabilities. *Sexuality and Disabilities, 9,* 323–335.

Barresi, J. (1994). Morton Prince and B. C. A.: A historical footnote on the confrontation between dissociation theory and Freudian psychology in a case of multiple personality. In R. M. Klein & B. K. Doane (Eds.), *Psychological concepts and dissociative disorders* (pp. 85–129). Hillsdale, NJ: Lawrence Erlbaum Associates.

Barrett, W. F. (1881, July 7). Mind-reading versus muscle-reading. *Nature, 24,* 212.

Beard, G. M. (1877). Physiology of mind-reading. *Popular Science Monthly, 10,* 459–473.

Beard, G. M. (1878). Mind-reading by the ear [Letter to the editor]. *Popular Science Monthly, 11,* 362–363.

Bell, C. (Ed.). (1902). *Spiritism, hypnotism and telepathy as involved in the case of Leonora E. Piper and the Society of Psychical Research.* New York: Medico-Legal Journal.

Bemporad, J. R. (1979). Adult recollections of a formerly autistic child. *Journal of Autism and Developmental Disorders, 9,* 179–197.

Benassi, V. A., Singer, B., & Reynolds, C. B. (1980). Occult belief: Seeing is believing. *Journal for the Scientific Study of Religion, 19,* 337–349.

Berger, C. L. (1992, Fall). Experiences with facilitated communication: The breakthrough. *The Advocate: Newsletter of the Autism Society of America,* pp. 17–18.

Berger, J. (1994, February 12). Shattering the silence of autism. *The New York Times,* pp. 21, 27.

Berry, D. C. (1994). A step too far? *Behavioral & Brain Sciences, 17,* 397–398.

Bikel, O., & Dretzin, R. (1995, October 24). *Frontline: The search for Satan.* New York: Public Broadcasting Service.

Biklen, D. (1990). Communication unbound: Autism and praxis. *Harvard Educational Review, 60,* 291–314.

Biklen, D. (1992). Autism orthodoxy versus free speech: A reply to Cummins and Prior. *Harvard Educational Review, 62,* 242–256.

Biklen, D. (1993). *Communication unbound: How facilitated communication is challenging traditional views of autism and ability/disability.* New York: Teachers College Press.

Biklen, D. (1995). Response to review of *Communication Unbound. American Journal on Mental Retardation, 99,* 450–451.

Biklen, D., & Duchan, J. F. (1994). "I am intelligent": The social construction of mental retardation. *Journal of the Association for Persons with Severe Handicaps, 19,* 173–184.

Binet, A. (1896). *Alterations of personality* (H. G. Baldwin, Trans.). New York: Appleton. (Original work published 1891)

Binet, A. (1896). *On double consciousness.* Chicago: Open Court. (Not published in French)

Binet, A. (1899). *The psychology of reasoning* (A. G. Whyte, Trans., from the 2nd French ed.). Chicago: Open Court. (French 2nd ed. published 1896)

Bligh, S., & Kupperman, P. (1993). Brief report: Facilitated communication evaluation procedure accepted in a court case. *Journal of Autism and Developmental Disorders. 23,* 553–557.

Bliss, E. L. (1980). Multiple personalities: A report of 14 cases with implications for schizophrenia and hysteria. *Archives of General Psychiatry, 37,* 1388–1397.

Boor, M., & Coons, P. M. (1983). A comprehensive bibliography of literature pertaining to multiple personality. *Psychological Reports, 53,* 295–310.

Boring, E. G. (1950). *A history of experimental psychology* (2nd., rev. ed.). New York: Appleton-Century-Crofts.

Boring, E, G. (1952). The validation of scientific belief. *Proceedings of the American Philosophical Society, 96,* 535–539.

Botash, A. S., Babuts, D., Mitchell, N., O'Hara, M., Lynch, L., & Manuel, J. (1994). Evaluations of children who have disclosed sexual abuse via facilitated communication. *Archives of Pediatric and Adolescent Medicine, 148,* 1282–1287.

Bowers, K. S. (1987). Revisioning the unconscious. *Canadian Psychology, 28,* 93–104.

Bowers, K. S. (1992). Imagination and dissociation in hypnotic responding. *International Journal of Experimental Hypnosis, 40,* 253–275.

Bowers, K. S., & Davidson, T. M. (1991). A neodissociative critique of Spanos's social-psychological model of hypnosis. In S. J. Lynn & J. W. Rhue (Eds.), *Theories of hypnosis: Current models and perspectives* (pp. 105–143). New York: Guilford.

Bowers, K. S., Farvolden, P., & Mermigis, L. (1995). Intuitive antecedents of insight. In S. M. Smith, T. B. Ward, & R. A. Finke (Eds.), *The creative cognition approach* (pp. 27–51). Cambridge, MA: MIT Press.

Boynton, J. L. (1994, Summer/Fall). Personal thoughts from someone who's been there—Experiences with facilitated communication. *The IARET Newsletter,* 2–4.

Bozzuto, J. C. (1975). Cinematic neurosis following "The Exorcist": Report of four cases. *Journal of Nervous and Mental Disease, 161,* 43–48.

Brown, Chip. (1995, July 30). The experiments of Dr. Oz. *The New York Times Magazine,* pp. 20–23.

Brown, Christy. (1970). *Down all the days.* Greenwich, CT: Fawcett.

Burkhardt, F., & Bowers, F. (1986). *The works of William James: Essays in psychical research.* Cambridge, MA: Harvard University Press.

By a personality (B) claiming to be co-conscious. (1908–1909). An introspective analysis of co-conscious life: (My life as a dissociated personality). *Journal of Abnormal Psychology, 3,* 311–334.

Campbell, J. L., & Hall, T. H. (1968). *Strange things.* London: Routledge & Kegan Paul.

Carlson, E. T. (1981). The history of multiple personality in the United States: I. The beginnings. *American Journal of Psychiatry, 138,* 666–668.

Carlson, E. T. (1984). The history of multiple personality in the United States: Mary Reynolds and her subsequent reputation. *Bulletin of the History of Medicine, 58,* 72–82.

Carpenter, W. B. (1852). On the influence of suggestion in modifying and directing muscular movement, independently of volition. *Proceedings of the Royal Institution, 1,* 147–156.

Cattell, J. M. (1896). Psychical research. *Psychological Review, 3,* 582–583.

Ceci, S. J., & Loftus, E. F. (1994). "Memory work": A royal road to false memories? *Applied Cognitive Psychology, 8,* 351–364.

Cesaroni, L., & Garber, M. (1991). Exploring the experience of autism through firsthand accounts. *Journal of Autism and Developmental Disorders, 21,* 303–312.

Chevreul, M-E. (1833). Lettre à M. Ampère sur une classe particulière de mouvements musculaires [Letter to Mr. Ampere on a particular class of muscular movements]. *Revue des Deux Mondes, 2,* 249–257.

Chomsky, N. (1965). *Aspects of a theory of syntax.* Cambridge, MA: MIT Press.

Christopher, M. (1970). *ESP, seers & psychics.* New York: Crowell.

Coon, D. J. (1992). Testing the limits of sense and science: American experimental psychologists combat spiritualism, 1880–1920. *American Psychologist, 47,* 143–160.

Coons, P. M., Bownan, E. S., Kluft, R. P., & Milstein, V. (1991). The cross-cultural occurrence of MPD: Additional cases from a recent survey. *Dissociation, 4,* 124–128.

Costa, A. B. (1962). *Michel Eugene Chevreul: Pioneer of organic chemistry.* Madison, WI: Department of History, University of Wisconsin.

Crossley, R. (1994). *Facilitated communication training.* New York: Teachers College Press.

Crossley, R., & McDonald, A. (1980). *Annie's coming out.* New York: Penguin.

Cummins, R. A., & Prior, M. P. (1992). Autism and facilitated communication: A response to Biklen. *Harvard Educational Review, 62,* 228–241.

Damgaard, J., Van Benschoten, S., & Fagan, J. (1985). An updated bibliography of literature pertaining to multiple personality. *Psychological Reports, 57,* 131–137.

Darley, J. M., & Fazio, R. H. (1980). Expectancy confirmation processes arising in the social interaction sequence. *American Psychologist, 35,* 867–881.

Daubert v. Dow Pharmacueticals, 61 USLW 4805 (June 28, 1993).

Davidson, D. (1982). Paradoxes of irrationality. In R. Wollheim & J. Hopkins (Eds.), *Philosophical essays on Freud* (pp. 289–305). Cambridge, UK: Cambridge University Press.

Dawes, R. M. (1976). Shallow psychology. In J. S. Carroll & J. W. Payne (Eds.), *Cognition and social behavior* (pp. 3–11). Hillsdale, NJ: Lawrence Erlbaum Associates.

Dement, W., & Kleitman, N. (1957). The relation of eye movements during sleep to dream activity: An objective method for the study of dreaming. *Journal of Experimental Psychology, 53,* 339–346.

Dennett, D. C. (1991). *Consciousness explained.* Boston: Little, Brown & Co.

Dessoir, M. (1886). Experiments in muscle-reading and thought-transference. *Society for Psychical Research, 4,* 111–126.

Dillon, K. M. (1993). Facilitated communication, autism, and Ouija. *Skeptical Inquirer, 17,* 281–287.

Dillon, K. M., Fenlason, J. E., & Vogel, D. J. (1944). Belief in and use of a questionable technique, facilitated communication, for children with autism. *Psychological Reports, 75,* 459–464.

Donnellan, A. M. (1996a). [Review of the book *Facilitated communication: The clinical and social phenomenon*]. *American Journal on Mental Retardation, 100,* 432–435.

Donnellan, A. M. (1996b). A comment on Spitz's comment. *American Journal on Mental Retardation, 101,* 100–103.

Downey, J. E. (1908). Automatic phenomena of muscle–reading. *Journal of Philosophy, Psychology, and Scientific Methods, 5,* 650–658.

Downey, J. E. (1909). Muscle-reading: A method of investigating involuntary movements and mental types. *Psychological Review, 16,* 257–301.

Downey, J. E., & Anderson, J. E. (1915). Automatic writing. *American Journal of Psychology, 26,* 161–195.

Doyle, A. C. (1930). *The edge of the unknown.* New York: Putnam's Sons.

Eagle, M. N. (1987). The psychoanalytic and the cognitive unconscious. In R. Stern (Ed.), *Theories of the unconscious and theories of the self* (pp. 155–189). Hillsdale, NJ: The Analytic Press.

Eberle, P., & Eberle, S. (1993). *The abuse of innocence: The McMartin preschool trial.* Buffalo, NY: Prometheus.

Einstein, A. (1970). Autobiographical notes. In P. A. Schilpp (Ed.), *Albert Einstein: Philosopher-scientist* (3rd ed., pp. 2–95). La Salle, IL: Open Court. (This chapter translated by P. A. Schilpp)

Electro-biology and mesmerism. (1853). *Quarterly Review, 93,* 501–557.

Ellenberger, H. F. (1970). *The discovery of the unconscious: The history and evolution of dynamic psychiatry.* New York: Basic Books.

Epstein, S. (1994). Integration of the cognitive and psychodynamic unconscious. *American Psychologist, 49,* 709–724.

Erdelyi, M. H. (1994). Dissociation, defense, and the unconscious. In D. Spiegel (Ed.), *Dissociation: Culture, mind, and body* (pp. 3–20). Washington, DC: American Psychiatric Press.

Erickson, M. H. (1937). The experimental demonstration of unconscious mentation by automatic writing. *Psychoanalytic Quarterly, 6,* 513–520.

Erickson, M. H., & Kubie, L. S. (1938). The use of automatic drawing in the interpretation and relief of a state of acute obsessional depression. *Psychoanalytic Quarterly, 7,* 443–466.

Erickson, M. H., & Kubie, L. S. (1939). The permanent relief of an obsessional phobia by means of communications with an unsuspected dual personality. *Psychoanalytic Quarterly, 8,* 471–509.

Eysenck, H. J. (1947). *Dimensions of personality.* London: Routledge & Kegan Paul.

Eysenck, H. J., & Furneaux, W. D. (1945). Primary and secondary suggestibility: An experimental and statistical study. *Journal of Experimental Psychology, 35,* 485–503.

Fahy, T. A. (1988). The diagnosis of multiple personality disorder: A critical review. *British Journal of Psychiatry, 153,* 597–606.

Faraday, M. (1853, July 2). Experimental investigation of table-moving. *Athenæum,* No. 1340, 801–803.

Fernald, D. (1993). *The Hans legacy.* Hillsdale, NJ: Lawrence Erlbaum Associates.

Festinger, L. (1957). *A theory of cognitive dissonance.* Evanston, IL: Row, Peterson & Co.

Festinger, L., Riecken, H. W., & Schachter, S. (1956). *When prophecy fails.* Minneapolis: University of Minnesota Press.

Fingarette, H. (1974). Self-deception and the "splitting of the ego." In R. Wollheim (Ed.), *Freud: A collection of critical essays* (pp. 80–96). Garden City, NY: Anchor Books.

Fisher, S., & Greenberg, R. P. (1977). *The scientific credibility of Freud's theories and therapy.* New York: Basic Books.

Fleming, M. Z., Shilony, E., Sanchez, E., Hiam, C. M., & Rodehaver, S. (1995, Spring). The construction of multiple personality: Citations in the popular and clinical press, 1899 to 1988. *History of Psychology Newsletter, 27,* 3–7.

Flournoy, Th. (1963). *From India to the planet Mars: A study of a case of somnambulism with glossolalia* (D. B. Vermilye, Trans.). New Hyde Park, NY: University Books. (Original work published 1900)

Försterling, F. (1988). *Attribution theory in clinical psychology* (J. Harrow, Trans.). New York: Wiley.

Foster, W. S. (1923). Experiments on rod-divining. *Journal of Applied Psychology, 7,* 303–311.

Fraser, G. A. (1994). Dissociative phenomena and disorders: Clinical presentations. In R. M. Klein & B. K. Doane (Eds.), *Psychological concepts and dissociative disorders* (pp. 131–151). Hillsdale, NJ: Lawrence Erlbaum Associates.

Freeborn, H. (1902, June 14). Temporary reminiscence of a long-forgotten language during the delirium of broncho-pneumonia. *The Lancet, 1,* 1685–1686.

Freeland, A., Manchanda, R., Chiu, S., Sharma, V., & Merskey, H. (1993). Four cases of supposed multiple personality: Evidence of unjustified diagnosis. *Canadian Journal of Psychiatry, 38,* 245–247.

Frye v. United States, 293 F. 1013 (D.C. Ct. App. 1923).

Fuller, R. C. (1986). *Americans and the unconscious.* New York: Oxford University Press.

G. Allan Roeher Institute. (1988). *Vulnerable: Sexual abuse and people with an intellectual handicap.* Ontario, Canada: Author.

Gallup, D. (Ed.). (1953). *The flowers of friendship: Letters written to Gertrude Stein.* New York: Alfred A. Knopf.

Galton, F. (1883). *Inquiries into human faculty and its development.* London: Macmillan.

Gardner, M. (1957). *Fads and fallacies in the name of science* (Rev. ed., formerly titled *In the name of science*). New York: Dover.

Gardner, M. (1981). *Science: Good, bad and bogus.* Buffalo, NY: Prometheus.

Gauld, A. (1968). *The founders of psychical research.* New York: Schocken Books.

Gilovich, T. (1991). *How we know what isn't so: The fallibility of human reason in everyday life*. New York: Free Press.

Goddard, H. H. (1926). A case of dual personality. *Journal of Abnormal and Social Psycholgy, 21*, 170–192.

Goldberg, T. E. (1987). On hermetic reading ability. *Journal of Autism and Developmental Disorders, 17*, 29–44.

Gollan, K. (Investigative reporter). (1996, July 29). *Autism—a special report*. Sidney, Australia: Australian Broadcasting Corp. [Radio transcript]. (Available from ABC Radio, The Health Report, GPO Box 9994, Sidney 2001, Australia)

Goode, D. (1994). Defining facilitated communication in and out of existence: The role of science in the facilitated communication controversy. *Mental Retardation, 32*(4), 307–311.

Goodwin, M. S., & Goodwin, T. C. (1969). In a dark mirror. *Mental Hygiene, 53*, 550–563.

Gould, S. J., & Vrba, E. S. (1982). Exaptation—a missing term in the science of form. *Paleobiology, 8*, 4–15.

Grandin, T., & Scariano, M. M. (1986). *Emergence: Labeled autistic*. Novato, CA: Arena.

Green, G. (1992, October). *Facilitated communication: Scientific and ethical issues*. Paper presented to the E. K. Shriver Center University Affiliated Program Service-Related Colloquium series, Waltham, MA.

Green, G. (1994). The quality of the evidence. In H. C. Shane (Ed.), *Facilitated communication: The clinical and social phenomenon* (pp. 157–225). San Diego, CA: Singular Publishing Group.

Green, G. (1995, August). *An ecobehavioral interpretation of the facilitated communication phenomenon*. Paper presented at the meeting of the American Psychological Association, New York City.

Green, G., & Shane, H. C. (1994). Science, reason, and facilitated communication. *Journal of the Association for Persons With Severe Handicaps, 19*, 151–172.

Greenwald, A. G. (1992). New look 3: Unconscious cognition reclaimed. *American Psychologist, 47*, 766–779.

Gurney, E. (1888). Note relating to some of the published experiments in thought-transference. *Proceedings of the Society for Psychical Research, 5*, 269–270.

Gurney, E., Myers, F. W. H., & Podmore, F. (1886). *Phantasms of the living* (Vols. 1–2). London: Trübner.

Hadamard, J. (1954). *The psychology of invention in the mathematical field*. New York: Dover. (Original work published 1949)

Haines, C. R. (1926). The dowser or water-diviner. *Journal of the American Society for Psychical Research, 20*, 611–617.

Hall, G. A. (1993). Facilitator control as automatic behavior: A verbal behavior analysis. *Analysis of Verbal Behavior, 11*, 89–97.

Hall, G. S. (1887). [Combined review of the journal *Proceedings of the English Society for Psychical Research, July, 1882, to May, 1887* and the book *Phantasms of the living*.] *American Journal of Psychology, 1*, 128–146.

Hall, G. S. (1923). *Life and confessions of a psychologist*. New York: D. Appleton.

Hall, T. H. (1964). *The strange case of Edmund Gurney*. London: Gerald Duckworth.

Hardyck, J. A., & Braden, M. (1962). Prophecy fails again: A report on a failure to replicate. *Journal of Abnormal and Social Psychology, 65*, 136–141.

Harriman, P. L. (1942a). The experimental induction of a multiple personality. *Psychiatry, 5*, 179–186.

Harriman, P. L. (1942b). The experimental production of some phenomena related to the multiple personality. *Journal of Abnormal and Social Personality, 37*, 244–255.

Harriman, P. L. (1943). A new approach to multiple personalities. *American Journal of Orthopsychiatry, 13*, 638–643.

Haskew, P., & Donnellan, A. M. (1993). *Emotional maturity and well-being: Psychological lessons of facilitated comunication*. Madison, WI: DRI Press.

Hebb, D. O. (1978). [Review of the book *Divided consciousness: Multiple controls in human thought and action*]. *American Journal of Psychology, 91*, 545–547.

Herman, J. H. (1992). Transmutative and reproductive properties of dreams: Evidence for cortical modulation of brain-stem generators. In J. S. Antrobus & M. Bertini (Eds.), *The neuropsychology of sleep and dreaming* (pp. 251–262). Hillsdale, NJ: Lawrence Erlbaum Associates.

Hermelin, B., & O'Connor, N. (1986). Idiot savant calendrical calculators: Rules and regularities. *Psychological Medicine, 16*, 885–893.

Hilgard, E. R. (1973). A neodissociation interpretation of pain reduction in hypnosis. *Psychological Review, 80*, 396–411.

Hilgard, E. R. (1977). *Divided consciousness: Multiple controls in human thought and action.* New York: Wiley.

Hilgard, E. R. (1991). A neodissociation interpretation of hypnosis. In S. J. Lynn & J. W. Rhue (Eds.), *Theories of hypnosis: Current models and perspectives* (pp. 83–104). New York: Guilford.

Hilgard, E. R. (1992). Divided consciousness and dissociation. *Consciousness and Cognition, 1*, 16–31.

Hilgard, E. R. (1994). Neodissociation theory. In S. J. Lynn & J. W. Rhue (Eds.), *Dissociation: Clinical and theoretical perspectives* (pp. 32–51). New York: Guilford.

Hilton, J. L., Darley, J. M., & Fleming, J. H. (1989) Self-fulfilling prophecies and self-defeating behavior. In R. C. Curtis (Ed.), *Self-defeating behaviors: Experimental research, clinical impressions, and practical implications* (pp. 41–65). New York: Plenum.

Hope, J. (1996, January). Urban New Agers have taken over the art of dowsing. *Smithsonian, 26*, 66–70, 72, 74–75.

Horevitz, R. (1994). Dissociation and multiple personality: Conflicts and controversies. In S. J. Lynn & J. W. Rhue (Eds.), *Dissociation: Clinical and theoretical perspectives* (pp. 434–461). New York: Guilford.

Houdini. (1924). *A magician among the spirits.* New York: Harper & Brothers.

Hudson, A. (1995). Disability and facilitated communication: A critique. In T. H. Ollendick & R. J. Prinz (Eds.), *Advances in clinical child psychology* (Vol. 17, pp. 197–232). New York: Plenum.

Hudson, A., Melita, B., & Arnold, N. (1993). Brief report: A case study assessing facilitated communication. *Journal of Autism and Developmental Disorders, 23*, 165–173.

Hull, C. L. (1933). *Hypnosis and suggestibility: An experimental approach.* New York: D. Appleton-Century.

Hunt, S. (1985). *Ouija: The most dangerous game.* New York: Harper & Row.

Jacobson, E. (1925). Progressive relaxation. *American Journal of Psychology, 36*, 73–87.

Jacobson, E. (1927). Action currents from muscular contractions during conscious processes. *Science, 66*, 403.

Jacobson, E. (1930a). Electrical measurements of neuromuscular states during mental activities: I. Imagination of movement involving skeletal muscle. *American Journal of Physiology, 91*, 567–608.

Jacobson, E. (1930b). Electrical measurements of neuromuscular states during mental activities: III. Visual imagination and recollection. *American Journal of Physiology, 95*, 694–702.

Jacobson, E. (1930c). Electrical measurements of neuromuscular states during mental activities: IV. Evidence of contraction of specific muscles during imagination. *American Journal of Physiology, 95*, 703–712.

Jacobson, E. (1931). Electrical measurements of neuromuscular states during mental activities: VII. Imagination, recollection and abstract thinking involving the speech musculature. *American Journal of Physiology, 97*, 200–209.

Jacobson, E. (1932). Electrophysiology of mental activities. *American Journal of Psychology, 44*, 677–694.

Jacobson, E. (1939). The neurovoltmeter. *American Journal of Psychology, 52*, 620–624.

Jacobson, E. (1940). The direct measurement of nervous and muscular states with the integrating neurovoltmeter (action potential-integrator). *American Journal of Psychiatry, 97*(1), 513–523.

Jacobson, E. (1951). Muscular tension and the estimation of effort. *American Journal of Psychology, 64*, 112–117.

Jacobson, E. (1967). *The biology of emotions: New understanding derived from biological and multidisciplinary investigations; first electrophysiological measurements.* Springfield, IL: Charles C. Thomas.

Jacobson, E. (1973). Electrophysiology of mental activities and introduction to the physiological process of thinking. In F. J. McGuigan & R. A. Schoonover (Eds.), *The psychophysiology of thinking* (pp. 3–31). New York: Academic Press.

Jacobson, E. (1982). *The human mind: A physiological clarification.* Springfield, IL: Charles C. Thomas.

Jacobson, J. W., & Mulick, J. A. (1994). Facilitated communication: Better education through applied ideology. *Journal of Behavioral Education, 4,* 95–107.

Jacobson, J. W., & Mulick, J. A. (1995, summer). Behavior modification & technologies against all odds: Merchandising a fad. *Psychology in Mental Retardation and Developmental Disabilities, 21,* 4–10.

Jacobson, J. W., Mulick, J. A., & Schwartz, A. A. (1995). A history of facilitated communication: Science, pseudoscience, and antiscience science working group on facilitated communication. *American Psychologist, 50,* 750–765.

James, W. (1886). Report of the Committee on Mediumistic Phenomena. *Proceedings of the American Society for Psychical Research, 1,* 102–106.

James, W. (1889). Notes on automatic writing. *Proceedings of the American Society for Psychical Research, 1,* 548–564.

James, W. (1890). A record of observations of certain phenomena of trance. *Proceedings of the Society for Psychical Research, 6,* 651–659.

James, W. (1892, October). What psychical research has accomplished. *Forum, 13,* 727–742.

James, W. (1896a). Address of the president before the Society for Psychical Research. *Science, New Series, 3,* 881–888.

James, W. (1896b). Psychical research. *Psychological Review, 3,* 649–652.

James, W. (1901). Frederic Myers's service to psychology. *Proceedings of the Society for Psychical Research, 17,* 13–23.

James, W. (1909, October). The confidences of a "psychical researcher." *American Magazine, 68,* 580–589.

James, W. (1950) *The principles of psychology* (Vols. 1–2). New York: Dover. (Original work published 1890)

Jastrow, J. (1892). Studies from the laboratory of experimental psychology of the University of Wisconsin—II. *American Journal of Psychology, 4,* 381–428.

Jastrow, J. (1900). *Fact and fable in psychology.* Boston: Houghton, Mifflin.

Jastrow, J. (1937, June). Chevreul as psychologist. *Scientific Monthly,* 487–496.

Johnson, C. (1994). My facilitated communication nightmare. *The IARET Newsletter, 6,* 5–7.

Johnson, H. M. (1911). [Review of the book *Clever Hans (the horse of Mr. von Osten): A contribution to experimental, animal, and human psychology*]. *Journal of Philosophy Psychology and Scientific Methods, 8,* 663–666.

Johnson, H. M. (1912). The talking dog. *Science, 35,* 749–751.

Johnston, M. (1988). Self-deception and the nature of mind. In B. P. McLaughlin & A. O. Rorty (Eds.), *Perspectives on self-deception* (pp. 63–91). Berkeley, CA: University of California Press.

Kelley, H. H., & Michela, J. (1980). Attribution theory and research. *Annual Review of Psychology, 31,* 457–501.

Keyes, D. (1981). *The minds of Billy Milligan.* New York: Bantam Books.

Kihlstrom, J. F. (1994). One hundred years of hysteria. In S. J. Lynn & J. W. Rhue (Eds.), *Dissociation: Clinical and theoretical perspectives* (pp. 365–394). New York: Guilford.

Kihlstrom, J. F. (1995). The rediscovery of the unconscious. In H. Morowitz & J. L. Singer (Eds.), *The mind, the brain, and complex adaptive systems* (pp. 123–143). Reading, MA: Addison-Wesley.

Kirmayer, L. J. (1994). Pacing the void: Social and cultural dimensions of dissociation. In D. Spiegel (Ed.), *Dissociation: Culture, mind, and body* (pp. 91–122). Washington, DC: American Psychiatric Press.

Kirsch, I. & Lynn, S. J. (1995). The altered state of hypnosis: Changes in the theoretical landscape. *American Psychologist, 50,* 846–858.

Kluft, R. P. (1994). Multiple personality disorder: Observations on the etiology, natural history, recognition, and resolution of a long-neglected condition. In R. M. Klein & B. K. Doane

(Eds.), *Psychological concepts and dissociative disorders* (pp. 9–50). Hillsdale, NJ: Lawrence Erlbaum Associates.

Krippner, S. (1994). Cross-cultural treatment perspectives on dissociative disorders. In S. J. Lynn & J. W. Rhue (Eds.), *Dissociation: Clinical and theoretical perspectives* (pp. 338–361). New York: Guilford.

Ladd, G. (1892). Contributions to the psychology of visual dreams. *Mind, 1,* 299–304.

Laycock, T. (1869). *Mind and brain* (2nd ed.). New York: D. Appleton.

Levine, K., Shane, H. C., & Wharton, R. H. (1994). Response to commentaries on risks of facilitated communication. *Mental Retardation, 32*(4), 317–318.

Lewicki, P., Hill, T., & Czyzewska, M. (1992). Nonconscious acquisition of information. *American Psychologist, 47,* 796–801.

Lewis-Fernández, R. (1994). Culture and dissociation: A comparison of *ataque de nervios* among Puerto Ricans and possession syndrome in India. In D. Spiegel (Ed.), *Dissociation: Culture, mind, and body* (pp. 123–167). Washington, DC: American Psychiatric Press.

Loftus, E. F. (1993). The reality of repressed memories. *American Psychologist, 48,* 518–537.

Loftus, E. F., & Klinger, M. R. (1992). Is the unconscious smart or dumb? *American Psychologist, 47,* 761–765.

Logan, E. B. (1994, June 26). Currents: Searching for hidden water the intuitive way. *The New York Times,* p. 41.

Makarushka, M. (1991, October 6). The words they can't say. *The New York Times Magazine,* pp. 33, 36, 70.

Margolin, K. N. (1994). How shall facilitated communication be judged? Facilitated communication and the legal system. In H. C. Shane (Ed.), *Facilitated communication: The clinical and social phenomenon* (pp. 227–257). San Diego, CA: Singular Publishing Group.

Marx, O. M. (1970). Morton Prince and the dissociation of a personality. *Journal of the History of the Behavioral Sciences, 6,* 120–130.

Matter of Luz P., 189 A.D.2d 274, 595 N.Y.S.2d 541 (1993).

Max, L. W. (1934). An experimental study of the motor theory of consciousness: I. Critique of earlier studies. *Journal of General Psychology, 11,* 112–125.

Max, L. W. (1935a). An experimental study of the motor theory of consciousness: II. Method and apparatus. *Journal of General Psychology, 13,* 159–175.

Max, L. W. (1935b). An experimental study of the motor theory of consciousness: III. Action-current responses in deaf-mutes during sleep, sensory stimulation and dreams. *Journal of Comparative Psychology, 19,* 469–486.

Max, L. W. (1937). Experimental study of the motor theory of consciousness: IV. Action-current responses in the deaf during awakening, kinaesthetic imagery and abstract thinking. *Journal of Comparative Psychology, 24,* 301–344.

McCabe, M. P., Cummins, R. A., & Reid, S. B. (1994). An empirical study of the sexual abuse of people with intellectual disability. *Sexuality and Disability, 12,* 297–396.

McCurdy, H. G. (1941). A note on the dissociation of a personality. *Character and Personality, 10,* 35–41.

McDougall, W. (1935). Forward. In J. B. Rhine, *Extra-sensory perception* (pp. xiii–xvii). Boston: Bruce Humphries.

McDougall, W. (1961). William McDougall. In C. Murchison (Ed.), *A history of psychology in autobiography* (Vol. 1, pp. 191–223). New York: Russell & Russell. (Original work published 1930)

McGuigan, F. J. (1971). Covert linguistic behavior in deaf subjects during thinking. *Journal of Comparative and Physiological Psychology, 75,* 417–420.

McGuigan, F. J. (1978). *Cognitive psychophysiology: Principles of covert behavior.* Englewood Cliffs, NJ: Prentice-Hall.

McGuigan, F. J. (1994). *Biological psychology: A cybernetic science.* Englewood Cliffs, NJ: Prentice-Hall.

McGuigan, F. J., & Schoonover, R. A. (Eds.). (1973). *The psychophysiology of thinking: Studies of covert processes.* New York: Academic Press.

McGuigan, F. J., & Tanner, R. G. (1971). Covert oral behavior during conversational and visual dreams. *Psychonomic Science, 23,* 263–264.

McLaughlin, B. P., & Rorty, A. O. (Eds.). (1988). *Perspectives on self-deception*. Berkeley, CA: University of California Press.

Meehan, J. (1904). The Berlin "thinking" horse. *Nature, 70,* 603.

Mellow, J. R. (1974). *Charmed circle: Gertrude Stein & company*. New York: Praeger.

Merrill, J. (1983). *The changing light at Sandover*. New York: Atheneum.

Merrill, J. (1993). *A different person: A memoir*. New York: Alfred A. Knopf.

Merskey, H. (1992). The manufacture of personalities: The production of multiple personality disorder. *British Journal of Psychiatry, 160,* 327–340.

Merton, R. K. (1948). The self-fulfilling prophecy. *Antioch Review, 8,* 193–210.

Meyers, J. E. B. (1994). The tendency of the legal system to distort scientific and clinical innovations: Facilitated communication as a case study. *Child Abuse & Neglect, 18,* 505–513.

Miller, G. A. (1956). The magical number seven, plus or minus two: Some limits on our capacity for processing information. *Psychological Review, 63,* 81–97.

Moore, O. K. (1966). Autotelic responsive environments and exceptional children. In O. J. Harvey (Ed.), *Experience structure and adaptability* (pp. 169–216). New York: Springer.

Moore, R. L. (1977). *In search of white crows: Spiritualism, parapsychology, and American culture*. New York: Oxford University Press.

Mountjoy, P. T., & Lewandowski, A. G. (1984). The dancing horse, a learned pig, and muscle twitches. *Psychological Record, 34,* 25–38.

Mühl, A. M. (1924). Automatic writing combined with crystal gazing as a means of recalling forgotten incidents. *Journal of Abnormal Psychology and Social Psychology, 19,* 264–273.

Mühl, A. M. (1930). *Automatic writing*. Dresden and Leipzig: Theodore Steinkopff.

Mühl, A. M. (1968). Automatic writing and hypnosis. In M. L. LeCron (Ed.), *Experimental hypnosis* (pp. 426–438). New York: Citadel. (Original work published 1948)

Murphy, G., & Ballou, R. O. (Eds.). (1960). *William James on psychical research*. New York: Viking.

Myers, F. W. H. (1884). On a telepathic explanation of some so-called spiritualistic phenomena. *Proceedings of the Society for Psychical Research, 2,* 217–237.

Myers, F. W. H. (1886a). Automatic writing—III: Physiological and pathological analogies. *Proceedings of the Society for Psychical Research, 4,* 209–261.

Myers, F. W. H. (1886b). Human personality in the light of hypnotic suggestion. *Proceedings of the Society for Psychical Research, 4,* 1–24.

Myers, F. W. H. (1889). Automatic writing—IV: The dæmon of Socrates. *Proceedings of the Society for Psychical Research, 5,* 522–547.

Needham, D. M. (1971). *Machina carnis: The biochemistry of muscular contraction in its historical development*. Cambridge, UK: Cambridge University Press.

Nemiah, J. C. (1984). The unconscious and psychopathology. In K. S. Bowers & D. Meichenbaum (Eds.), *The unconscious reconsidered* (pp. 49–87). New York: Wiley.

Nieves, E. (1993, March 30). Woman upheld in abuse case feels vindicated. *The New York Times,* pp. B1, B4.

Nieves, E. (1994, December 3). After 10 years, prosecutors drop charges of sex abuse. *The New York Times,* pp. 25, 29.

Nisbett, R. E., & Wilson, T. D. (1977). Telling more than we can know: Verbal reports on mental processes. *Psychological Review, 84,* 231–259.

Novikova, L. A. (1961). Electrophysiological investigation of speech (H. Asher, Trans.). In N. O'Connor (Ed.), *Recent Soviet psychology* (pp. 210–226). New York: Liveright.

Ofshe, R. J. (1992). Inadvertent hypnosis during interrogation: False confession due to dissociative state; mis-identified multiple personality and the Satanic cult hypothesis. *International Journal of Clinical and Experimental Hypnosis, 40,* 125–155.

Oppenheim, R. C. (1974). *Effective teaching methods for autistic children*. Springfield, IL: Charles C. Thomas.

Palfreman, J. (1994). The Australian origins of facilitated communication. In H. C. Shane (Ed.), *Facilitated communication: The clinical and social phenomenon* (pp. 33–56). San Diego, CA: Singular Publishing Group.

Perry, C., & Laurence, J.-R. (1984). Mental processing outside of awareness: The contributions of Freud and Janet. In K. S. Bowers & D. Meichenbaum (Eds.), *The unconscious reconsidered* (pp. 9–48). New York: Wiley.

Pfungst, O. (1907). *Das Pferd des Herrn von Osten (der Kluge Hans), ein Beitrag zur experimentellen Tier- und Menschen-Psychologie.* [The horse of Mr. von Osten (Clever Hans), a contribution to experimental animal and human psychology]. Leipzig: Barth.

Pfungst, O. (1911). *Clever Hans (the horse of Mr. von Osten): A contribution to experimental animal and human psychology.* (C. L. Rahn, Trans.) New York: Henry Holt. (Original work published 1907) (Reissued by Holt, Rinehart and Winston in 1965, edited and with an Introduction by Robert Rosenthal).

Prince, M. (1925). Automatic writing combined with "crystal gazing." *Journal of Abnormal and Social Psychology, 20,* 34–42.

Prince, M. (1992). *The dissociation of a personality: A biographical study in abnormal psychology.* New York: Classics of Psychiatry & Behavioral Sciences Library. (Original work published 1906)

Prior, M., & Cummins, R. (1992). Questions about facilitated communication and autism. *Journal of Autism and Developmental Disorders, 22,* 331–337.

Prizant, B. M., Wetherby, A. M., & Rydell, P. J. (1994). Implications of facilitated communication for education and communication enhancement practices for persons with autism. In H. C. Shane (Ed.), *Facilitated communication: The clinical and social phenomenon* (pp. 123–155). San Diego, CA: Singular Publishing Group.

Randi, J. (1982). *Flim-flam!: Psychics, ESP, unicorns and other delusions.* Buffalo, NY: Prometheus.

Reber, A. S. (1992). An evolutionary context for the cognitive unconscious. *Philosophical Psychology, 5,* 33–51.

Reber, A. S. (1993). *Implicit learning and tacit knowledge: An essay on the cognitive unconscious.* New York: Oxford University Press.

Rechtschaffen, A. (1973). The psychophysiology of mental activity during sleep. In F. J. McGuigan & R. A. Schoonover (Eds.), *The psychophysiology of thinking: Studies of covert processes* (pp. 153–205). New York: Academic Press.

Rhine, J. B., & Rhine, L. E. (1929a). An investigation of a "mind-reading" horse. *Journal of Abnormal and Social Psychology, 23,* 449–466.

Rhine, J. B., & Rhine, L. E. (1929b). Second report on Lady, the "mind-reading" horse. *Journal of Abnormal and Social Psychology, 24,* 287–292.

Riddick, T. M. (1952). Dowsing—an unorthodox method of locating underground water supplies or an interesting facet of the human mind. *Proceedings of the American Philosophical Society, 96,* 526–534.

Rimland, B. (1990a). Autistic crypto-savants. *Autism Research Review International, 4*(1), 3.

Rimland, B. (1990b). Surprising success reported with facilitated communication. *Autism Research Review International, 4*(4), 1–2.

Rimland, B. (1992a). Editor's note. *Autism Research Review International, 6*(2), 6.

Rimland, B. (1992b). Facilitated communication: Now the bad news. *Autism Research Review International, 6*(1), 3.

Rimland, B. (1993a). Facilitated communication: A light at the end of the tunnel? *Autism Research Review International, 7*(3), 3.

Rimland, B. (1993b). Facilitated communication update: The paradox continues. *Autism Research Review International, 7*(2), 7.

Romanes, G. J. (1881). "Thought-reading." *Nature, 24,* 171–172.

Rorty, A. O. (1988). The deceptive self: Liars, layers, and lairs. In B. P. McLaughlin & A. O. Rorty (Eds.), *Perspectives on self-deception* (pp. 11–28). Berkeley: University of California Press.

Rosenthal, R. (1966). *Experimenter effects in psychological research.* New York: Appleton-Century-Crofts.

Rosenthal, R., & Jacobson, L. (1968). *Pygmalion in the classroom: Teacher expectation and pupils' intellectual development.* New York: Holt, Rinehart & Winston.

Rosenthal, R., & Rubin, D. B. (1978). Interpersonal expectancy effects: The first 345 studies. *The Behavioral and Brain Sciences, 1,* 377–415.

Rosenzweig, S. (1987). Sally Beauchamp's career: A psychoarchaeological key to Morton Prince's classic case of multiple personality. *Genetic, Social, and General Psychology Monographs, 113*(1), 5–60.

Rosenzweig, S. (1994). *The historic expedition to America (1909): Freud, Jung and Hall the King-Maker* (Rev. ed. Originally published as *Freud, Jung, and Hall the King-Maker*). St Louis: Rana House.

Ross, D. (1972). *G. Stanley Hall: The psychologist as prophet*. Chicago: University of Chicago Press.

Ross, L. (1977). The intuitive psychologist and his shortcomings: Distortions in the attribution process. In L. Berkowitz (Ed.), *Advances in experimental social psychology* (Vol. 10, pp. 173–219). Orlando: Academic Press.

Rozin, P. (1976). The evolution of intelligence and access to the cognitive unconscious. In J. M. Sprague & A. N. Epstein (Eds.), *Progress in psychobiology and physiological psychology* (Vol. 6, pp. 245–280). New York: Academic Press.

Rüegg, J. C. (1986). *Calcium in muscle activation: A comparative approach*. Berlin: Springer-Verlag.

Ryan, T. A., Cottrell, C. L., & Bitterman, M. E. (1951). A reply to Jacobson. *American Journal of Psychology, 64*, 117–121.

Sanford, E. C. (1914a). Der Kluge Hans and the Elberfeld horses. *American Journal of Psychology, 25*, 131–136.

Sanford, E. C. (1914b). Psychic research in the animal field: Der Kluge Hans and the Elberfeld horses. *American Journal of Psychology, 25*, 1–31.

Sarbin, T. R. (1981). On self-deception. In T. A. Sebeok & R. Rosenthal (Eds.), *The Clever Hans phenomenon: Communication with horses, whales, apes, and people* (pp. 220–235). New York: New York Academy of Sciences.

Schneck, D. J. (1992). *Mechanics of muscle: Second edition*. New York: New York University Press.

Scientific critics. Notes. (1904, September 22). *Nature, 70*, 510.

Schreiber, F. R. (1973). *Sybil*. Chicago: Regnery.

Sears, R. R. (1947). *Survey of objective studies of psychoanalytic concepts* [A report prepared for the Committee on Social Adjustment]. New York: Social Science Research Council. Ann Arbor, MI: Edwards Brothers.

Sebeok, T. A., & Rosenthal, R. (Eds.). (1981). *The Clever Hans phenomenon: Communication with horses, whales, apes, and people*. New York: New York Academy of Sciences.

Sebeok, T. A., & Umiker-Sebeok, J. (1979, November). Performing animals: Secrets of the trade. *Psychology Today*, 78–79, 81–82, 91.

Sellin, B. (1995). *I don't want to be inside me anymore: Messages from an autistic mind* (A. Bell, Trans.). New York: Basic Books. (Original work published 1993)

Shane, H. C. (Ed.). (1994). *Facilitated communication: The clinical and social phenomenon*. San Diego, CA: Singular Publishing Group.

Shanks, D. R., & St. John, M. F. (1994). Characteristics of dissociable human learning systems. *Behavioral & Brain Sciences, 17*, 367–447.

Shaw, W. A. (1940). The relation of muscular action potentials to imaginal weight lifting. *Archives of Psychology, 35*(247), 1–50.

Shepard, L. (Ed.). (1978). *Encyclopedia of occultism & parapsychology* (Vols. 1–2). Detroit, MI: Gale Research Co.

Shepard, R. N. (1981). Psychophysical complementarity. In M. Kubovy & J. R. Pomerantz (Eds.), *Perceptual organization*. Hillsdale, NJ: Lawrence Erlbaum Associates.

Shepard, R. N., & Podgorny, P. (1978). Cognitive processes that resemble perceptual processes. In W. K. Estes (Ed.), *Handbook of learning and cognitve processes: Vol. 5. Human information processing* (pp. 189–237). Hillsdale, NJ: Lawrence Erlbaum Associates.

Sherry, D. F., & Schacter, D. L. (1987). The evolution of multiple memory systems. *Psychological Review, 94*, 439–454.

Shevrin, H., & Dickman, S. (1980). The psychological unconscious: A necessary assumption for all psychological theory? *American Psychologist, 35*, 421–434.

Siegel, B. (1995). Brief report: Asessing allegations of sexual molestation made through facilitated communication. *Journal of Autism and Developmental Disorders, 25*, 319–326.

Simon, E. W., Toll, D. M., & Whitehair, P. M. (1994). A naturalistic appoach to the validation of facilitated communication. *Journal of Autism and Developmental Disorders, 24*, 647–657.

Simon, E. W., Whitehair, P. M., & Toll, D. M. (1995). Keeping facilitated communication in perspective. *Mental Retardation, 33*(5), 338–339.

Simon, E. W., Whitehair, P. M., & Toll, D. M. (1996). A case study: Follow-up assessment of facilitated communication. *Journal of Autism and Developmental Disorders, 26*, 9–18.

Singer, B., & Benassi, V. A. (1981). Occult beliefs. *American Scientist, 69*, 49–55.

Skinner, B. F. (1934, January). Has Gertrude Stein a secret? *Atlantic Monthly*, 50–57.

Skinner, B. F. (1957). *Verbal behavior.* New York: Appleton-Century-Crofts.

Smith, M. D., & Belcher, R. G. (1994). Facilitated communication and autism: Separating fact from fiction. *Journal of Vocational Rehabilitation, 4*(1), 66–74.

Snow, R. E. (1969). Unfinished Pygmalion [Review of the book *Pygmalion in the classroom: Teacher expectation and pupils' intellectual development*]. *Contemporary Psychology, 14*, 197–199.

Sobsey, D., Gray, S., Wells, D., Pyper, D., & Reimer-Heck, B. (1991). *Disability, sexuality, and abuse: An annotated bibliography.* Baltimore: Brookes.

Solomons, L. M., & Stein, G. (1896). Normal motor automatism. *Psychological Review, 3*, 492–512.

Spanos, N. P. (1994). Multiple identity enactments and multiple personality disorder: A sociocognitive perspective. *Psycholological Bulletin, 116*, 143–165.

Spanos, N. P., & Burgess, C. (1994). Hypnosis and multiple personality disorder: A sociocognitive perspective. In J. S Lynn & J. W. Rhue (Eds.), *Dissociation: Clinical and theoretical perspectives* (pp. 136–155). New York: Guilford.

Spanos, N. P., & Chaves, J. F. (1991). History and historiography of hypnosis. In S. J. Lynn & J. W. Rhue (Eds.), *Theories of hypnosis: Current models and perspectives* (pp. 43–78). New York: Guilford.

Spanos, N. P., Weekes, J. R., Menary, E., & Bertrand, L. D. (1986). Hypnotic interview and age regression procedures in the elicitation of multiple personality symptoms: A simulation study. *Psychiatry, 49*, 298–311.

Spiritualism and its recent converts. (1871). *Quarterly Review, 131*, 301–353.

Spitz, H. H. (1986). *The raising of intelligence: A selected history of attempts to raise retarded intelligence.* Hillsdale, NJ: Lawrence Erlbaum Associates.

Spitz, H. H. (1993). The role of the unconscious in thinking and problem solving. *Educational Psychology, 13*, 229–244.

Spitz, H. H. (1995). Calendar calculating *idiots savants* and the smart unconscious. *New Ideas in Psychology, 13*, 167–182.

Spitz, H. H. (1996). Comment on Donnellan's review of Shane's (1994) "Facilitated communication: The clinical and social phenomenon." *American Journal on Mental Retardation, 101*, 96–100.

State v. Warden. No. 70377, Supreme Court of Kansas. 891 P.2d 1074 (Kan. March 10, 1995).

Stehli, A. (1991). *The sound of a miracle: A child's triumph over autism.* New York: Doubleday.

Stein, G. (1898). Cultivated motor automatism: A study of character in its relation to attention. *Psychological Review, 5*, 295–306.

Stein, G. (1933). *The autobiography of Alice B. Toklas.* New York: Vintage Books.

Stein, G. (1937). *Everybody's autobiography.* New York: Random House.

Stevenson, R. L. (1897). *Across the plains: With other memories and essays.* New York: Charles Scribner's Sons.

Stevenson, R. L. (1898). The strange case of Dr. Jekyll and Mr. Hyde. In *The novels and tales of Robert Louis Stevenson* (Vol. 7). New York: Charles Scribner's Sons. (Original work published 1886)

Stoyva, J. M. (1965). Finger electromyographic activity during sleep: Its relation to dreaming in deaf and normal subjects. *Journal of Abnormal Psychology, 70*, 343–349.

Stratton, G. M. (1921). The control of another person by obscure signs. *Psychological Review, 28*, 301–314.

Suryani, L. K., & Jensen, G. D. (1993). *Trance and possession in Bali: A window on western multiple personality, possession disorder, and suicide.* New York: Oxford University Press.

Sutherland, S. (1992). *Irrationality: The enemy within.* London: Constable and Company.

Szempruch, J., & Jacobson, J. W. (1993). Evaluating facilitated communications of people with developmental disabilities. *Research in Developmental Disabilities, 15*, 253–264.

Tanner, A. (1994). *Studies in spiritism.* Buffalo, NY: Prometheus. (Original work published 1910)

Taylor, W. S., & Martin, M. F. (1944). Multiple personality. *Journal of Abnormal and Social Psychology, 39*, 281–300.

Thigpen, C. H., & Cleckley, H. M. (1984). On the incidence of multiple personality disorder. *International Journal of Clinical and Experimental Hypnosis, 32*, 63–66.

Thompson, T. (1994). [Review of the book *Communication unbound*]. *American Journal on Mental Retardation, 98*, 670–673.

Thorndike, R. L. (1968). [Review of the book *Pygmalion in the classroom: Teacher expectation and pupils' intellectual development*]. *American Educational Research Journal, 5*, 708–711.

Thorson, A. M. (1925). The relation of tongue movements to internal speech. *Journal of Experimental Psychology, 8*, 1–32.

Treffert, D. A. (1989). *Extraordinary people: Understanding "idiot savants."* New York: Harper & Row.

Truitt, J. (1952, December 22). Talking horse. *Life, 33*, 20–21.

Tucker, M. A. (1896–1897). Comparative observations on the involuntary movements of adults and children. *American Journal of Psychology, 8*, 394–404.

Vogt, E. Z., & Hyman, R. (1979). *Water witching U.S.A.* (2nd ed.). Chicago: University of Chicago Press.

Volkmar, F. R., & Cohen, D. J. (1985). The experience of infantile autism: A first-hand account. *Journal of Autism and Developmental Disorders, 15*, 47–54.

Watson, J.B. (1913). Psychology as a behaviorist views it. *Psychological Review, 20*, 158–177.

Weitzenhoffer, A. (1953). *Hypnotism: An objective study in suggestibility.* New York: Wiley.

Weitzenhoffer, A. (1989). *The practice of hypnotism: Vol. 1. Traditional and semi-traditional techniques and phenomenology.* New York: Wiley.

Whitehurst, G. J., & Crone, D. A. (1944). Social constructivism, positivism, and facilitated communication. *Journal of the Association for Persons With Severe Handicaps, 19*, 191–195.

Whyte, L. L. (1960). *The unconscious before Freud.* New York: Basic Books.

Williams, D. (1992). *Nobody nowhere.* New York: Avon Books.

Williams, L. M. (1994a). Recall of childhood trauma: A prospective study of women's memories of child sexual abuse. *Journal of Consulting and Clinical Psychology, 62*, 1167–1176.

Williams, L. M. (1994b) What does it mean to forget child sexual abuse? A reply to Loftus, Garry, and Feldman (1994). *Journal of Consulting and Clinical Psychology, 62*, 1182–1186.

Wolfensberger, W. (1994). The "facilitated communication" craze as an instance of pathological science: The cold fusion of human services. In H. C. Shane (Ed.), *Facilitated communication: The clinical and social phenomenon* (pp. 57–122). San Diego, CA: Singular Publishing Group.

Woodworth, R. S., & Schlosberg, H. (1954). *Experimental psychology* (Rev. ed.). New York: Henry Holt.

Woody, E. Z., & Bowers, K. S. (1994). A frontal assault on dissociated control. In S. J. Lynn & J. W. Rhue (Eds.), *Dissociation: Clinical and theoretical perspectives* (pp. 52–79). New York: Guilford.

Wulff, S. B. (1985). The symbolic and object play of children with autism: A review. *Journal of Autism and Developmental Disorders, 15*, 139–148.

Yapko, M. D. (1994). *Suggestions of abuse.* New York: Simon & Schuster.

Author Index

A

Aldridge-Morris, R., 144
American Psychiatric Association, 130n
Anderson, J. E., 90
Antrobus, J. S., 113
Arnold, N., 17
Aronson, E., 166
Aserinsky, E., 113

B

Babuts, D., 12–13
Baladarian, N. J., 16
Ballou, R. O., 83
Barresi, J., 132, 140, 142
Barrett, W. F., 68, 78
Bean, N. P., 140–142
Beard, G. M., 57–58, 60
Belcher, R. G., 50
Bell, C., 84
Bemporad, J. R., 20
Benassi, V. A., 169
Berger, C.L., 24n
Berger, J., 158
Berry, D. C., 125
Bertrand, L. D., 155
Bikel, O., 147
Biklen, D., 2, 3–4, 5, 6, 8–9, 12, 20, 47–48, 49,
      50, 73, 161, 163–164, 166–167
Binet, A., 55n, 111, 128–129, 132–133, 134
Bitterman, M. E., 110
Bligh, S., 18
Bliss, E. L., 131
Boor, M., 143n
Boring, E. G., 1, 36, 38, 38n, 88n
Botash, A. S., 12–13
Bowers, F., 38n, 81n, 83, 84, 86
Bowers, K. S., 122, 124, 126, 153
Bowman, E. S., 144
Boynton, J. L., 168
Bozzuto, J. C., 146
Braden, M., 166
Brown, Chip, 56
Brown, Christy, 2
Burgess, C., 153
Burkhardt, F., 38n, 81n, 83, 84, 86

C

Campbell, J. L., 79
Carlson, E. T., 131
Carpenter, W. B., 58, 62–64, 66–67, 102–103
Cattell, J. M., 82
Ceci, S. J., 150
Cesaroni, L., 20
Chaves, J. F., 155
Chevreul, M. E., 54–55, 64, 66, 68, 121
Chiu, S., 144
Chomsky, N., 118–119
Christopher, M., 37, 38, 39, 42, 51, 74n
Cleckley, H. M., 145–146, 151
Cohen, D. J., 20
Coon, D. J., 84
Coons, P. M., 143n, 144
Costa, A. B., 54n, 55, 67
Cottrell, C. L., 110
Crone, D. A., 167
Crossley, R., 2–3, 9, 44–45, 46, 49, 50
Cummins, R. A., 3n, 6, 17
Czyzewska, M., 125–126

D

Damgaard, J., 143n
Darley, J. M., 162
Daubert v. Dow Pharmaceuticals, 15n
Davidson, D., 173
Davidson, T. M., 153n
Dawes, R. M., 160
Dement, W., 113
Dennett, D. C., 130, 170
Dessoir, M., 56, 59–60
Dickman, S., 124
Dillon, K. M., 8, 74
Donnellan, A. M., 13–14, 45–46
Downey, J. E., 60–62, 90, 122
Doyle, A. C., 38, 80–81
Dretzin, R., 147
Duchan, J. F., 166–167

E

Eagle, M. N., 124
Eberle, P., 13
Eberle, S., 13

Subject Index

A

Abnormal psychology, 132, 135, 142
Action potentials, 114
  sleep/dreaming and, 111–112
Adaptation, 122, 160
  evolution and, 161, 170
  unattended motor activity and, 123–124
  unconscious processes and, 123
Altered states of consciousness (ASC), 77,
    see also Clairvoyance; Consciousness;
    Mediums; Mystical phenomena; Pos-
    session; Spiritualism; Trance
  interpretation of, 129
  W. James and, 81–82, 88
American Academy of Child and Adoles-
    cent Psychiatry, 166
American Academy of Pediatrics, 166
American Association on Mental Retarda-
    tion, 166
American Institute for Scientific Research, 38n
American Journal of Psychology (Hall), 86
American Psychological Association, 166
  Working Group on Investigation of
    Memories of Childhood
    Abuse, 149
American Society of Dowsers, 73
American Society for Psychical Research,
    38, 81, 82, 85, 86, 139, *see also* Society
    for Psychical Research
American Speech-Language-Hearing Asso-
    ciation, 166
Amnesia, 97, 129, 131, 132
Ampère, André M., 54, 64
Anxiety, 172
Apparitions, 87
Apraxia, 3
Athenæum, 64
Atlantic Review, 69
Atoms, 118
Attribution theory, 161n
Autism, 7, *see also* Autistic people
  cognitive potential and, 3, 20, 23
  exceptionality and, 19–20
  Makarushka on, 1
  motor problems and, 2, 5, 21
  personal recollections and, 20–21
  ritual movements and, 1

sound hypersensitivity and, 21
Autistic people, *see also* Autistic savants
  autobiographies of, 20–21
  Birger Sellin, "not everyone is right for
    it", 21–22
Autistic savants, 19–20
Automatic impulse, 76
Automatic reading, 89
Automatic speaking, 89, 99
Automatic writing, 141, *see also* Automat-
    isms; Hypnosis; Planchette;
    Telepathy
  case of Mrs. Keech, 162–163
  dissociation and, 130–133
  Downey and, 90–91
  facilitated communication and, 98, 99,
    100, 157
  involuntary muscle movements and, 76,
    91, 98–99, 100, 133
  M. Erickson/Kubie papers and, 94–97
  M. Erickson's studies, 93–95
  Mühl's studies, early memories and,
    92–93, 99
  multiple personality and, 76, 114–115
    Harriman's study, 97–98
  Myers and, 76–77, 81
  Ouija board and, 75–76
  potential perils, 97–98
  script memories and, Prince on, 92
  secondary personality and, 89, 96
  Solomons & Stein's study, 89–91
  spiritualism and, 77, 88
  Stein's study, 89–90
  subordinate systems and, 153
  unconscious processes and, 91, 92, 94,
    102, 122
  W. James and, 88–89, 91
Automatisms, 77, 138, *see also* Motor auto-
    matisms; Verbal automatisms
Autonomic nervous system, 108
Autonomous activity, 122
Awareness, *see* Conscious awareness; Learn-
    ing

B

Barber, Theodore, 153
Barrett, William, on telepathy, 78